Ninety-nine More Maggots, Mites, and Munchers

Ninety-nine More
Maggots, Mites, and Munchers

May R. Berenbaum

Illustrations by John Parker Sherrod

University of Illinois Press   Urbana and Chicago

Dedicated to Hannah and Adam—who have a greater
appreciation for insects than their parents did at their age.

© 1993 by the Board of Trustees of the University of Illinois
Manufactured in the United States of America
1 2 3 4 5 C P 5 4 3 2 1

This book is printed on acid-free paper.

Library of Congress Cataloging-in-Publication Data

Berenbaum, M. (May)
    Ninety-nine more maggots, mites, and munchers / May R. Berenbaum ;
illustrations by John Parker Sherrod.
       p.   cm.
    Includes bibliographical references and index.
    ISBN 0-252-02016-2 (cl : acid-free paper).—ISBN 0-252-06322-8
(pb : acid-free paper)
    1. Insects—Popular works.   2. Insect pests—Popular works.
I. Title.   II. Title: 99 more maggots, mites, and munchers.
QL467.B474 1993
595.7—dc20   92-34639
                                                        CIP

Contents

Preface

At the end of the book *Ninety-nine Gnats, Nits, and Nibblers* I wrote that books about insects have great sequel potential—after all, there are upward of a million species of described insects. Thus, it wasn't difficult to find ninety-nine more to write about. Why I decided to write a sequel is an entirely different question. I have to admit, the decision wasn't really based on a flood of cards, letters, and phone calls from readers desperately demanding more. Basically, writing about insects is kind of habit-forming. After the first book came out, I began to feel guilty about all of the species—even entire orders—that I had neglected to mention. This book, then, is as much to do the insects justice as it is to do the readers a service. Although the cast of characters is entirely new, the format and approach are basically the same as before, with one exception. In this book, there is more emphasis on the obscure and unusual—insects that even hardcore entomologists may be unlikely to encounter (unless they happen to be looking under a sweat bee's wing, inside a spider's egg case, underneath a dead chipmunk, in a slime flux on a tree, or up a reindeer's nose, among other exotic locales).

As before, I have many people to thank, without whose help this book would not have been completed. My colleagues in the Department of Entomology at the University of Illinois at Urbana-Champaign never cease to amaze me with their wide-ranging knowledge and unerring ability to provide critical references or astute personal recollections at a moment's notice. I would particularly like to thank Dr. Ellis MacLeod in this regard, who, among other things, shared unpublished drawings of berothids. The continued support and enthusiasm of Judy McCulloh at the University of Illinois Press helped to make this book a reality. John Sherrod's whimsical illustrations and visual insights enliven the text immeasurably. My parents, Morris and Adrienne Berenbaum, have always been embarrassingly proud of my meager accomplishments and have always served as a source of motivation and inspiration for me. Of course, I would especially like to thank my husband, Richard Leskosky—fount of incredibly obscure and interesting information, brutally honest critic, most enthusiastic booster, and best friend. Because of Richard, there's Hannah, our amazing and beautiful daughter, who has made life more joyful than I had ever imagined possible. By the time Hannah was only twenty months old, she could already recognize and name, albeit not always in a manner consistent with contemporary taxonomy, a "bee," a "moth," an "ant," and a "ladybug." Only 999,996 more to go, sweetheart.

Parts List and Assembly Instructions
(Arthropod Anatomy and Physiology)

Remarkably, despite the fact that there are over a million species of insects in the world, the class Insecta is not a club that just anyone can join. Rules for membership are, at least at first glance, basically straightforward. Insects belong to the phylum Arthropoda, animals with jointed legs, whose bodies are composed of segments and who have external (exo-) skeletons. Within the phylum, insects are arthropods whose segments are arranged into three major body regions.

At the front end are the segments that are fused to form a head. Attached to the head are various and sundry mouthparts, which are actually thought to be modified jointed appendages. Mouthparts can take on a bewildering diversity of forms, even within a single order of insects. Among the more commonplace are mouths that chew, mouths that rasp, mouths that rasp and tear, mouths that pierce and suck, and mouths that soak up fluids like a sponge. The diversity of mouthparts reflects the extraordinary diversity of materials that insects regard as edible.

Also attached to the head are assorted sensory structures (a logical place for such equipment, since the head end generally arrives before the rest of the body in new places). Most adult insects have a pair of compound eyes—that is, eyes that are composed of many individual light-sensing units called ommatidia. Usually situated between the eyes is a single pair of antennae. Antennae come in a variety of shapes and sizes, and variously resemble feathers, combs, saws, wires, clubs, and other small household tools and appliances. Generally, antennae are covered with sensory hairs, although the type of sensory hairs varies with the species. The radarlike antennae of male mosquitoes, for example, are sensitive to the buzzing sound made by female mosquitoes (as are many a sleepless human in the summertime), while the radarlike antennae of male luna moths are sensitive to the pheromones (or sexual scents) released by female luna moths.

The second cluster of segments in an insect body constitutes the thorax. Three segments, each bearing a pair of walking appendages, make up the thorax. Thus, insects have six legs. Too many legs can bar an arthropod from membership in the class Insecta. Members of the class Arachnida, for example, have eight, not six, legs. Thus, spiders, mites, ticks, scorpions, daddy-long-legs, and other eight-legged armor-plated types are most emphatically not insects. Even if the leg infraction were to be overlooked, these arthropods fail to meet insect standards by one body region. In place of the insectan head, thorax, and abdomen, arachnids and many other noninsect arthropods have only two body regions—a combined head-and-thorax (or cephalothorax) and an abdomen.

Not all insects walk—some crawl, some run, some hop, and some propel themselves forward in fashions not easily described in words—and their legs are modified accordingly. Keeping track of six legs is no small task. Most walking insects move the first and third legs on one side and the middle leg on the opposite side off the ground at the same time and then alternate with the middle leg on one side and first and third legs on the opposite side. The end result is sort of a zigzag, but it gets them behind the refrigerator or up your leg when called upon to do so.

Wings are also uniquely insectan thoracic appurtenances. Insects, alone among all animals, sport wings that are not derived from walking appendages (thus, unlike birds and bats, they didn't have to give up any of their many legs to fly). Most insects have two pairs of wings, one on the middle thoracic segment (mesothorax) and one on the last thoracic segment (metathorax). Wings also come in all shapes and sizes. In fact, the names of many insect orders refer to distinctive characteristics of the wings. There are, among others, hairy-winged (Trichoptera), sheath-winged (Coleoptera), membranous-winged (Hymenoptera), and fringe-winged (Thysanoptera) insects. Wings also differ in the way they fold up when not in use. Dragonflies, damselflies, and mayflies, for example, have to hold their wings outstretched or upright all the time. Just about every other kind of insect can lay its wings flat or tuck them away. This wingfolding is no small accomplishment, inasmuch as it allows insects access into cracks and crevices, where an inordinate number of species have developed a comfortable lifestyle. One never has to worry about a dragonfly, with its permanently outstretched wings, crawling into a box of cereal or slipping inconspicuously under the sofa.

Although insects vary in how they put their wings away, there is considerably less variation when it comes to using them. Flying is one of the more challenging things an insect is called upon to do during its adult life. Among other things, for small animals, air resistance and turbulence are formidable obstacles. Most insects have mechanisms for coupling the two pairs of wings, so that the downstroke of one pair won't create turbulence for the second pair. Bees, for example, use a series of hooks and catches; moths and butterflies use overlapping lobes or hook-and-eye devices. Dragonflies, conspicuous exceptions, flap each pair independently in an alternating pattern; when they glide, however, they can lock all four into position by muscular action. Each pair of these wings is moved by thoracic muscles that attach directly to the wings. The majority of insects flap their wings in figure-eight fashion, akin to the way oars are used to push through the water; after the power downstroke, the wings are rotated on the upswing to cut down on friction. In these insects, the wings are moved indirectly; muscles alternately elevate or lower the thoracic wall, to which the wings are attached. One distinct advantage of indirect flight musculature over direct flight musculature is that insects can take advantage of the elasticity of the thoracic wall to get a few extra wingbeats in for each muscle contraction. Other insects operate their wings via fibrillary muscles, which contract and relax many times for every nerve impulse they receive, allowing such wings to beat several hundred times a minute.

The last group of segments in an insect body makes up the abdomen. The abdomen, usually eleven or so segments, houses the digestive organs. The basic insect alimentary plan is simple. The gut is basically a long tube, running from mouth to anus. It's divided into three sections—foregut, midgut, and hindgut—which are separated by all types of sphincters and valves. In the foregut, food is usually broken up into smaller pieces; in the midgut, digestive and detoxification enzymes break down pieces into their biochemical components for absorption; and in the hindgut, water is resorbed and wastes are packaged for excretion.

The abdomen also contains the reproductive apparatus, including the genitalia, thought by some to be modified appendages. Insect genitalia are so staggeringly diverse that they are carefully dissected out and scrutinized by insect taxonomists, not for cheap thrills but for finding anatomical traits for distinguishing among closely related species. Popular some time ago was a theory (called the lock-and-key hypothesis) that insects actually recognize each other during mating by the size and shape of their genitalia.

So, those are the rules for membership—head, thorax, and abdomen, one pair of antennae, and one or two pairs of wings. It's apparent, though, that some rule bending is going on among the ranks. The wing requirement, for example, is waived for all immature stages—no immature insect ever has wings. For that matter, the wing requirement is waived for some adult insects as well. Adult fleas don't have wings—but they're clearly related to winged insects, since they still have remnants of flight muscles in the thorax. Mouthparts come and go, as well. Adult giant silk moths have no functional mouthparts at all—they consume what they need during their larval stage (during which time they consume about 86,000 times their own weight in foliage and increase their size by 4,000-fold). Even digestive organs come and go—mayflies, which spend less than one day in the adult stage, not only lack functional mouthparts, they lack a functional gut as well. The rules are basically guidelines, and there are still creatures whose status is hotly debated among entomologists. Collembolans, or springtails, for example, are six-legged arthropods with one pair of antennae. What's the problem, you ask? Collembolans are indeed considered by some to be insects. They have no wings, however, and there's no indication that they or any close relatives ever had wings. At the moment, collembolans are placed by some in their own class, and by others in the subclass Apterygota (from the Latin meaning "wingless") of the class Insecta.

One of the reasons that it's so hard for people to classify insects is that they are in so many ways so different from us. External differences are obvious and are clearly recognized by most people. Insects have an embarrassing surfeit of legs, for one thing. Their skeletons are on the outside rather than the inside of their bodies, where skeletons of all self-respecting vertebrates are found. There's not much in the face of an insect that looks familiar. They have no neck, no throat, no nose, no recognizable ears, no eyelashes, and no eyebrows (so, to be "beetle-browed" is not apt at all).

Internally, insects are even more radically different from humans. Among other things, their whole body plan is upside down. Humans, like all other species of the vertebrate, have a nerve cord running down the length of their backs (through, what else, the backbone). Insect nerve cords run along their bellies. Moreover, there are two nerve cords, connected by bridges along the length of the body. Since their nerve cords are not in the right place, it stands to reason that their hearts are not in the right place, either. The heart is a long tube extending down the back of the body. It doesn't exactly beat, either, at least in the same way vertebrate hearts beat. Unlike our circulatory system, in which blood moves in a neat and orderly fashion through an elaborate series of tubes and channels, the insect circulatory system is open—blood just sort of stands around in the body cavity (called, not inappropriately, a hemocoel, or blood cavity), sloshing leisurely from the neck area backward every time the heart muscles contract. Thus, although there is a plethora of "wrists" at which to take an insect pulse, such an effort is destined to come to naught. Insect blood cells don't carry oxygen, as do our hemoglobin-rich red blood cells. Oxygen is delivered throughout the body through a series of pipes, called tracheae, that open directly to the outside world through little portholes, or spiracles.

All in all, it would appear that insects are about as different as animals can be from humans and still be of this planet. Far more subtle than the differences, however, are the remarkable similarities between humans and insects, similarities that go unnoticed probably by most people and undoubtedly by most insects. Although an insect's nervous system is constructed differently in overall design, insect nerve cells operate in basically the same way as do human nerve cells. Like insects, humans are segmented animals with jointed appendages, and muscular systems move appendages in both humans and insects in fundamentally the same fashion. Many of the digestive and detoxification enzymes of insects are similar to those of humans, and many aspects of reproductive physiology operate on the same principles (in fact, amazingly, male mammals and insects are distinctive in the animal world in possessing intromittent sexual organs).

Perhaps the most startling similarities, however, are the ecological ones. Humans and insects have similar tastes in habitats and habits. They move into our houses because they enjoy the same temperatures and humidities; they attack our crops and infest everything in our kitchens and cupboards because they like the same kind of food. They even share our weaknesses and vices—*Drosophila melanogaster* infests wineries because it's hopelessly hooked on alcohol, and *Tribolium confusum*, the confused grain beetle, can be found happily chewing its way through bales of marijuana held in storage in police vaults (although the "confusion" in its name alludes to different circumstances). One of the reasons insects are so prominent and pestiferous is that they are intent on sharing much of the planet that we have staked out for our own. For my money, it's worth getting to know insects better if only because we have so much in common with them. Who knows what deep insights into one's own psyche one might gain by studying the habits of say, a *real* louse, social butterfly, gadfly, firebrat, or borer? I hope readers find relatively few of the latter within these pages.

A Word about References

This book contains all kinds of information, so it's not surprising that all kinds of sources were used to put this book together. Following each chapter is a listing of the major (and most accessible) references used in writing that chapter. In addition, for basic information three books were always kept within reach. These were:

Borror, D. J., D. Delong, and C. A. Triplehorn. 1976. *An Introduction to the Study of Insects.* 4th ed. New York: Holt Rinehart and Winston.

Metcalf, C. L., W. P. Flint, and R. L. Metcalf. 1962. *Destructive and Useful Insects.* New York: McGraw-Hill.

Swann, L. A., and C. S. Papp. 1972. *The Common Insects of North America.* New York: Harper and Row.

Besides these basic texts, I used various technical journals, specialized books, bulletins, and experiment station reports, as well as popular newspapers and magazines, in order to obtain maggot, mite, and muncher minutiae. As always, I am indebted to the staff of the Biology Library and the Natural History Survey Library at the University of Illinois for lending their expertise and support and for assisting unstintingly in the search for all sorts of peculiar sources of information. I also exploited the collective wisdom, experience, and libraries of my friends and colleagues in the Department of Entomology and at the Natural History Survey. Their vast knowledge could easily fill a library; unlike most libraries, however, the information they possess was obtainable in pleasant conversation rather than in exhaustive computerized database searches and endless walks down dimly lit stacks of journals. For this wonderful information exchange, I am most grateful.

Chapter 1

Homebodies

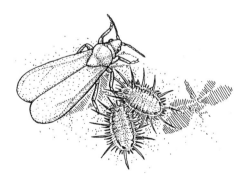

ASIAN COCKROACHES

Some animals are just inherently more newsworthy than others. For a dog to make headlines, it has to do something heroic, like pull a drowning boy out of a lake or awaken people in a burning building and lead them to safety. For a *cockroach* to make headlines, all it has to do is show up somewhere it's never been seen before. *Blattella asahinai*, for example, has recently made most of the major wire services, not to mention the grocery store tabloids, simply because it's an Asian cockroach that, like many immigrants in the history of the United States, sees our nation as a land of opportunity.

Blattella asahinai was first identified in Lakeland, Florida, in February 1985. The species created more than a few problems for entomologists and pest control operators alike, among other reasons because it's morphologically almost indistinguishable from *Blattella germanica*—the German cockroach, or croton bug—a longtime resident of North America. Both species are about ½ to ⅗ an inch in length and both are light brown with darker brown longitudinal stripes on the pronotum (the

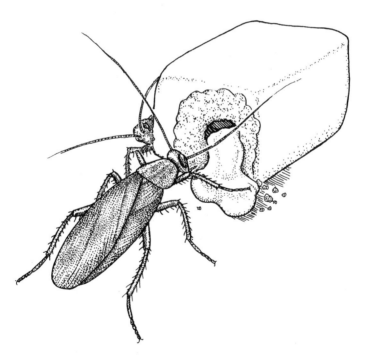

Asian cockroaches: "Creme filling? For this I gave up sushi?"

shield behind the head). Both carry around their egg cases, each containing thirty to forty eggs, until just before the eggs are ready to hatch. There are a few subtle but significant differences, however. The Asian species, known previously only from Okinawa, China, Sri Lanka, Thailand, India, Burma, and the Andaman Islands, is slightly lighter in color than is the German cockroach and its wings are slightly longer, in fact, long enough in the female to extend beyond the tip of the abdomen to cover the egg case from above.

This last morphological difference accounts for a major behavioral difference between the new Asian and the familiar German cockroach. *Blattella asahinai* is eminently more flightworthy than is its near relative. A German cockroach, if pressed or in mortal danger, can bumble off a few feet in no particular direction; but the Asian cockroach, with its longer wings, can take off and land with precision and can cover distances of 120 feet or more in the process.

Another behavioral difference promises to make the Asian cockroach an unwelcome addition to the North American fauna. While most cockroaches are almost entirely nocturnal and shun any kind of light (which at least makes them inconspicuous), Asian cockroaches get geared up around dusk, just about the time families are gathering for dinner or sitting down to watch the six o'clock news. Not only do they *not* avoid light, they actively seek it out, and they fly toward white walls and illuminated buildings whether they're welcome or not.

At the moment, *Blattella asahinai* is found only in a 300-square-mile area of central Florida. With its ability to fly and its rapid reproductive rate (it reaches sexual maturity in only six to seven weeks, almost a month faster than German cockroaches), it's highly likely that, as Florida goes, so goes the nation. If they have trouble making it on their own, they'll undoubtedly get assistance from tourists and campers in Florida who return to their place of origin with cockroaches in suitcases or camping equipment. To complicate matters, males of the introduced Asian species can breed with females of the established German cockroach and produce fertile offspring (although, apparently, efforts in the opposite direction are unsuccessful). The habits of the hybrids are anybody's guess.

Indeed, if any group of insects has taken advantage of America's melting-pot tradition, the cockroaches have. Just about all of the more conspicuous species have arrived here from other countries and in no time at all have settled in and assimilated, even adopting as their own "the wretched refuse of our teeming shores" (with apologies to Emma Lazarus).

4

BOXELDER BUGS

The boxelder bug, *Leptocoris trivittatus*, doesn't ask for much in life. In spring, all a boxelder bug needs to find true happiness is a boxelder tree (*Acer negundo*), preferably one just beginning to bud out with a fresh growth of leaves. The boxelder tree is the one place that female boxelder bugs can feel confident about depositing their eggs, since boxelder leaves, flowers, and seeds are the only things that the hatching nymphs require to make them grow fat and happy. This predilection for boxelder explains why boxelder bugs are found primarily in the Midwest (particularly in the Mississippi Valley), although they range from the eastern United States west to British Columbia and south to California. Boxelder is a prairie tree that tolerates midwestern climatic extremes better than many lesser species and thus is widely planted as a shade tree in the central states.

Like all true bugs (in the order Hemiptera), boxelder bugs use their long slender mouthparts to pierce plant tissue and suck up plant sap. Even the adults, which are winged and fully capable of flying off in search of other fare, are for the most part content to suck the sap of boxelder parts throughout the summer months. Come fall, all a box-

Boxelder bugs: "It's a nice place to overwinter, but I wouldn't want to live here."

5

elder bug needs to complete its days in sublime contentment is a nice warm place to pass the cold winter months in comparative comfort.

Given the few simple needs and desires of boxelder bugs, it's a little surprising how unpopular they are among people best acquainted with them. They don't really even cause much damage to boxelder trees (although relentless sap-sucking can bring about leaf malformations). Boxelder bugs get into trouble because they share one of their simple needs—a warm place to spend the winter—with humans, and, since their specifications are about the same, their choice of overwintering sites is usually somebody's house.

Every year in early fall, boxelder bugs gather in huge numbers, massing in the sun-facing side of trees, fences, rocks, or buildings before collectively taking off and taking over doorframes, windowledges, and any other port of entry into an inviting, warm house. Once inside, boxelder bugs pose no risk to anybody—they apparently don't even eat or drink till spring. Aesthetically, they're even rather appealing—about a half inch in length and elliptical in shape, they're basically black with a natty red trim along the edge of the wings, wing veins, and the sides of the body (colors that coordinate nicely with many interior decorating schemes). Unlike other plant-feeding bugs, such as the leaf-footed bugs, the seed bugs, and the aptly named stink bugs, boxelder bugs and their relatives in the family Rhopalidae don't even smell bad. Although they're called the "scentless plant bugs," rhopalids do indeed possess scent glands on the upper and lower surfaces of their abdomens. These glands release not noxious fumes resembling emissions from a toxic waste dump but rather (in the words of one author) "pleasant-smelling monoterpenes." In fact, the male *Leptocoris* is said to "smell like roses"—kind of a six-legged air freshener.

Nonetheless, people dislike boxelder bugs with a passion usually reserved for arthropods that spread incurable diseases. This vehemence seems attributable entirely to the gatecrashing habits of the boxelder bugs, entering a house uninvited and, worse yet, staying the entire winter. What's more, they bring all their friends and relatives with them, so the tally of uninvited homesteaders can number in the hundreds in any one home.

Boxelder bugs can suffer rather severe mortality over the winter at the hands (and feet) of their unwilling hosts—far out of proportion to the magnitude of their offenses. This imbalance was recognized by one Bill Holm, who wrote an entire book of poetry inspired by the boxelder bug (not inappropriately, since its scientific name, *Leptocoris trivittatus*, is a perfect trochaic tetrameter). In "The Boxelder Bug Prays," he writes:

> I want so little
> for so little time,

A south window,
A wall to climb.
The smell of coffee,
A radio knob,
Nothing to eat,
Nothing to rob,
Not love, not power,
Not even a penny.
Forgive me only for
being so many.

CELLAR SPIDERS

The expression "you are what you eat" is most appropriate to describe *Pholcus phalangioides*, otherwise known as the cellar spider or the daddylonglegs spider. Its two most easily recognizable attributes are pretty much summed up by its common names—*P. phalangioides* is the nondescript brownish elongate spider in cellars all over the world, dangling upside down in its sparse, rather casual web by eight very long and skinny legs. Like most standard-issue spiders, *Pholcus phalangioides* builds a web to snare the occasional unsuspecting arthropod. When an unfortunate insect hits the web, *Pholcus phalangioides* quickly wraps the morsel snugly with silk, using its second and third pairs of legs to rotate the prey alternately toward and away from its own body and its fourth pair of legs to draw out silk from the spinnerets on its abdomen. Particularly large prey are further secured by cross-ties and suspension lines anchored to upper parts of the web. After two or three minutes of wrapping, *Pholcus phalangioides* takes a few bites and then alternates biting with wrapping at a leisurely pace till replete.

Unlike most spiders, however, *Pholcus phalangioides* occasionally gets the urge to go out to eat. *Pholcus* and its relatives in the family Pholcidae are relatively unusual among spiders in that they leave their own webs to forage in the webs of other spider species, not to steal prey but to eat the occupant. Araenophagy (spider eating) is not al-

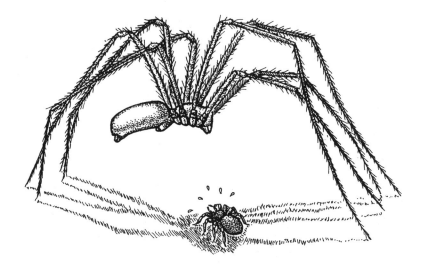

Cellar spiders: "Lucky for me I like drumsticks."

together without risks—after all, virtually all spiders are equipped with venom and are prepared to use it. *Pholcus phalangioides* has thus incorporated the element of surprise into its hunting strategy. Upon entering an alien web, *Pholcus phalangioides* undergoes a series of behaviors vaguely reminiscent of demonic possession—twitching its abdomen, bouncing in place or while walking forward, shivering, and tetanically tensing by contracting its long legs in toward its body, pulling silk strands along with it. Rather than sending the web occupant rushing off to call the proper authorities, this bizarre behavior actually whets its appetite. All of this moving and shaking convinces the resident spider that a helpless victim has been snared in the nether reaches of its web. It then eagerly scurries across its web in anticipation of a meal—which it becomes, for the waiting pholcid.

Pholcus phalangioides is well endowed for home invasion; with its extraordinarily long legs, it's able to span with ease the gaps in webs with widely spaced threads. Moreover, *Pholcus* literally walks on tiptoe (or tip-tarsus), only touching sticky webs with the extreme tips of its long legs. If the tip should happen to stick to the silk, the long leg has the leverage necessary to yank it free. Pholcids thus have free run of most spider webs, although they do have some trouble in webs of cribellate spiders, which have an extra spinning organ that attaches thousands of nonsticky catching threads to each silk strand.

Pholcids jump up and down on occasions other than mealtime. Courtship, for example, is characterized by stiff-legged jerky movements by the male and (in at least one species) upward abdominal thrusts by the female. After the female mates, eggs are produced by more abdominal thrusts and are collected by the third leg pair, enclosed in a silken sac, and attached to the chelicerae, or jaws. After two to three weeks the hatching spiderlings escape from the eggs by flexing their long skinny legs.

When threatened by a potential enemy in their own webs, pholcids capitalize on their long legs not to run away—as would most self-respecting spiders with any shred of the instinct for self-preservation—but to vibrate. When disturbed, pholcids anchor themselves to their webs by their claws and immediately begin swinging their bodies around in circles so rapidly that they seem to disappear. It's obvious, then, that when danger threatens, a pholcid doesn't need to be reminded to "shake a leg."

CHEESE SKIPPERS

It is a regrettable but true entomological observation that some holes in Swiss cheese may not have been intended by the cheesemaker. Cheese, smoked meats, dried fish, and other high-protein, high-cholesterol items in pantries and cupboards are prone to infestation by *Piophila casei*, the cheese skipper. Adult cheese skippers are shiny bronze or black two-winged tiny flies with yellow feet and faces; at no more than a sixth of an inch or so in length, they are not terribly likely to attract much notice. Before humans made an appearance on earth, *Piophila casei* and its relatives in the Piophilidae spent much of their adult lives searching out dead animals in the stage of decomposition between fresh-succulent and dried-mummified. Females lay about five hundred or more eggs in such material; these hatch into yellowish white maggots tapered in good maggot fashion toward what would be the head end if they had heads. These maggots feed by stripping whatever shards of flesh remain clinging to skeletons after blow flies and their ilk have worked over a carcass.

Feeding on dead animals is hard work—they are, after all, few and far between and can be slim pickings, depending on the competition.

Cheese skippers: "Come on, Gramps, tell us how you used to work in the Egyptian wing at the British Museum."

It must then have been a red-letter day in *Piophila casei* history when some nameless fly discovered that *Homo sapiens*, a cohabitant of planet Earth, actually stockpiles and stores dead animals in superabundance. Dried cured meats like ham or bacon are, like it or not, actually very similar to what *Piophila casei* is accustomed to eating. Cheese, a dried form of animal protein cured by microbial action, is even more to its liking—no nasty fur or bones to contend with. Thus, when humans started bringing home the bacon, they discovered that they brought home cheese skippers with it.

The powerful mouthhooks of the maggots permit them to tunnel through dry, hard proteinaceous material without so much as a by-your-leave. They will, however, leave upon provocation. The name "skipper" refers to the remarkable ability of *Piophila casei* larvae to propel themselves up to six inches straight in the air. Six inches may not seem like much of an accomplishment to you until you consider that the maggots are only ⅓ inch long, tops, and that they have absolutely no legs at all. Most animals use legs as levers for locomotion; that option being unavailable, cheese skippers resort to another time-honored invention, the spring. A maggot intent on skipping bends itself into a circle until its mouthparts hook into two projections at the tip of the abdomen. When the abdominal muscles contract and the maggot releases its hold on its tail, the force of the contraction propels the maggot up into the air.

The cheese skipper is not alone among the Diptera in being able to skip; at least thirty-two species in five families can hop to it. Most of these larvae, however, leap as they emerge from the tree trunk or leaf mine in which they've been feeding to find a safe spot in the soil to pupate. Speed is of the essence, since a long, slow, legless crawl across the ground leaves a maggot vulnerable to both predators and desiccation. *Piophila casei* is the best known among skipping Diptera since it performs not in the relative isolation of a forest glade but rather in the brightly illuminated kitchens of horrified homeowners. Its behavior is also the most puzzling among the skipping Diptera since, as Oldroyd writes, "*Piophila casei* is notorious for eating out a cavity in, say, a large ham, without showing any trace on the surface; what use is the power to leap inside a ham?"—a question bound to leave philosophers puzzling for years to come.

To some extent, the modern larder has cooled cheese skipper ardor—the maggots have no tolerance for refrigeration or even mildly warm temperatures, in excess of 145 degrees Fahrenheit. The refrigerator and the fondue pot are no doubt cheese skipper nightmares. Modern hygiene, too, has almost made *Piophila casei*, which used to delight in infesting meat particles clinging to uncleaned meat or cheese slicers, an endangered species. But *Piophila casei* has an unlikely ally in the form of the so-called gourmet. The cheese skipper's habit of burrowing under the surface of hams or cheeses has led at times to its being accidentally ingested; some people, for whatever reason, steadfastly maintain that the experience is highly desirable and that maggoty cheese is an incomparable delicacy. The practice, however, is not to be recommended. The larvae are extraordinarily resistant to stomach acid and their strong mouthparts can lacerate stomach linings and cause physical harm. They can also cause psychological distress, to say the least, as they are passed out, still alive, at the end of the digestive process. So if a self-proclaimed gourmet offers you a chunk of suspicious-looking Swiss or cheddar, you'd be well advised to do the skipping (before *Piophila casei* can) and avoid the whole thing altogether.

COCKROACH PARASITES

Whatever its other shortcomings may be, a wise cockroach knows not to count its eggs before they hatch. Although as a group cockroaches have overcome sprays, dusts, powders, pounding feet, and hurled imprecations, they haven't quite figured out how to cope with their major enemies—the chalcidoid wasps, sometimes less than two millimeters (¹⁄₁₀ inch) in length, that parasitize their egg capsules.

Take *Supella longipalpa*, the brown-banded cockroach, a domiciliary species as entomologists like to say (meaning that you can find it in your Shredded Wheat box or behind your kitchen clock). Female brown-banded cockroaches package their eggs in a tough leathery capsule called an ootheca. With a noticeable dearth of maternal concern, they attach their oothecae to a surface (often inside a dark drawer or cupboard) with a mucilaginous substance and give them not another thought. There, after the biblical forty days and forty nights, the eggs develop, ostensibly undisturbed, and finally hatch. *Comperia merceti*, a chalcidoid wasp ranging in size from 1.5 to 2.5 millimeters, makes a living finding little cockroach nurseries and laying eggs in them. These tiny wasps wander around houses day and night, barber-pole-striped antennae incessantly tapping the ground, in search of oothecae. Once an ootheca is discovered, the female checks it out, tapping with her antennae for up to half an hour, occasionally stopping to dismount,

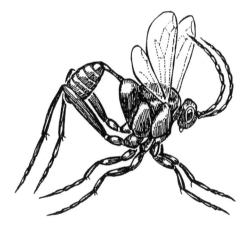

Cockroach parasites: "I hope there is such a thing as reincarnation—anything would be an improvement . . ."

move a centimeter or two away, and stand motionless for one to five minutes, antennae clamped together, before resuming her inspection.

Once the egg case passes muster, oviposition begins. Egglaying by the wasp can take almost an hour. From three to fifteen wasps eventually result from a single round of oviposition. Development takes about thirty-three days to complete, about a week less than the baby cockroaches would have needed had they not been eaten by wasp grubs.

Comperia merceti is indeed hell on six legs as far as brown-banded cockroaches are concerned. In some places in Hawaii, nearly 100 percent of all egg cases are parasitized. But there's only so much a tiny wasp can do. Among other things, not all cockroach species are as accommodating as the brown-banded cockroach. Some tropical species, like *Blaberus craniifer* and *Leucophaea maderae*, actually carry their oothecae inside their abdomens for the entire incubation period, so that nymphs hatch inside their mother's body. Needless to say, this arrangement makes life difficult for the egg-eating parasite. Other domiciliary cockroaches much larger than the brown-banded, such as the Oriental (*Blatta orientalis*) and the American (*Periplaneta americana*) cockroaches, deposit their oothecae on the ground before the eggs hatch but, for tiny *Comperia merceti*, their cases are too tough to crack.

Lest these species get too smug, it should be noted that there's more than one way to skin a cockroach. The imported ensign wasp, *Evania appendigaster*, is huge by chalcidoid standards, reaching a forewing length of seven millimeters ($\frac{1}{3}$ inch). This large all-black species specializes on the egg cases of the larger household cockroaches. Upon locating an egg case, the female lies on her side along the long axis of the case, braces her legs against it, and penetrates the tough exterior with her ovipositor in fifteen to thirty minutes. Only a single egg is laid. The grub that hatches is equipped with sharp, serrated mandibles to allow it to saw through the leathery egg shells inside the case. After five molts and feasting on eggs in between, the grub pupates and finally emerges as an adult, chewing its way out through the remnants of the ootheca.

Ensign wasps (or Evaniidae) owe their common name to the unusual appearance of the abdomen, which attaches high on the thorax instead of at the normal location low down between the third pair of legs. Moreover, the tail end is laterally flattened and almost triangular in shape, resembling a small hand flag. From the cockroach point of view, however, this is one flag even the American cockroach won't stand to salute.

14

DEATH-WATCH BEETLES

Metaphorical language notwithstanding, things really do crawl out of the woodwork every now and then. More often than not, what crawls out are beetles in the family Anobiidae, variously called furniture beetles, powder post beetles, and a few other more picturesque things. Adults, which are seldom seen, emerge from the wood in the spring or early summer. They're rather unprepossessing as beetles go, generally $\frac{1}{10}$ to $\frac{3}{10}$ inch in length, mostly brown or black in color, and vaguely humpbacked when seen in profile. Eggs are generally laid in wood pores; unlike termites, furniture beetles can infest freestanding wood that is not in direct contact with soil. After the eggs hatch, the whitish tiny grubs construct numerous galleries from $\frac{1}{16}$ to $\frac{1}{4}$ inch across, which end up packed with finely powdered dry droppings. These beetles spend their larval days tunneling through seasoned wood, neatly reducing it to fine sawdust and perforating the surface

Death-watch beetles: "Come on, let's really give them something to think about."

with numerous small shot holes. Throughout the winter, however, the growing larvae play carpenter mostly unobserved.

Anobiids are major structural pests for several reasons. First and foremost is the fact that they can live and breed successfully for many generations without giving themselves away. Thus, they can infest lumber and deign to make an appearance only after it has been converted to chairs, tables, wheel spokes, shovel handles, two-by-fours, wall paneling, floorboards, or handcarved duck decoys. Often the only visible sign of their presence comes when structural timbers give way and an infested chair, wall, or floor collapses.

Despite the depredations of anobiids, much of their bad reputation is a bit overblown. Take *Testobium rufovillosum*, known as the death-watch beetle. Its presence in a house was supposed to portend death. This idea arose not so much from the fact that the larvae assiduously chew though wood but rather from a peculiar behavior the adults engage in when it comes time for courtship. Female *Testobium rufovillosum* make a distinctive tapping sound by knocking their heads against the sides of their burrows. This sound supposedly attracts male beetles. The behavior isn't unprecedented among house-dwelling insects; there is a psocid or booklouse that makes a similar tapping sound by rapping a thickened knob near its tail against a resonating surface.

These sounds may be siren songs to male insects but they have scared the heck out of male and female people alike for centuries. Death-watch beetles are at least partly responsible for some of the evening sounds traditionally attributed to ghosts in haunted houses. One nineteenth-century author remarked, "The fate of many a nervous and superstitious patient has been accelerated by listening, in the silence and solitude of night, to this imagined knell of his approaching dissolution."

The biological basis for this bizarre behavior on the part of the death-watch beetle is at the moment unknown. Perhaps this beetle makes sounds because, to insects that tunnel through wood for a living, life would otherwise just be "boring."

DRUGSTORE BEETLES

Changing times require changing language, and one such updated expression may be "snug as a bug in a drug." The drugstore beetle, *Stegobium paniceum*, eats just about anything that is stored dry on a shelf, from macaroni to medicine. It appears to have no cultural biases either and it's as comfortable infesting instant custard as it is consuming a steady diet of cayenne pepper. The drugstore beetle has apparently been getting into people's pantries for millennia. Remains of *Stegobium paniceum* were found in a vase in the tomb of King Tutankhamen that had been sealed for over three thousand years. Evidently, even royalty couldn't rid themselves of the pest.

One reason that the drugstore beetle is so adept at what it does is that it's easily overlooked. Full grown, it measures a mere $1/10$ inch in length. As tiny beetles go, *S. paniceum* is fairly nondescript, light brown, humpbacked in shape, covered with a fine coat of hair, and otherwise undistinguished except for the fact that it's eating your Raisin Bran. Eggs about $1/50$ inch long are laid on virtually any dry food material.

Drugstore beetles: "Only if you smoke 'em."

17

Since each female can lay up to one hundred eggs, what the drugstore beetle lacks in size it can quite readily make up for in number. After about a week at room (or pantry) temperature, the eggs hatch and the yellowish white hairy grubs go to work. They pupate in one or two months inside a silken tube bedecked with bits of food material and emerge several days later as adults to seek out new treats to eat. Undisturbed, these beetles can undergo up to six generations a year.

S. paniceum is not alone in its closet peregrinations. Its close relative, the cigarette beetle, *Lasioderma serricorne*, shares a similar lifestyle, with the notable exception that it has an extraordinary predilection for package and chewing tobacco, cigars, and cigarettes—despite the fact that tobacco contains large quantities of nicotine, a substance used as a commercial insecticide for over 250 years. *L. serricorne* is also known to infest furniture, particularly furniture upholstered with straw, hair, or tow (and in fact it's sometimes called the towbug). The cigarette beetle is similar in appearance to the drugstore beetle but can be distinguished by its redder tint and by the lack of grooves on the wing covers. The grubs are also considerably more hirsute than are drugstore beetles.

While it's nice to feel that one has some of the same problems as Egyptian royalty, the feeling palls in the face of the unanticipated shortage of every ingredient in a recipe. About the only way to control drugstore and cigarette beetles is to get rid of existing infestations and prevent new ones. Spilled food on shelves should be removed and all new items should be stored in tightly sealed containers, preferably metal or glass (cardboard presents no challenge to these beetles). Contaminated food can be recovered by heating in an oven for thirty minutes at 130 degrees Fahrenheit or by freezing at 0 degrees for four days or more. The threat of drugstore beetles, then, can be eliminated just by exercising a little "shelf-control."

GREENHOUSE WHITEFLIES

In winter, when the vegetation lies buried beneath a blanket of white, a greenhouse is a pleasant respite from the realities of winter—that is, unless the vegetation in the greenhouse happens to buried beneath a blanket of whiteflies. The greenhouse whitefly, *Trialeurodes vaporariorum*, is a tiny aphidlike insect with a prodigious capacity for reproduction. Like other members of the family Aleyrodidae, adult greenhouse whiteflies have four membranous wings dusted with a white waxy powder. At 6/100 inch in length, the greenhouse whitefly is a midsized member of the family. *T. vaporariorum* is not exactly a household name, but it is a greenhouse-hold name worldwide; the insect infests greenhouses throughout the Western Hemisphere, Europe, New Zealand, and Australia. Where the climate is accommodating, as in Hawaii, greenhouse whiteflies can even establish themselves in the great outdoors. One secret of their success is that they'll eat almost anything that's put in front of them and are a particular nuisance on tomatoes, lettuce, cucumbers, and ornamentals.

The damage they cause to vegetables indoors and out is not so much a matter of direct injury but rather the insult they add to it. Greenhouse whiteflies, like aphids, have needlelike piercing stylets for mouthparts, which they use to tap into the vascular sap. Since sap is pretty dilute as far as insect required daily allowances are concerned, the insects

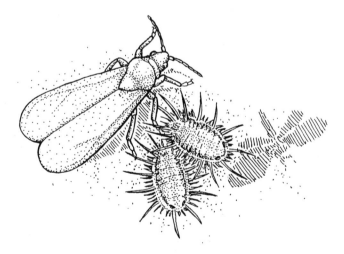

Greenhouse whiteflies: "This is the life, sitting around sucking sap . . . Say, what was that passing shadow?"

have to pump through vast quantities of sap to sustain themselves. The excess simply passes out the other end in the form of a sugary secretion called honeydew. In a heavy infestation, honeydew liberally coats the leaves of whatever plants the whiteflies are plumbing and provides a perfect medium for supporting the growth of sooty mold, a fungus that blackens the leaf surfaces of the plants, generally reducing their health and well-being in the process.

Female greenhouse whiteflies lay abundant quantities of eggs, up to five hundred or more over their lifetime. The eggs are characteristically deposited in a circle; since the female can't be bothered to stop eating as she lays eggs, she inserts her stylets into a convenient spot and pivots her body around her mouthparts as she oviposits. Each egg is placed on top of a long slender stalk. The eggs hatch in six to eight days and the emerging nymphs are pale green, flat, semitransparent, and equipped with alternating long and short waxy filaments. After their first molt, the nymphs lose their antennae and all of their legs. After about two to three weeks of necessarily staying in the same place (lacking any appendages to carry them elsewhere) and avidly sucking plant sap, the nymphs molt into a resting stage, during which transformation into adulthood takes place over a period of twelve to sixteen days. Emerging whiteflies, equipped again with antennae and legs and for the first time with wings, resume the sap-sipping routine. All life stages of the greenhouse whitefly can be found at any given time in an infested greenhouse.

Greenhouse whiteflies are not, however, without their worries. Chief among these is *Encarsia formosa*, a parasitic wasp in the family Aphelinidae that is totally devoted to greenhouse whiteflies. Female wasps lay their eggs inside the nymphs or resting stages. The whitefly slowly blackens and, after four weeks, what emerges is not a greenhouse whitefly but rather a parasitic wasp. *Encarsia formosa* has been released inside greenhouses around the world to wreck havoc with the private lives of greenhouse whiteflies.

As for the private life of *Encarsia formosa*, it's unusual even by insect standards. Males are extremely rare and can be found only when whitefly populations are very high. Unlike their mates, male wasps do not parasitize greenhouse whiteflies. Actually, they parasitize females of their own species by developing inside the bodies of distaff greenhouse whiteflies (a practice known as adelphoparasitism). While in human terms, living off one's spouse is deplored, casting aspersions is of little use. After all, people in glass houses (or greenhouses) shouldn't throw stones.

MEDITERRANEAN FLOUR MOTHS

If you think you're on top of the latest trends for getting into bran in a big way, you're at least a hundred years behind *Anagasta kuehniella,* the Mediterranean flour moth. Mediterranean flour moths have been getting into bran—as well as flour meal, breakfast foods, corn, whole grains, dried fruits, nuts, and almost everything else in the cupboard—since they were first discovered in this country around 1889. Nobody's closet is safe; Mediterranean flour moths have even been found nibbling pollen stored by fellow insects in beehives.

As its name suggests, the Mediterranean flour moth is a native of Europe; it was discovered in flour mills in Germany in 1877. It was far from a welcome discovery (except perhaps from the point of view of the entomologist who got to lay claim to discovering a new species), since the creamy white larvae, ornamented with a few black spots and a pinkish hue, make a practice of spinning little silken tubes in which to hide while they nibble on flour and grain parts. Although individual caterpillars are small and easily overlooked—they're only a half inch long at maturity—collectively they can bring a flour mill to a grinding halt. Masses of flour webbed together in chutes and elevators can clog and stop machinery. Shortly after its discovery in this country, the Mediterranean flour moth rocketed to fame as the most serious pest of commercial flour mills.

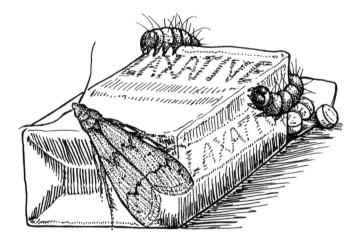

Mediterranean flour moth: "Constipation? Not as long as we stick to whole grains!"

Fame, however, is fleeting, and today the Mediterranean flour moth is more likely to cause only a moment's consternation to a homeowner than it is to cause the economic ruination of a captain of industry. Modern fumigation methods have all but eliminated *Anagasta kuehniella* from the mills. Human fumigators aren't the only force of nature with which Mediterranean flour moths have had to contend, however. A sack of flour is fraught with perils. Refrigeration, for example, spells death to this refugee from the milder climates of Europe. *Anagasta kuehniella* is also susceptible to infection by *Bacillus thuringiensis*, a bacterium that specializes in turning caterpillars into pulpy goo (*B. t.*, as it's known commercially, was first discovered in this species in Germany). There are also parasitic wasps such as *Venturia canescens* that make a practice of inserting their eggs into the bodies of unsuspecting caterpillars, so that their offspring can consume the inner organs of their host at their leisure.

If it seems that finding a caterpillar in a flour bin is a little like finding a needle in a haystack, *Venturia canescens* does a little detective work in finding its prey. As they feed, the larvae of the Mediterranean flour moth produce chemical secretions from their mandibular glands, marking their little pile of flour as already occupied. What was designed as a warning to other caterpillars to go elsewhere for dinner, however, is an engraved dinner invitation for parasitic wasps, who can also detect the chemical. The wasps simply follow the scent to its source and chow down (proving that there are worse things than having to share your dinner with a member of your own family).

Adult Mediterranean flour moths are at best unprepossessing in appearance. The wings, with a span of an inch or less, are brownish gray in color and marked with zigzagging black lines at the tip. At rest, the moths have the distinctive habit of elevating the front end of their bodies. What makes a Mediterranean flour moth even more difficult to recognize is that it often flies about in the company of a number of its near relations—*Ephestia elutella* (the tobacco moth), *Cadra cautella* (the almond or fig moth), and *Cadra figulilella* (the raisin moth). All are members of the same family (the Pyralidae) and are so similar in appearance and habits that they were once all considered to be members of the same genus.

One way these moths recognize each other in the dark recesses of closets, boxes, or flour mills is by chemical communication. Females of each species produce a unique blend of attractants or pheromones. To make sure no mistakes are made, males of these species produce pheromones as well. While females simply expose the glands at the tip of their abdomens and allow the winds to waft away their pheromones, males are a bit more aggressive—they approach the females, expose the glands on their forewings, line up head to head with the females, whip their abdomens up and around, and strike the females repeatedly about the head and thorax with their abdomens. This is not some form of ritualized spouse abuse—the males have glands on the tips of their abdomens and use this action as a way of bringing them close to a female's antennae. So, you can't really blame them for getting rambunctious—anybody who *eats* his oats is probably entitled to *feel* his oats now and then.

ODD BEETLES

Entomologists as a group are hard to impress; the bizarre is more or less the order of the day. *Thylodrias contractus*, however, is so peculiar even entomologists refer to it simply as the "odd beetle." *Thylodrias contractus* didn't even have an approved common name until 1917; the literature on this insect invariably includes such adjectives as "remarkable," "peculiar," curious," "queer," astonishing," "anomalous," "unique," "strange," and "extraordinary," and, only one year after it was discovered in the United States, it appeared on the cover of *Entomological News* as the most interesting insect of the year.

What is known about the life cycle of the odd beetle is certainly odd, although it's even odder that so little is known at all about it, given that it seems to be found only in human habitations and has no more natural habitat to speak of. It shows up most frequently in the drawers, shelves, and cupboards of entomologists (it was known briefly as the tissue paper bug), although this probably reflects the fact that only when it is found in the drawers, desks, shelves, and cupboards of entomologists is it ever recognized to be *Thylodrias contractus*. Nobody

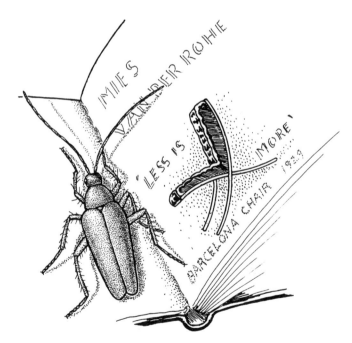

Odd beetles: " 'Think small'—I like this guy!"

knows for sure what it eats, although captive individuals feed readily on dry cooked beef liver and dead insects; one expects that odd beetles are more likely to encounter the latter than the former in the drawers, desks, and shelves of entomologists, but one can never be too sure. Odd beetles are believed to have originated in Asia (larval skins have been found in Iran in archaeological excavations of sites that are about four thousand years old), but they now can be found throughout North America and Europe as well.

Taxonomically, odd beetles have been placed in the family Dermestidae, which, containing such oddities as the larder beetles, hide beetles, and carpet beetles, seems about the right place for it. Classifying *Thylodrias contractus* is difficult because no two investigators describe it the same way. Everyone agrees that female odd beetles are wingless, but males have been described with hind wings longer than the elytra (or hardened forewings), a bit shorter than the elytra, as little tiny stubs, and as missing altogether. Adult males are said to range in size from 2 to 4.5 millimeters and females from 3.6 to 5 millimeters. The larval stage of the odd beetle is probably the least unorthodox life stage. Like many dermestids, the grubs are crescent-shaped and equipped with long reddish brown hairs that form rows at the posterior edge of all but the last two abdominal segments.

If the larva is the least unorthodox stage, the pupa is easily the most peculiar. Pupation occurs partly inside the old larval skin, which splits along the back from the head only as far as the fifth abdominal segment. The shiny, creamy white pupal skin is covered with long, fine yellow hairs. A thick tuft of coarse brown hairs near the tail end anchors the pupa in place in the larval skin. It's not easy to say how long it takes an odd beetle to go from normal egg and larvahood through bizarre pupation and adulthood. It seems to vary from about 280 days to over three years. Larvae on a subsistence diet are supposed to be able to survive up to five years. Odd beetles under less than ideal conditions also engage in the rather odd practice of retrogressive molting. Instead of growing larger with each molt, they get smaller and smaller with each molt until they molt into miniature adults, which is an odd end, indeed.

SCALE INSECTS

As temperatures and leaves begin to fall outdoors, people tend to focus their attention once again on their houseplants. Occasionally, houseplants, particularly ferns, die in a heartrending and seemingly inexplicable manner. Their foliage turns yellow, leaves drop right and left, and in general all is not well with their world. Close inspection, however, can reveal numerous brownish raised spots all over the undersides of leaves and along the stems. Appearances notwithstanding, this particular plague is insectan in origin. Scale insects are among the greatest scourge to houseplants and greenhouse plants. There are over twenty species making a living in this manner and they can be divided into two groups. Armored scales or members of the family Diaspididae are characterized by a hard shell made of wax and cast skins that can be lifted off the body. The shells are enlarged as the insects rotate their bodies and exude wax. This group includes in its ranks the oleander scale, the greedy scale, the California red scale (a major citrus pest), the rose scale, and the fern scale. Members of the second group are called the tortoise scales, not inappropriately—the protective shell that covers the body is convex like a turtle's shell. Also, turtle-fashion, the shell can't be removed from the body. These include the soft scale, the hemispherical scale, the black scale, and the long scale.

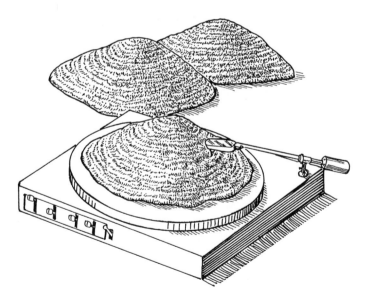

Scale insects: "Darn, Bernie's skipping again."

The life cycle of the scale is hardly worthy of emulation by human standards. Most come from eggs deposited underneath the mother's shell for protection, although some scale insects go in for live birth (no great accomplishment for humans but a rarity among insects). After they hatch, the young nymphs, called crawlers, crawl out from under their mother, find a nice spot, and insert their slender mouthparts into the plant. Then, they sit and suck. As they suck, they undergo two to three molts, progressively losing seemingly vital body parts, including eyes, legs, and antennae. The cast skins from each molt are incorporated into the protective shell covering the insect. For females, things remain pretty much as they are, but males undergo an additional molt in which they develop new legs, eyes, antennae, and wings. Once equipped, they go off in search of females. Most of the time, they haven't got far to go—females are totally motionless and in some species the ratio of males to females is around 1:5,000, so the challenge is, to say the least, minimal. In any event, after mating, the male dies and ceases to be of interest to anyone. The female, however, continues to breed and to produce up to a thousand eggs until she dies (ostensibly from exhaustion or boredom).

Not all scale insects are enemies of humanity. *Laccifer lacca* is a scale insect from India whose waxy platelike shell is the source of shellac. The common name *lakh* derives from the Hindi word for "100,000" and refers to the huge aggregations that these insects form on their host trees (reaching densities of 150 per square inch). The coalesced shells are collected, ground, filtered, and formed into flat sheets, the "shell-lac" of commerce. Lac's uses, even in today's synthetic society, are many due to its remarkable properties. It's resilient, resistant to solvents, nonpoisonous, odorless, and unlike synthetics completely biodegradable. For these reasons, it's been used in electrical apparatus, sealing wax, shoe polish, printing ink, furniture polish, billiard balls, chocolate glazes, and, ironically, insecticide sprays. Its most important use historically was in the record industry. From 1921 to 1928, 18,000 tons of shellac went into making 260 million records in Europe. World War II effectively put an end to the shellac record industry. Synthetic substitutes that were technically superior to shellac were developed when shellac supplies were cut off. About the only place where shellac records are still made is India, where there's so much shellac available that there's a premium on using it. It's an active cottage industry and many people even today make their living gathering and processing *Laccifer lacca;* these individuals can truly by said to be working "for scale."

References

Aldrich, J. R. 1988. Chemical ecology of the Heteroptera. *Ann. Rev. Ent.* 33:211–38.

Blatchley, W. S. 1926. *Heteroptera or True Bugs of Eastern North America.* Indianapolis: The Nature Publishing Co.

Busvine, J. R. 1966. *Insects and Hygiene.* London: Methuen and Co.

Cowan, F. 1865. *Curious Facts in the History of Insects.* Philadelphia: J. B. Lippincott.

Foelix, R. F. 1982. *Biology of Spiders.* Cambridge, Mass.: Harvard University Press.

Jackson, R. R., and R. J. Brassington. 1987. The biology of *Pholcus phalangioides* (Araneae: Pholcidae): predatory versatility, araenophagy and aggressive mimicry. *J. Zool.* 211:227–38.

Johnson, W. T., and H. H. Lyon. 1976. *Insects that Feed on Trees and Shrubs.* Ithaca, N.Y.: Comstock Publishing Assn.

Kearney, P. W. 1958. Shellac. In *Illustrated Library of the Natural Sciences,* ed. E. M. Weyer, 1543–51. N.Y.: Simon and Schuster.

Matheson, R. 1950. *Medical Entomology.* Ithaca, N.Y.: Comstock Publishing Assn.

Maughan, O. E. 1978. The biology and behavior of *Pholcus muriacola. Am. Midl. Nat.* 100:483–87.

Mertins, J. W. 1981. Life history and morphology of the odd beetle, *Thylodrias contractus. Ann. Ent. Soc. Am.* 74:576–81.

Oldroyd, H. 1964. *The Natural History of Flies.* London: Weidenfeld and Nicolson.

Phelan, P. L., and T. C. Baker. 1987. Evolution of male pheromones in moths: reproductive isolation through sexual selection? *Science* 235:205–7.

Smith, K. V. G. 1980. *Insects and Other Arthropods of Medical Importance.* London: British Museum.

Chapter 2

Farm Workers

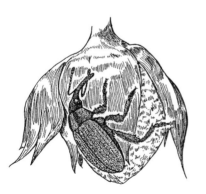

ANGOUMOIS GRAIN MOTHS

While there are thousands of individuals in major urban areas of our country interested in investing in grain futures, there are millions of individuals (specifically, of *Sitotroga cerealella*) in rural areas of our country actively *infesting* in grain futures, without ever paying a broker's fee. *Sitotroga cerealella*, the Angoumois grain moth, is probably the most serious grain pest among the various and sundry moths that make their living infesting stored products. It was first noticed in the United States in 1728, damaging grain in North Carolina, presumably introduced from Europe in wheat brought by settlers. Its rather exotic common name derives from the fact that the species first attracted scientific attention by devastating the province of Angoumois, France, around 1736 and was as a result the subject of a rather lengthy monograph by two representatives of the French Royal Academy of Sciences several years later (entitled *History of an Insect which Devours the Grain of Angoumois*).

Sitotroga cerealella is, for a small brown moth, fairly distinctive in appearance. With a wingspan of about ½ inch, and a buff-brown color interrupted by a few dark spots, it superficially resembles many of the other small buff-brown moths infesting stored grain. However, close inspection reveals a characteristic fringe of hairs on both front and hind wings and an unmistakable shape to the hind wing—that of a finger pointing in accusation (perhaps like the finger of its countryman Émile Zola).

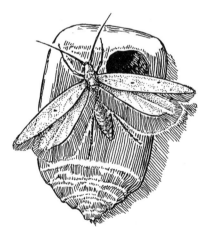

Angoumois grain moths: "*Mon dieu!* American food, it just cannot compare to *la cuisine française.*"

The moth is the only stage of *Sitotroga cerealella* likely to be even remotely familiar to anyone but the most devoted entomologists, since all the other life stages are inconspicuous, to say the least. Females lay eggs on grain not only in storage but also in the field as it is ripening. On corn ears, the eggs are shoved deep down between kernels; on wheat in the field or in shocks, the eggs are laid on the heads. As for stored grain in bins, eggs are simply laid on kernels in the surface layer. A single female can lay anywhere from forty to four hundred whitish eggs, which turn red as they mature in anywhere from four days to a month. Upon hatching, the tiny caterpillar, whitish in color with a yellow head, constructs a silken sheath and then bores a hole into a kernel of grain. Once ensconced inside, it will continue to feed unobtrusively for four more instars, or developmental stages. Generally in wheat, there is only one caterpillar per kernel; in corn, occasionally two or more will bunk together. Since sorghum kernels are too small to hold even a single caterpillar, *S. cerealella* gathers several kernels into a ball, all tied with silk, and feeds inside the ball.

Development inside the kernel condo takes from five to seven weeks, depending on temperature (the species is rather sensitive to cold). When ready to pupate, the caterpillar constructs an escape hatch—a circular "window" partially cut out of the external surface of the kernel. The larva then spins a cocoon to line its feeding chamber and pupates. When the moth emerges, it escapes from the kernel with ease through the prefabricated escape hatch.

Sitotroga cerealella is indeed a major cause of injury to stored grain but it is also a major source of insult to grain handlers by contributing to a skin condition known as straw, hay, or grain itch. While *S. cerealella* isn't directly responsible, it may as well be, since it is the major host for the mite *Pyemotes tritici*, the grain or straw itch mite. Up until 1882, it was assumed that the mites that infested people who handled straw or grain fed on straw or grain, a not unreasonable assumption. F. M. Webster, however, by careful scrutiny determined that *Pyemotes tritici* was not a harmless vegetarian gone astray on a human arm or leg, but was rather a career carnivore accustomed to consuming the flesh and fluids of Angoumois grain moth larvae. Infestations by the mites, which come in contact with humans accidentally, although temporary, are nonetheless irritating, characterized by intense itching often over the entire body. Vesicular (blisterlike) eruptions appear twelve to sixteen hours after the initial infestation and are accompanied by headache, fever, joint pain, and even nausea and vomiting. In view of the assocation between itch mites and Angoumois grain moths, perhaps the safest way to handle grain is through a broker on the Board of Trade, after all.

BLUEGRASS BILLBUGS

Bluegrass as a musical genre has its fans, but in pastures it has no greater fan then *Sphenophorus parvulus*, the bluegrass billbug. The bluegrass billbug is one of several species of curculionids, or snout beetles, that make their living feeding on stalks of tender young seedlings at or below the ground level. *Sphenophorus parvulus* is partial to Kentucky bluegrass but will also obligingly feed on timothy, redtop, corn, wheat, and other small grains. As is the case for most snout beetles, the bluegrass billbug's most distinctive feature is its snout, which is long, curved, and about one-third as long as the remainder of the quarter-inch body. The bluegrass billbug uses the tiny mouthparts at the tip of the snout to excavate a hole in the stem of a grass plant, into which an egg is deposited. The chunky, white legless grubs hatch in one to two weeks and go about the business of hollowing out the pith and root crown of the hostplant. Full-grown larvae pupate in the stem or soil. After pupation, the adults emerge in about eight days and resume the attack on the grasses. The whole process can be completed in less than a month and a half. Since adult beetles feed on the developing leaves layered in the center of the young plant, those plants that survive damage show a characteristic transverse row of identical holes at ap-

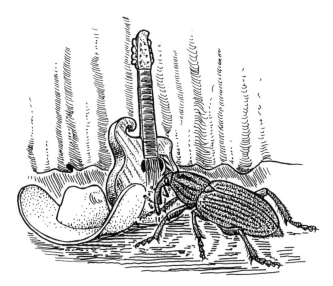

Bluegrass billbugs: "I love that high, lonesome sound."

proximately the same spot across the leaves, somewhat akin to paper dolls, beetle-style.

Despite the fact that they undergo only one generation a year, billbugs can cause considerable damage. Adults and larvae can stunt and even kill young corn plants and reduce yields in hayfields, pasture crops, and sodlands. Fans will be relieved to hear, however, that name notwithstanding, bluegrass of the "Monroe" variety is resistant to "Bill"-bugs.

BOLL WEEVILS

Imagine if you can a force of nature so awesome and so immutable that it can close down factories, depreciate land values, disrupt railroad business, cause bank failures, and create massive unemployment and homelessness. Now imagine that this force of nature is only a quarter of an inch long, tannish to brown in color, covered with yellowish scaly hairs, and equipped with a slender curving snout about half the length of its body. This agronomic nightmare is the notorious cotton boll weevil. *Anthonomus grandis* has earned the dubious title of "most costly insect in the history of American agriculture." The boll weevil wasn't always the scourge of American cotton farmers; in fact, before about 1892 it was known in the United States only by a few entomologists enamored of beetles in the family Curculionidae (commonly called weevils).

The boll weevil was first collected near Vera Cruz, Mexico, in the 1830s and was thought to be indigenous to tropical Mesoamerica, feeding on wild cotton and its relatives in the plant family Malvaceae. By 1880, however, it was observed feeding on cultivated cotton in Mexico and by 1892 it crossed the Rio Grande River and first set foot (or all

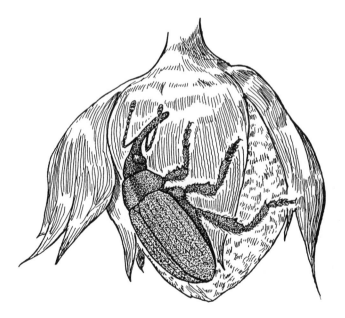

Boll weevils: "Nothing beats three squares a day."

35

six feet) on American soil. Since the beetles are capable of flying sixty or more miles in search of food, conquering the cotton belt of North America provided little challenge to *Anthonomus grandis*. By 1903 it reached Louisiana; four years later it was found in Oklahoma, Arkansas, and Mississippi. Alabama and Florida fell victim by 1913, and by 1916 it reached the Atlantic coast. Its westward movement was somewhat slower; although it reached Arizona by 1920, it didn't make it to California for another sixty years.

Everywhere the boll weevil went, disaster followed in its wake. Its feeding habits are the source of all the trouble. Females use their long slender snouts to burrow into the blossom buds, or squares, of cotton. They then lay their eggs in the puncture and move on in search of more squares. The hatching grubs feed inside the squares on the floral parts and soon clean out the bud. After five to seven days and several molts, the grub pupates inside the cavity it has formed by its incessant feeding; the walls of the cavity are lined with excrement that has been compacted by the movements of the larva in the square. Late in development, boll weevil grubs release pectinases, enzymes that cause the cotton square to open, discolor, and fall to the ground. Between one and two weeks after the square hits the ground, a mature weevil emerges, ready to mate and lay eggs within the week.

The fact that female boll weevils lay only one or two eggs per square and lay up to three hundred eggs over their lifetime is bad news for cotton farmers. Moreover, in the warmer parts of their range, boll weevils undergo up to seven generations. Thus, only a year after it was first found in western Mississippi, it was responsible for a 63 percent decline in cotton production in the state. The only thing in nature that puts a stop to the destruction is winter. When the weather turns cold, the amazingly prolific reproductive organs of adult weevils shrivel up and the beetles hide out under leaf litter in woods, along fences, and in other protected places. As for *unnatural* things that put a stop to the boll weevil, today about 40 percent of all agricultural insecticides used in the United States are sprayed onto cotton primarily to control boll weevils. Despite the chemical arsenal, the little weevil still causes as much as $200 to $300 million annually in losses and adds an average of 3½ to 4 cents to every 60 cents per pound of cotton.

The boll weevil has had major political, scientific, and social impact over and above its agricultural impact. The town of Enterprise, Alabama, which teetered on the edge of collapse when boll weevils decimated its economic base of cotton, resorted to diversification of crops to pull out of its economic doldrums and years later erected a statue of the weevil in the town square (as opposed to the cotton square) in gratitude for its newfound economic stability. And the boll weevil has even made a musical contribution, by serving as the inspiration for the famed "Ballad of the Boll Weevil." As the chorus relates,

> Oh the boll weevil is a little black bug,
> Come from Mexico they say,
> Come all the way from Texas,
> Just-a-lookin for a place to stay,
> Just-a-lookin for a home,
> Just-a-lookin for a home.

Unfortunately, from the perspective of cotton farmers all across America, the boll weevil has found a home to its taste and appears in no hurry to relocate.

CABBAGEWORMS

If familiarity does indeed breed contempt, then *Pieris rapae*, the cabbage white butterfly, is the most contemptible of butterflies. Not only is it on the wing from early morning to dusk, it flies from late March through mid-October, even in the northern reaches of New England. It is as familiar to New Yorkers as to Californians and, in fact, can be found in every state of the Union. The butterfly is equally at home in rural meadows and in the thick of downtown traffic, where it offers city dwellers an entomological respite from cockroaches, bedbugs, fleas, and other urban offenses. In impeccable butterfly fashion, these little insects, rarely measuring more than an inch or so from head to tip of abdomen, flit from flower to flower sipping nectar, their creamy white wings suffused with yellow and adorned with black tips and one or two black spots on the forewing. Yet for those familiar with the life history of the cabbage white, the sight of this butterfly engaging in activities that might otherwise inspire a flood of poetic sentiments brings only resentment and ill temper. While incurable romantics maintain that butterflies are here to spread joy and contentment, the more entomologically minded realize the cabbage white is here to spread its offspring—the all-too-familiar cabbageworm—over the face of the continent.

Anyone who has ever attempted to grow cole crops (cabbages and their relatives in the plant family Cruciferae) in a home garden has

Cabbageworms

most probably encountered the cabbageworm—an inch-long, velvety green caterpillar with a narrow lemon-yellow stripe along its back. Those who missed the caterpillar can easily find ample evidence of its existence, in the form of riddled leaves, half-eaten heads of broccoli, cabbage, or cauliflower, and, to add insult to injury, round fecal pellets accumulating at the junction of leaf petiole and stem. Each year, these caterpillars cause a tremendous amount of damage, not only to home gardens, but to commercial farms as well. They feed on almost any member of the family Cruciferae, including cabbage, cauliflower, broccoli, kale, collards, brussels sprouts, turnips, horseradish, and mustards. In addition, they have been found on plants from two other families, mignonette (*Reseda* spp.) and capers (*Capparis* spp.).

The plants that fall prey to the cabbageworm's appetite share a chemical similarity. All contain compounds called glucosinolates, or mustard oil glycosides. These are the compounds that, under certain conditions (such as cooking), release odorous, sulfur-containing mustard oils—the chemicals responsible for, among other things, the odor of boiling cabbage. To most organisms, mustard oils are deadly toxic; indeed, during World War I, they formed the basis for poison gas and even today find use as emetics. But the cabbageworm dotes on them, and in fact *Pieris rapae* won't begin to eat unless it detects the compounds in its food. When mustard oils or their glycosides *are* present, however, there's no stopping the caterpillars. Even raising the concentrations of mustard oils in the leaves of the plants they feed on does not deter them; if anything, it stimulates them to eat even more. The adult butterflies are also attracted to mustard oil glycosides. Female *P. rapae* have receptors for the compounds located on their front legs (and possibly on their ovipositors) and thus are stimulated to lay eggs on plants that will be suitable for their ravenous but fussy offspring.

The ubiquity of the cabbage white butterfly is deceptive; only 120 years ago, the butterflies were completely unknown on this continent. In 1860, William Couper, a taxidermist and amateur entomologist, captured one near his home in Quebec. He was elated because, at that time, the cabbage white butterfly was known only in Europe. After correspondence with other entomologists, Couper decided that the caterpillars must have come over from Europe on a cargo ship of some sort, smuggling themselves into North America inconspicuously ensconced in cabbage heads or similar produce. Cabbage whites wasted no time in establishing themselves across the continent. By 1890, they occupied every one of the contiguous United States. Their surreptitious entry into the States and spectacular invasion afterward may merit them the appellation of "spies who came in from the cole."

CORN EARWORMS

Helicoverpa zea has as many aliases as Jesse James and enjoys a reputation to match. Its potential hostplant range includes over one hundred plants in twenty-nine families and thus is known by whatever damage it happens to be inflicting at any particular time and place. Its most common moniker—certainly well earned—is "corn earworm." *H. zea* is beyond doubt the most important pest of corn in the United States; it has been estimated that about two million acres of corn annually go to feed the corn earworm. In the East, among truck farmers, *H. zea* is known as the tomato fruitworm or vetchworm; in the Southwest it is called the cotton bollworm, in which guise it regularly inflicts massive losses upon cotton growers not only by voraciously consuming leaves and fruits but by indiscriminately spreading various fungal and bacterial plant rots as well. *H. zea* has an unerring taste for economic crops; it is the principal insect pest of soybeans in the South and can frequently convert a field of lush growth into a stark assemblage of stripped stems.

Even scientifically, the name of the insect has been much bandied about. It's been described variously through history as *Bombyx obsoleta*, *Phalaena zea*, *Heliothis umbrosus*, *H. armigera*, [form] *ochracea*, *Heliothis zea*, and various combinations and permutations in the genera *Chloridea* and *Noctua*. For the moment, *"Helicoverpa zea"* holds sway. One pos-

Corn earworms: "I was thinking of having you for dinner later in the week."

sible explanation for the nomenclatural confusion is the irritating variability of *H. zea*. The moths, approximately ¾ inch in length with a 1½ inch wingspan, defy characterization. They vary in color from dusky beige to yellow to green to grey to reddish brown. The markings are anything but distinctive—generally, there are several indistinct black or grey streaks scattered over the forewing surface. The mature larvae are equally variable—they run the gamut from beige to cream to yellow, pink, green, or black, with or without alternating light and dark longitudinal stripes along the sides. About the only consistent characteristic distinguishing the larvae is the presence of tiny sharp spines covering the skin, even of the youngest larvae. In the formative stages, the caterpillars are slightly more uniform. Female moths lay from three hundred to three thousand tiny eggs, which resemble off-white slightly flattened globes in shape. The newly hatched larvae are white, about 1 to 1.2 millimeters in length, with black heads and legs. As they progress through five, or more rarely six, larval molts, they assume a variety of patterns and colors. Pupation takes place after two to four weeks, depending on temperature and humidity, inside a silk-lined cell excavated by the caterpillar two to four inches below the soil surface. In addition to constructing a cell, the caterpillars also build a smooth passageway to just below the soil surface, to allow the moth to tunnel upward and emerge after seven to twenty-five days.

Every year, adults emerge from overwintering pupae beginning in March in the south through May in the northern extremes of the range. *H. zea* doesn't overwinter in areas where the frost line is below two to four inches (five to ten centimeters)—the buried pupae cannot tolerate freezing. This corresponds to a region extending from central Virginia through St. Louis to Topeka—roughly paralleling forty degrees north latitude. However, regions north of the line are not immune from attack. Enterprising moths fly north each spring and reach southern Canada by midsummer to breed. By virtue of such zeal, *H. zea* has extended its range in the Western Hemisphere from southern Canada to Montevideo, Uruguay, and west to Hawaii. In the southern part of the United States, *H. zea* breeds continuously, averaging seven generations a year. In the Corn Belt, it breeds more conservatively, only two or three times a season.

In corn, caterpillars burrow into the central whorl and feed on the succulent unfurled leaves. The emerging leaves, thus damaged, appear ragged—hence, yet another appellation of *H. zea*, the ragworm. As the season progresses, ears begin to silk and the silk is an overwhelming feeding and oviposition stimulus for caterpillars and moths respectively. Caterpillars feed voraciously on silk, moving through the silk to the ear, where they commence wholesale destruction of the kernels and reduce the ear tip to brown mush. Sweet corn is a particular favorite of *H. zea* and even nongardeners have certainly encountered *H. zea* in the form of unwelcome extra protein in fresh corn purchased at roadside stands or supermarkets. When infesting field corn, *H. zea* feeds *under* the hardened kernels on the softer germ.

Corn is frequently the preferred host of *H. zea* and in some areas female moths raised on corn lay up to twice as many eggs as compatriots raised on other hosts. In a pinch, however, cotton, soybeans, lima beans, alfalfa, and tomatoes will suffice. So, for that matter, will peanuts, potatoes, eggplant, chrysanthemums, gladiolus, and geraniums. There are few plants that do not suit the taste of *H. zea*. In general, they are partial to feeding on fruits and have the annoying habit of traveling from fruit to fruit, destroying far more than they consume. In this way, they can destroy up to 80 percent of tomato fruits in a given area.

Natural enemies are extremely important in the regulation of earworm populations. *H. zea* is a staple item in the diet of birds (over twenty species are recorded as feeding on *H. zea*), toads, spiders, predacious bugs, lacewings, ladybird beetles, and wasps. Voles, mice, and moles feed on the buried pupae. In addition, *H. zea* is parasitized by a number of insects, including *Trichogramma* spp., tiny wasps that parasitize the eggs. *Trichogramma* has been used successfully in inundative release biological control programs; mass release of approximately 200,000 to 300,000 wasps per acre reduces *H. zea* damage substantially. *H. zea* also falls prey to a number of diseases, particularly in wet weather; these include fungi, microsporidia, and even nematodes.

Heliocoverpa zea, however, is probably its own worst enemy. The caterpillars are exceedingly cannibalistic, with the result that one rarely, if ever, finds more than one corn earworm in an ear of corn. Cannibalism, social repercussions notwithstanding, is detrimental from an epidemiological standpoint—the habit facilitates the transmission of many of the diseases that disable the earworm. In this respect, *H. zea* differs from its close relative, *Heliothis virescens*. *H. virescens*, known as the tobacco budworm (a onetime alias of *H. zea*) or false budworm, is altogether a more temperate insect. While it can feed and develop on a number of plants, *H. virescens* concentrates its attentions on tobacco. In North Carolina, where both species are firmly established, entomologists consider *H. virescens* a "gentleman" in comparison to *H. zea*. It's not altogether surprising to find moderation in a close relative of such menace; after all, Frank James quietly turned himself in to authorities after his brother Jesse perished in a blaze of gunfire.

CORNFIELD ANTS AND CORN ROOT APHIDS

If you have a nervous feeling whenever summer begins, it may be because you have ants in your plants—in particular, *Lasius alienus americanus*, the cornfield ant, in your corn. Cornfield ants are in and of themselves nothing to get agitated about—they're light to dark brown soft-bodied ants about an inch long who for the most part go about their business of consuming insects (alive or dead) or gathering nectar to pass the time. They probably wouldn't attract any attention at all if it weren't for the company they keep. Cornfield ants have an obsession in life—they are pathologically fond of honeydew, the sugary secretion produced by aphids and other sucking insects that tap the sugar-rich vascular sap of plants.

Cornfield ants go to great lengths to insure themselves of a steady supply of honeydew. In the fall, they assiduously collect the shiny blackish oval eggs of the corn root aphid, *Anuraphis maidiradicis*, and painstakingly watch over them through the winter months. When spring arrives and the eggs begin to hatch, the ants then transport the tiny bluish green wingless nymphs to the roots of smartweed and other weeds, often traveling distances of 150 feet or more to find choice pasturage. All the aphid has to do on arrival is plug into the selected food supply, eat, and grow, which they do, obligingly producing honeydew all the while. After two to three weeks, the aphids reach ma-

Cornfield ants and corn root aphids: "Would you like your aphid for here or to go?"

turity and the adult females can reproduce parthenogenetically, or without benefit of mating. The parthenogenetic females have dispensed not only with mates but with the bother of laying eggs, and nymphs are produced full-blown right off the bat. The cornfield ants dutifully distribute these offspring in and around the roots of smartweed, corn, cotton, and other grasses and weeds and wait another eight to fourteen days to start in all over again. Since each female aphid can generate forty to fifty offspring at a clip and since this sort of thing can happen at least a dozen times each summer, cornfield ants can quickly engineer themselves a virtually inexhaustible supply of honeydew, and cornfields are quickly infested with hordes of tiny little aphids.

The corn root aphid is almost entirely dependent, as it were, on the kindness of strangers. For most of its life cycle the wingless insects depend on the ants to feed them, transport them, and protect them from their enemies. They do display one brief period of independence in late summer when a winged sexual generation appears. These individuals, with black heads, near-black legs and antennae, and a light green abdomen marked with small dark spots, can actually fly away and find food on their own. The independence, however, wanes shortly after they mate and lay eggs. The only place corn root aphid eggs can safely pass the winter is in the nest of a cornfield ant underground so, once finished with their fling with freedom, the prodigal aphids settle back into their dependent domesticity for the winter.

The cornfield ants' remarkable achievements in raising aphids have hardly endeared them to people who are in the business of raising corn. Sap feeding by the corn root aphid begins to stunt the growth of corn before it reaches even a foot in height. In dry years, serious infestations cause yellowing and reduce yields. Moreover, the aphid, which can't even get around on its own, nevertheless acts as a principal vector or carrier of maize dwarf mosaic virus of corn. Control of the corn root aphid is aimed mostly at controlling the brains of the outfit, the cornfield ants. Although ants nest too deeply through the winter to be bothered by normal plowing at six-inch depth, by mid-March they start to move up in the world, at which point plowing and disking can do them in. Eliminating weed hosts can also cut down on ants, who will transport hungry nymphs to greener pastures to keep the honeydew flowing.

This sort of roundup and relocation is analogous to the cattle drives of the Old West, in which cattle were moved to winter foraging grounds hundreds of miles from their summer range. Such drives were long, arduous undertakings for cowhands. They must be equally difficult for the cornfield ants. One wonders if the West would have been won if cowboys had to carry their cows everywhere they went.

44

CORN ROOTWORMS

You call it "corn," the Native Americans called it "maize," but six beetles in the genus *Diabrotica* call it "dinner." Collectively, *Diabrotica virgifera* and its close relatives are known as corn rootworms since in their larval stages they focus their culinary attention not on the sweet tender kernels of corn but rather on the roots. Large populations can seriously undermine the integrity of the support system of corn and cause the whole stem to buckle or lodge, giving rise to the "goosenecks" and "leaners" of rootworm insecticide commercial fame. Adult corn rootworm beetles are variously solid yellowish green (as is the case for *Diabrotica barberi*, the northern corn rootworm) or yellowish green with black stripes down the center and sides of the wing covers, or elytra, in the case of *D. virgifera*, the western corn rootworm. Unlike the larvae, the adults consume corn the more traditional way, nibbling on tender young kernels, although they are not averse to partaking of pollen, silks, and, at least for *D. virgifera*, the foliage.

Corn rootworms have been holding their own versions of sweetcorn festivals and making a nuisance of themselves in the process for thousands of years. Archaeological evidence indicates that Mesoamerican

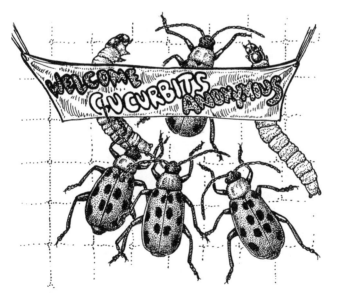

Corn rootworms: "I've tried to quit, but I just can't."

45

farmers five thousand years ago traditionally planted corn in hills, presumably to prevent lodging brought about by rootworm damage. However, such was not always the case. Three closely related species, *D. barberi*, *D. lemniscata*, and *D. cristata*, are found only in relict prairie habitats, where they feed on the roots of perennial grasses. Since they are so particular as to what they eat, these beetles lay their eggs in September and October in and around plants with permanent root systems that will assuredly be around next year to support the hatching grubs. Corn, which in its present domesticated form lives only a year, was not a sufficiently reliable hostplant until humans took up the practice of planting acres of it year after year in the same place. In fact, one of the most effective control measures for corn rootworm is simply to rotate crops—plant soybeans next year where you planted corn this year. Hatching grubs emerge, search in vain for corn roots, and starve to death, no doubt wondering what their mothers were thinking when they oviposited where they did.

Although the predilection of corn rootworms for corn may seem perfectly normal to us, it's something of an aberration in the tribe Luperini, the section of the family Chrysomelidae to which corn rootworms belong. For species in the tribe with known hostplants, over 80 percent feed not on corn and other plants in the grass family but rather on plants in the Cucurbitaceae, the cucumber family. Among these, there are even some beetles that will feed on almost anything. *Diabrotica undecimpunctata*, the spotted cucumber beetle, feeds (name notwithstanding) on potatoes, peanuts, and many other garden crops, including corn (and is known in certain circles as the southern corn rootworm).

In a family with such disparate appetites, it's most unusual that virtually everybody has a taste for cucurbitacins—extremely bitter chemicals produced almost exclusively by plants in the cucumber family. Even we humans, with our notoriously poor powers of perception, can detect cucurbitacins dissolved in water at concentrations down around one part per billion. Although we find cucurbitacins repulsive (and in fact toxic at relatively low concentrations), diabroticite beetles find them to be positively irresistible. They literally can't stop eating anything they can sink their mandibles into that has even a trace of cucurbitacins. Gorging on cucurbitacin-rich fruits, adults will even ignore their own sex pheromones. This fondness for a chemical found only in cucurbits, even in species otherwise restricted to grasses, suggests that the earliest ancestors of the tribe fed on Cucurbitaceae. For thousands of generations, a compulsion for cucurbitacins has been passed on, even to species no longer dependent on the cucurbits for sustenance. And you thought it was tough to give up smoking.

CUTWORMS

When it comes to excelling at a particular skill, nobody can cut the mustard—or any other plant—like cutworms do. Cutworms are a motley group of caterpillars in an even motlier family of moths, the Noctuidae. Noctuids include in their ranks some of the economically most important pests in the United States and are known variously as loopers, armyworms, borers, fruitworms, or cutworms, according to their habits. The cutworms are so named because of their habit of cutting seedlings and young plants at the base, leaving behind a garden full of tiny stubble.

There are basically four types of cutworms. The climbing cutworms climb up onto the plant to eat leaves, flowers, and stems. This group includes the variegated cutworm, *Peridroma saucia,* one of the most widely distributed of the cutworms. The surface-feeding cutworms, most versatile in the group, can not only cut down small plants near the base but can eat foliage and burrow into fruit as well. The dingy cutworm and the granulate cutworm fall into this category. The subterranean cutworms live virtually their whole lives underground and

Cutworms: "Think this is what Mom had in mind when she said 'Finish your vegetables'?"

nibble off plants just above the crown. They're restricted by and large to arid areas, especially in the southwestern United States.

Finally, the tunnel-making cutworms construct passageways underground into which they drag cut seedlings to consume at their leisure. The black cutworm, *A. ipsilon*, is the epitome of tunnelmakers. *Agrotis ipsilon* is one of the most destructive of all cutworms, and gardeners in the United States, Canada, Mexico, South America, Europe, Africa, and Australia have good reason to be nervous when they set out bedding plants. Black cutworms spend the winter as pupae underground. In early spring, the moths emerge and mate and then the females set off in search of places to deposit their eggs—all two thousand of them— mostly one or a few at a time on leaves and stems near the ground. The adult cutworm is a nondescript brown moth. The forewings, spanning 1½ to 2 inches, are narrow and dark and usually marked with three black lines. The hind wings in contrast are pale, almost clear.

The cutworm is the original thief in the night. The females lay eggs at night. After hatching three to six days later, the caterpillars do their dirty work at night. The newly hatched caterpillars first scrape the leaf surface; as they grow, they start to eat holes in leaves and, in the final instars, they take up the habit to which they owe their names—cutting down plants at or near the base and dragging them underground to their lairs. The caterpillars are unmistakable if you happen to be gardening late at night and catch a glimpse. They're gray, brown, or black and "greasy" looking (they're sometimes called the greasy cutworms, an appropriate name for a slippery character). One thing that makes cutworms so destructive is that they cut down many more plants than they can possibly eat and leave the remainder out on the surface. Another thing is their almost total lack of selectivity—they feed on just about anything anyone is likely to plant in the garden, including beans, broccoli, corn, cabbage, peas, tomatoes, potatoes—you name it, they'll maim it. Still another problem is that up to four generations a year can complete development, so seedlings are never really safe at any time of the growing season.

Controlling the black cutworm in the home garden is relatively straightforward. The old trick of sinking a tin can (like a soup can) with top and bottom removed around bedding plants or seedlings of concern is still effective—it presents enough of a barrier to convince the cutworms to move elsewhere. If your stock of cans runs short, call your county extension agent before trying an insecticide. Insecticides vary in effectiveness with the species of cutworm and with environmental conditions. In any case, it seems that the only kind of cutting *Agrotis ipsilon* is reluctant to do is to cut it out and leave the gardens alone.

FLEA BEETLES

Garden plants have a way of finding any number of ignominious ways to die before harvest. Occasionally they look as if some tiny neighbor took a miniature shotgun and blasted them into oblivion. This sort of damage occurs to eggplant, cabbage, broccoli, potatoes, spinach, sweet potatoes, beans, and a host of other plants. The agents responsible are not gun-toting garden-haters but rather are flea beetles. The flea beetles are rather distinctive members of the Chrysomelidae, a huge family of plant-feeding beetles whose ranks include such garden nemeses as the Colorado potato beetle, the corn rootworm, the spotted cucumber beetle, and the asparagus beetle. In the flea beetles, the hind legs are characterized by an enormously enlarged basal segment. This enables them to indulge in the behavior that earned them their name: they jump (like fleas). The resemblance to fleas is more than just behavioral. At sizes starting at ¹⁄₂₀ inch and topping out at ¹⁄₅ inch, they're about the same size as fleas, too. There are distinctive differences, however. First, fleas are flattened from side to side (the better to slide through hairs on an animal's coat) and flea *beetles* are flattened top to bottom. Second, adult fleas are almost invariably found in association with

Flea beetles: "Man, I can't see the spinach for the weeds!"

warm-blooded animals; flea beetles associate with plants and only by accident with an occasional hot-blooded gardener. Finally, while adult fleas suck, flea beetles chew—hence the tiny little holes in the leaves of just about everything in the garden.

It's not a single flea beetle species that attacks all the garden plants; there are hundreds of species, each with discriminating tastes. Beetles in the genus *Epitrix* feed on practically all members of the family Solanaceae, including, besides weedy species like the nightshades and horse nettle, garden plants like potatoes, eggplants, and tomatoes. They are about 1/20 inch in length, shiny black, and very fast. The larvae live underground and tunnel through the roots, often causing considerable damage to potatoes and other underground tubers. Species in the genus *Phyllotreta*, in contrast, restrict themselves to plants in the family Cruciferae—so there go the cabbages, radishes, broccoli, brussels sprouts, horseradish, turnips, and cauliflower. They're a little more ornate, with pale yellow stripes on a black background. Members of the genus *Disonycha*, bluish black with yellow shields, are giants as the flea beetles go, averaging about 1/5 inch in length. They're most frequently found on Chenopodiaceae—that is, spinach, beets, and lambs' quarters. The larvae of the spinach flea beetles live inside the leaves, tunneling out the leaf guts and leaving in their wake thin papery-brown blotches.

Not all flea beetles are quite so conservative in their tastes. Some feed on a tremendous variety of trees, shrubs, and herbs. In such cases, it's generally the adult with the catholic tastes; the immatures, stuck inside roots or inside leaves, don't get out much. One such example is *Psylliodes convexior*. The larvae feed on the roots of hops and the adults feed on the foliage of many plants. *Psylliodes convexior* is commonly known as the hop flea beetle, which, but for the larval host, would sound like a redundancy.

Flea beetles cause garden problems out of all proportion to their diminutive size. For many species, including strawberry, grape, potato, eggplant, corn, and sweet potato flea beetles, individuals pass the winter as full-grown adults and are thus ready, willing, and able to get a jump on feeding (as it were) as soon as seedling plants make their appearance first thing in the spring. As a result, flea beetles create havoc in seedling beds and on transplanted bedding plants. Injury by flea beetles tends to be greatest in wet or cold spring seasons, when the growth of plants is slowed down to the extent that the beetles can overwhelm them. Moreover, flea beetles as a group tend to associate with several very unsavory plant pathogens and cause additional damage to vegetation by serving as vectors, or carriers, of plant diseases. Probably the worst offender on this count is *Chaetocnema pulicaria*, the corn flea beetle, which is the chief vector for Stewart's disease, a bacterial wilt that affects primarily corn (although the beetles feast freely on beets, cabbage, oats, millet, sorghum, and a host of other plants as well). The wilt bacteria actually live in the guts of the flea beetles, where they pass the winter in comparative warmth and safety. *Epitrix cucumeris*, the potato flea beetle, not only defoliates potato plants but also can infect them with early potato blight. All told, flea beetle infestation can reduce yields up to 25 percent or more, which is pretty impressive for insects barely big enough to cover the head of a pin.

Controlling the flea beetles is problematical. The concealed larvae are protected from insecticide dusts and sprays and the adults are so mobile that repeated applications are invariably required. Rotenone dusts work fairly well. Diatomaceous earth is an inert material, obtained from deposits of the silica-containing skeletons of minute algae. When dusted on plant tissues, it can adhere to and abrade the waxy layer of a beetle's exoskeleton, causing the beetle to expire by desiccation. In general, diatomaceous earth is relatively nontoxic to non-insect life forms. Weeding the garden is another option for controlling flea beetles, as many of the species build up their populations on weeds during their first generation in the spring and cause major damage to garden plants only during the second generation.

Removing weeds, however, is a two-edged sword because several studies have demonstrated that, for flea beetles restricted to only a single family of plants, damage is greatly reduced in weedy garden plots. Evidently, flea beetles that feed exclusively on plants in the Cruciferae, or cabbage, family orient to and recognize their dinners by detecting the distinctive odor of glucosinolates, chemicals produced in great abundance only by crucifers and a few related plant families. When garden plots are weedy, the Gemisch of odors from the various and sundry plant species is sufficiently disorienting or disgusting to the beetles that they head for headier pastures. A laissez-faire approach to weeding around your cabbage, collards, kale, kohlrabi, broccoli, cauliflower, mustard, horseradish, turnips, and radishes, then, may be not only an effective control measure against flea beetles but also an easy one to follow rigorously. Perhaps, however, the very best solution hasn't been devised yet—equipping gardeners with tiny shotguns to give the beetles a dose of their own medicine.

JAPANESE BEETLES

Most immigrants to the northeastern United States arrived at Ellis Island in New York harbor. The Japanese beetle, however, docked a few miles south; it was first discovered in Riverton, New Jersey, in August 1916. Hailing from one of the main islands in the Japanese archipelago, it probably arrived, uninvited, in the soil clinging to nursery stock.

When the beetles were first discovered, every effort was made to eradicate them. In 1917, plans called for establishing a barrier zone one-half to one mile wide around the infested area, in which economically unimportant plants were cut and burned and all others sprayed. Hand collection of adults and sodium cyanide fumigation to kill the larvae were planned. Despite the fact that, in 1918, 1.5 million beetles were collected and killed, the beetles increased their New Jersey real estate interests from 2.5 to 48 acres. The eradication program was abandoned by 1920, at which point the beetles had more than doubled their acreage to encompass over 100 acres. Today, Japanese beetles can be found in almost every state east of the Mississippi and they are making inroads into Missouri and Minnesota.

One reason for the astounding success of the Japanese beetle in America is its versatility. The adults can feed on almost three hundred species of woody and weedy plants and they can eat many different plant parts on any particular plant—they eat flowers, skeletonize leaves,

Japanese beetles

and gouge, peel, and devour fruits with equal facility. Among the victims, to mention but a few, are shade trees such as maples, sycamores, and oaks; ornamentals such as rose, honeysuckle, and azalea; fruit trees like apple, cherry, and peach; vines and bushes like raspberry and grape; flowers such as zinnias, geraniums, and marigolds; field crops like soybean, clover, and corn; garden crops like cantaloupes, beans, and asparagus; and weeds such as smartweed, mallow, and dock.

In the central part of their range, adults first emerge from their subterranean chambers in mid-June and continue to emerge until late October, with a peak in mid-July. After a week or so of gluttony, the mated females return to the soil, preferably moist, sunny loam, and burrow down from two to five inches. The female then excavates a cell and lays one to four spherical to elliptical white eggs inside. In her three-to-four-week lifespan, a female is capable of laying up to fifty eggs. The eggs hatch in approximately two weeks, producing tiny white C-shaped larvae commonly called white grubs. These increase in size almost two hundred times, before they pause for pupation.

All this growth requires energy, and the grubs are just as destructive as their folks are. They live in the soil and feed on the roots of plants, particularly grasses. As the grass dies and the turf loosens, pastures, lawns, cemeteries, parks, and golf courses turn from green to brown. Population densities in places to *Popillia japonica's* liking can exceed five hundred grubs per square yard. The grubs don't restrict themselves to grasses and can wreak havoc with the roots of vegetables and nursery stock as well. After about four months of feeding, the larvae enter a resting stage and sit out the winter in their underground cells. In the following spring, they complete development, pupate, and emerge again as adults.

The Japanese beetle has managed to make itself sufficiently unpopular to inspire people to seek means of destroying it. Since the beetle presents no major economic problems in Japan, entomologists traveled there in hopes of finding a natural enemy to import. They found a couple dozen and imported them all, but none took too well to life in these United States; only two wasps remain as permanent residents and they aren't terribly effective as control agents. Far more effective, however, was a homegrown cure—milky disease, a bacterial infection caused by two species of *Bacillus* bacteria (*B. popillae* and *B. lentimorbus*). These pathogens were discovered not in Japan but in New Jersey in 1933. One dead beetle can release two billion spores into the soil, and the spores remain viable there for years. Milky-disease spores are now produced commercially and can be purchased by homeowners anxious to eliminate their undesirable alien insects.

SPIDER MITES

When it comes to house plants, "mite" doesn't make right, especially if the "mite" in question is *Tetranychus urticae*, the two-spotted spider mite. Called a spider mite by virture of its silk-spinning prowess, *T. urticae* is most often recognized by the damage it leaves in its wake. Plants infested with spider mites die a slow and horrible death. At first, white spotting appears on the foliage. Gradually, as mites continue to feed, the leaves turn brown as up to one-third of the chlorophyll content is sucked out. Without chlorophyll, photosynthesis is reduced and eventually the entire plant shrivels and dies. Few houseplants are immune from the onslaught. Some, like the smooth hard-leaved palms, bear the damage well; other, like chrysanthemums, asparagus ferns, and carnations, die in a particularly poignant manner. Out of doors, the two-spotted spider mite is no less of a menace, as it is equally at home on tree fruits, vegetable crops, forage plants, and florist and ornamental crops.

Despite the fact that it is tiny, vexatious, and a menace to plant life, the spider mite is not an insect at all but rather is an arachnid, a class

Spider mites: "My hero? Why, Mitey Mouse, of course!"

distinguished from the insects at least in part by the fact that members have two instead of three principal body regions. This distinction is a nicety lost on most people since the spider mite is barely visible to the human eye. Females measure in at $1/50$ to $1/60$ of an inch in length, and males are even smaller at $1/80$ of an inch. At those dimensions, another distinctive feature is difficult to discern; as adults, spider mites have not six legs, as do all self-respecting insects, but instead have eight legs, as do spiders, mites, ticks, and other members of the class Arachnida. When they first hatch, however, spider mite larvae possess only six legs. After hatching, the young mites eat for a few days, rest for a few days, and acquire their fourth pair of legs after the first larval molt. As eight-legged protonymphs, spider mites feed for a few days, rest for a few days, and molt again to the deutonymph stage. The process of eating and resting is repeated one last time until the final molt into adulthood. The whole affair takes about one to three weeks, depending on temperature and humidity, with about half of that period devoted to systematically robbing plants of their vital fluids.

An adult *T. urticae* can be distinguished from other almost invisible mite scourges of houseplants by the two dark spots on its abdomen, which ranges in color from yellow to green to orange to brown. The spots are actually not pigmented but are macerated houseplant visible through the almost transparent body wall. Like the immature spider mites, the adults are plant feeders, but much of their time is taken up with the complicated business of reproduction. There is such intense competition among the males for females with which to mate that male mites seek out female deutonymphs before they are even ready to molt into maturity, and spin webs around them to stake out a claim. The males stand guard over the developing deutonymphs to assure that they have the first opportunity to come courting. Confrontations over females can get ugly—males frantically spin silk over the legs and mouthparts of opponents in order to render them helpless and send them into ignominious defeat. Generally, the male that spins the most silk the fastest is the winner of such confrontations.

The females are less frenetic about the process of reproducing. If males are in short supply, the female is capable of arrhenotokous reproduction, a sexual parlor trick shared with bees, wasps, and a few other insects. When sperm is available, fertilized eggs develop into female offspring; in the absence of male input, unfertilized eggs can develop into perfectly normal male offspring. Female *T. urticae* lay eggs continuously throughout their two-month lifespan, averaging two to six per day. The eggs are attached to the ubiquitous webbing, which provides protection against general predators, a favorable humidity regime, and an anchor to prevent wind and rain from displacing the developing larvae.

Like many of their relatives in the class Insecta, mites have a short generation time and can produce prodigious quantities of offspring, a combination of traits that predisposes them, like insects, to develop resistance to pesticides. Satisfactory chemical control, both indoors and outdoors, is a tricky business and depends to a large extent on prudent selection and alteration of chemical types. To date, one of the most effective ways to deal with the two-spotted spider mite involves an application of the "fight-fire-with-fire" principle. Nothing can track the population growth of a mite better than another mite, and among *T. urticae*'s mortal enemies are the predaceous phytoseiid mites, including *Amblyseius fallacis* and *Metaseiulus* (=*Typhlodromus*) *occidentalis*. These mites have reproductive abilities on a par with their prey and are among the very few predators to develop resistance to pesticides. The phytoseiids are rather particular about what they eat and have hit upon some ingenious ways to find their dinners. Since they don't have eyes, they locate their tiny prey by scent. *M. occidentalis* can detect a chemical cue inadvertently laid down in the silk by *T. urticae* and can follow the trail to the source like miniaturized bloodhounds.

Other nonchemical alternatives to controlling spider mites include gentle spraying with water to break up the all-important webbing. Spraying should not be done indiscriminately, since many houseplants cannot tolerate frequent drenching. Several insecticidal soaps have shown promise as effective control agents that are relatively nontoxic to houseplant and homeowner alike. Perhaps most effective of all are sanitation and quarantine. Carefully inspect any plants for signs of spider mite injury before bringing them home—webbing and browning of leaves are dead giveaways of infestation. Shaking the plant over a white piece of paper is an effective diagnostic device—if the dust that falls onto the paper begins to crawl, don't bring the plant home. When it comes to *Tetranychus*, prevention is the only way to change "mite" to "might have been."

References

Branson, T. F., and J. L. Krysan. 1981. Feeding and oviposition behavior and life cycle strategies of *Diabrotica:* an evolutionary view with implications for pest management. *Env. Ent.* 10:826–31.

Burke, H. R., W. E. Clark, J. R. Cate, and P. A. Fryell. 1986. Origin and dispersal of the boll weevil. *Bull. E.S.A.* 32:228–38.

Cotton, R. T. 1943. *Insect Pests of Stored Grain and Grain Products.* Minneapolis: Burgess Publishing Co.

Gould, F., G. Holtzman, R. L. Rabb, and M. Smith. 1980. Genetic variation in predatory and cannibalistic tendencies of *Heliothis virescens* strains. *Ann. Ent. Soc. Amer.* 73:243–50.

Ladd, T. L. 1976. *Controlling the Japanese Beetle.* Washington, D.C.: U.S. Department of Agriculture.

Little, V. A. 1983. *General and Applied Entomology.* New York: Harper and Row.

Sabelis, M. W., and H. E. van de Baan. Location of distant spider mite colonies by phytoseiid predators: demonstration of specific kairomones emitted by *Tetranychus urticae* and *Panonychus ulmi. Ent. Exp. Appl.* 33:303–14.

Scudder, S. H. 1889. *The Butterflies of the Eastern United States and Canada.* Cambridge, Mass.: By the Author.

Sturm, M., and W. L. Sterling. 1986. Boll weevil mortality factors within flower buds of cotton. *Bull. E.S.A.* 32:239–47.

Treat, A. E. 1975. *Mites of Moths and Butterflies.* Ithaca, N.Y.: Cornell University Press.

Chapter 3

Field hands

Black blow flies

Daddy-long-legs (harvestmen)

Garden spiders

Ladybugs

Mantispids

Milkweed bugs

Minute pirate bugs

Mourning cloaks

Question marks and commas

Spring azures

Thrips

BLACK BLOW FLIES

The black blow fly, *Phormia regina*, has a secret as dark as its metallic bluish-green body. Often called the bluebottle fly, *P. regina* is a familiar sight throughout North America and northern Europe. Beginning in early spring each year, the rather large bristly flies, topping off at just under half an inch in length, can be frequently found visiting all sorts of flowers and in fact are rather important as pollinators of several economically important crop plants, including carrots, onions, and strawberries. But when the urge to lay eggs strikes a female black blow fly, she turns away from flowers and fields and sets out in search of meat—dead meat.

Larvae of the black blow fly are the whitish, pointy-headed maggots that inevitably are found writhing and wriggling in dead things. Female *P. regina* are exceedingly sensitive to odors of decay and are among the first insects to arrive at a carcass, often within hours of the moment of death. Females deposit masses of eggs and the maggots develop rapidly, reaching maturity in anywhere from ten days to three weeks, depending on temperature and humidity. The teeming masses of maggots of this and related species in the family Calliphoridae are what cause a corpse to appear "fly-blown." When the maggots are ready to pupate, they burrow into the ground; if winter is approaching, they'll stay underground as pupae (encased in their hardened last larval skin, or puparium) until spring heralds the approach of new flowers and fresh meat.

Black blow flies: "The person in question is sitting right there, Your Honor!"

Since blow flies are among the only animals in the world that can break down collagen, the refractory material that makes up much of vertebrate connective tissue, they provide a valuable service to the rest of us on the planet by clearing away tons of dead bodies every year. They're useful in other ways, too. Calliphorids are so reliable in their quest for dead meat that they're actually used by the police to estimate time of death (or PMI, post-mortem interval). As long as local weather conditions are known, a forensic entomologist can, by estimating the age of larvae and/or pupae, calculate within several hours when a female blow fly deposited eggs on a body—that is, when the victim was murdered. Blow fly behavior is so strictly regulated that accurate guesses can even be made as to whether a body was originally placed in sun or shade, or whether death occurred during the day or night.

This use of blow fly behavior to track down a killer is not exactly a modern concept. Probably the earliest recorded example can be found in a Chinese manual on forensic medicine published in the thirteenth century. After a person had been murdered with a sickle, local farmers were rounded up and asked to lay their sickles on the ground. Flies settled on only a single, presumably bloodstained, sickle, prompting its owner, confronted by so many six-legged witnesses, to confess his crime. Today, the testimony of forensic entomologists is admissible in court and has been instrumental in hundreds of convictions. A fly's testimony, then, can be quite damaging to an accused murderer; it tells the truth even if no one ever figures out which leg it should raise and which should be placed on the Bible.

DADDY-LONG-LEGS (HARVESTMEN)

Although there are arthropods with *more* legs, there are certainly no species with more *conspicuous* legs than the phalangids. Phalangids are otherwise known as daddy-long-legs, a name that, paternity aside, aptly describes the eight extremely long, slender appendages that characterize every member of the order Phalangida. The lack of a waistlike constriction between the cephalothorax and the abdomen, as well as a few other anatomical niceties, distinguishes daddy-long-legs from spiders, eight-legged arachnids that don't go to such lengths in the leg department.

The study of phalangids, according to Savory in 1928, "is a study of legs." Those long gams have been a source of fascination to less well endowed humans for hundreds of years. The redoubtable Dr. Robert Hooke estimated in 1658 that a phalangid with legs "an hundred and fifty times the strength of a man would not keep the body from falling on the breast," were his legs of equivalent length. Aside from the rather pedestrian function, as it were, of elevating its body off the ground and propelling it forward, the legs of a daddy-

Daddy-long-legs (harvestmen): "Okay, okay, I give up . . . it's not worth an arm and a leg!"

long-legs contribute in a number of more remarkable ways to daily life. Legs, for example, figure prominently in the love life of phalangids. Male *Leiobunum longipes* demonstrate their superior strength to potential mates by engaging in leg-pulling contests in which one male positions himself above a competitor, grabs a leg with his chelicerae (or jaws), and yanks—either by jerking up and down or by rotating rapidly three to five times in a clockwise direction. This confrontation continues until the lesser contender loses a leg and leaves the scene. Breaking off a leg can take as many as twenty of these Olympic-quality bouts.

The male daddy-long-legs uses his legs not only in combat with other males but in courtship with females as well. The male approaches the female and immobilizes her by grabbing her body with his palpi behind her second pair of legs. He uses *his* second pair of legs as a distant early warning system, to detect the approach of potential intruders; with his first pair of legs, he restrains the female's first pair of legs so she stays in position; and the remaining two pairs of legs are used to hold himself upright during the entire encounter, which can take anywhere from a few seconds to over two hours, depending on his skill and her cooperation. After the fact, the male uses his legs to form a cage over the female, preventing her escape and compelling her to oviposit before seeking out the attention of other daddy-long-legs to father her children.

The legs of daddy-long-legs are also important in allowing them to escape from their multitudinous enemies, which include spiders, centipedes, assassin bugs, fish, toads, shrews, badgers, foxes, and a few birds. Their first line of defense when disturbed is to secrete noxious and distasteful secretions from the base of their second pair of legs. If the predator is undeterred, a phalangid can then flee. This process usually begins with vigorous bobbing up and down, with ever-increasing velocity, and terminates with the phalangid stepping out and away from danger. If a phalangid is grabbed while trying to escape, it has one remaining trick up its sleeve (or rather, up its trouser leg)—it simply sheds the immobilized appendage via a virtually bloodless process called autotomy.

Long legs are not entirely without drawbacks, however. One of the greatest challenges of the life of a phalangid is molting or shedding its exoskeleton, something it is called upon to do no fewer than seven times after egg hatch. Prior to molting, a phalangid typically anchors itself, usually by a pair of front legs and a pair of back legs, to a rough surface from which it can dangle, taking advantage of gravity to withdraw its long legs from their old skin. It then begins to twist and jerk, alternately flexing and relaxing its muscles. The process of withdrawing the legs from their old exoskeleton has been likened in human terms to taking off a jacket when the sleeves are tied to your pants legs. The phalangid grabs each leg with its chelicerae and palpi and pulls it free, taking care to keep the newly extricated and as yet unsclerotized leg from adhering to its neighbors. Each leg is passed through the mouthparts for cleaning and drying. The phalangid must hang motionless until its new exoskeleton hardens; when the process is complete, the new improved legs are almost 50 percent longer than before.

The long legs of daddy-long-legs, with their tendency to autotomize, also leave them peculiarly vulnerable to mindless cruelty. Pulling the legs off daddy-long-legs has long been a pastoral pastime of people the whole world over. In fact, in Montgomeryshire in the United Kingdom, leg pulling is even accompanied by a nursery rhyme:

> Old Harry long legs
> Cannot say his prayers.
> Catch him by the right leg,
> Catch him by the left leg
> And throw him downstairs.

As the rhyme is recited, the legs are systematically removed and the dismembered body tossed onto the ground. This sort of treatment sheds an entirely new light on the implications of being "footloose."

GARDEN SPIDERS

Ludovico Castelvetro, a sixteenth-century literary critic, established himself as an iconoclast among his peers with the publication of his *Poetica d'Aristotele vulgarizzata et sposta*, a commentary on the *Poetics* of Aristotle. The accepted Humanist tradition of the day was for poets to emulate (or imitate) the style and substance of previous masters of the art form, rather than to discover "by and for themselves the essential principles of their arts" (Hathaway 1962). The standard analogy used at the time was to liken those who borrow from previous traditions to the honey bee, which sucks nectar from many flowers to produce sweet honey, and to liken those who insist on creating from within, ignoring tradition, to the silkworm, which creates silk from substances within its own body. Castelvetro was one of only a tiny minority that came out in favor of the silkworm rather than the bee.

Castelvetro could have greatly strengthened his analogy if he had drawn a comparison using another silk-producing arthropod in place of the silkworm. While it is true that silkworms (caterpillars of the

Garden spiders: "What do you mean, do I believe in an all-consuming passion?"

Japanese mulberry silkmoth *Bombyx mori*) can and do produce silk, they do so for only part of their lives and for only a few specific purposes—notably, to spin themselves a cocoon in which to pupate in warmth and safety. Spinning silk for such a purpose isn't even unique to the silkworm (or the order Lepidoptera)—immature bees, ants, wasps, lacewings, and even fleas can spin silken cocoons. When it comes to creative silk-spinning, however, the spiders have no equals. Silk is used for everything from capturing prey to courtship to cocoon construction to communication.

Spider silk is produced in silk glands located in the abdomens of all species of spiders. Each gland connects to an appendage called a spinneret, a flexible spigotlike device. Most spiders have three pairs of spinnerets (except the very primitive, who have more, and the very advanced, who have fewer); different glands spin different types of silk. All silk, however, basically consists of a protein called fibroin. As fibers go, silk is very strong for its weight—a strand would have to be over fifty feet long before it would break under its own weight. It's also a very elastic fiber, capable of stretching up to 30 percent of its length (more impressive than nylon, which has only half the stretchability).

The form of spider silk that is probably most familiar is the orb web. Orb webs are spun by most of the twenty-five hundred members of the family Araneidae (sometimes called Argiopidae) and by species in a handful of other spider families (including the Uloboridae, the Tetragnathidae, and the Theriosomatidae). The most familiar of the familiar orbweavers is probably *Araneus diadematus*, the garden spider, which, as the common name suggests, can be found in gardens all across the Northern Hemisphere. *A. diadematus* is also known to some as the cross or diadem spider due to the conspicuous white cross on its abdomen (actually, the result of the accumulation of crystals of guanine, a waste product that is highly reflective).

The web of the garden spider is classic in design. At the center of the web is a central hub, a meshwork of fibers surrounded by a strengthening spiral. This spiral is in turn surrounded by a "free zone," lacking spirals; in this space, the spider can move from one side of its web to the other freely and quickly. Emanating from the central hub, crossing the free zone, are twenty-five to thirty dry radial threads separated from each other by a twelve to fifteen degree angle. These radial threads connect to a few strong frame threads that form the outline of the web. From the outside of the web running to the free zone are the viscid or sticky spirals (the last threads to be added to the web, spun from the outside inward). On these threads the spider deposits a thin sticky coating, which under tension breaks up into a series of droplets. These are the threads in which passing insects get entangled.

In general, the garden spider sits in the hub of its orb, legs outstretched to detect any movement in the web that might indicate the presence of a potential meal. If for some reason she must leave the hub, she spins a signal thread that guides her return in the event of an insect visitor. When an insect is discovered, the spider runs toward it along a radial thread and immediately begins to wrap it with silk to restrain it. Here's where having eight legs comes in handy; the insect is grasped with the third pair of legs while the fourth pair of legs draws silk from the spinnerets and the first and second pairs hold the spider in place on the web. After the prey is secured, it is bitten and injected with paralytic venom; after a few more wraps, it is snipped out of its place of capture in the web and carried to a more convenient location for future consumption.

Spiders rarely get stuck in their own webs—being both architect and builder has some advantages in knowing where the trouble spots are. Orbweavers generally travel through their webs on the dry radial threads rather than on the sticky spirals. They are greatly assisted in their travels by their anatomy. Garden spiders, like other araneids, have an extra hooklike tarsal claw (in addition to the customary pair) that faces a set of stiff, saw-toothed bristles. The bristles guide the strands of silk onto the unpaired claw, which is twisted for a better purchase on the cable. In addition, spider legs are coated with an oily substance that cuts down on sticking.

Orb webs are primarily aerial filters that intercept unwary flying or jumping insects. Garden spiders are extremely catholic in their taste as regards the class Insecta, although they are known to cut out and drop prey that are distasteful (which they detect through chemical sensors on their legs, as they wrap and before they bite). Except for the frame threads, *A. diadematus* spins a completely new web on a daily basis, conserving on protein by consuming and recycling the old web. Sites that are not providing enough careless insects can thus be quickly abandoned for more promising locations.

In addition to serving as a kitchen and dining room, the orb web is also a bedroom for courting spiders. A female garden spider reaches maturity, and a length of about half an inch, after eight molts; the male, only one-quarter the size of his prospective mate, requires only six molts to come of age. As an adult, the male garden spider no longer spins an orb web; for food, he eats silk and occasionally wrapped prey from the webs of the females he courts. He spins a small silken pad called a sperm web, ejaculates into it, and then soaks it up into his pedipalp. Thus armed, he goes off to find the orb web of a female (how he finds the web is something of a mystery; the prevailing idea is that the silk contains a sexual signal or pheromone that alerts the male as to its location).

Once a male garden spider finds a female, he approaches her with caution, spinning a mating thread and tugging on it to attract her attention and perhaps to distinguish himself from struggling prey. Once she is within reach, he grabs her abdomen with his front legs; if she's in the mood, she acquiesces by hanging quietly upside down (bringing to mind a rude limerick about a certain young lady from Norway . . .). After jumping up and down several times, for reasons about which one can only speculate, he quickly inserts his pedipalp and discharges its contents, a process requiring a brief fifteen seconds. Given the opportunity, a male will repeat the process, spinning a second sperm web and inserting the other palp. It's not an undertaking without risk, however. Females have been known to lose interest *in flagrante delecto* and decide that sex is a poor substitute for a snack. In one study, 25 percent of males attempting to copulate were consumed before they managed to insert even a single palp.

After mating, the female garden spider can begin to lay eggs. She vacates her web in order to search for a safe spot to prepare an egg cocoon—often under loose bark or soil. She deposits some three hundred to eight hundred eggs, glues them together, and covers them with a blanket of coarse yellow silk, to which she attaches bits of debris. This covering not only protects the eggs from passing predators but also anchors the egg mass in place and keeps the eggs warm. The following spring, the hatching spiderlings, which molt once in the cocoon before they even eat, spin thin threads to catch the breeze, and sail off to start spinning their own webs.

While the number of uses to which spiders put silk is impressive, humans have been pretty creative as well. Historically, spider silk, like the silk from *Bombyx mori*, has been used for fabric, although spiders have not proved as adaptable or as prolific as silkworms. Today, spider silk's greatest commercial value comes from its use in the crosshairs of gunsights; few other fibers are as sturdy yet thin and elastic. Spider silk is the fiber of choice for use in gunsights of highpowered telescopic rifles. Such a use is perhaps not so original after all—spiders have been using their silk to bring down "big game" before humans ever hit upon the concept.

LADYBUGS

The common names that people bestow upon insects rarely reflect deep abiding respect or affection for the recipient. What isn't simply descriptive is often downright unflattering—among the choicer epithets are "thief ant," "firebrat," "insidious flower bug," "stink bug," and "ugly-nest caterpillar," to name a few. One group that is curiously exempt from this nomenclatural nastiness is the family Coccinellidae. Coccinellids are, as beetles go, rather unprepossessing in appearance—hemispherical in shape, rarely much more than half an inch in length, and ranging in color from solid conservative black to bright orange or red with upward of a dozen black spots on the elytra, or wing covers.

In a rare display of global consensus, these beetles are almost universally named in honor of a deity. In an exhaustive compilation by one A. W. Exell of some 250 names in almost 50 languages, the author writes, "With regard to the religious element in the names we get: the Virgin (with variations) 63, God (with variations) 52. There is then a great drop to St. Catherine who scores 6 and Heaven also 6. At the bottom of the list come the Devil, Jesus and the Pope who score 1

Ladybugs: "We were thinking of buying a ski condo, but once we hit the mountains all Bert wants to do is diapause."

each. Various saints have small scores (St. John 3)." In the United States, coccinellids are known as ladybugs or (more rarely) ladybird beetles, ostensibly in honor of the Virgin Mary. Other, less frequently encountered but more colorful names in English include "God's little cows," Cowlady," and "Bishop is burning."

Considering that the vast majority of the million-plus named arthropod species are resolutely nondenominational, it's all the more impressive that a religious affiliation has been established with coccinellids on at least five continents. Most likely it was the actions, rather than the appearance, of ladybugs that earned them their ecumenical status. Despite their unprepossessing, almost clownish, appearance, ladybugs are actually ravenous killers, specializing on soft-bodied, slow-moving helpless prey, particularly aphids, scale insects, mealybugs, and other homopterans. Even ladybug larvae, bizarre spindleshaped grubs bedecked with various sorts of spines, lobes, and sundry other fleshy projections, spend their days mowing down masses of unsuspecting prey sitting and sucking plant sap.

To early agriculturalists, whose crops were undoubtedly ravaged by homopterans and the many plant diseases they carry, the appearance of coccinellids in the fields must truly have seemed a godsend. Thus, in Sanskrit, coccinellids are known as "Indra's cowherds" (Indra being a Vedic god); as new religions arose, the names were revised accordingly. In modern, more practical days, ladybugs have proved to be an economic windfall, if not a religious experience, for American agriculture. Ladybugs provided the test case that demonstrated the feasibility of biological control—importation of a natural enemy to control an introduced pest insect. What launched biological control into scientific circles was an infestation in California of cottony-cushion scale on citrus. *Icerya purchasi* was first noticed in Menlo Park around 1868; by 1885, it was a threat to the brand-new citrus industry. C. V. Riley, then state entomologist for Missouri, suggested in 1872 that, since the pests were Australian in origin, there were undoubtedly predators there accustomed to eating them. By 1878, as chief entomologist for the United States Department of Agriculture, he was in a position to send Albert Koebele to Australia as State Department representative at the International Exposition in Melbourne (no foreign travel was allowed for USDA employees) for the express purpose of searching for natural enemies of cottony-cushion scale.

In Australia, Koebele located a parasitic fly, *Cryptochaetus iceryae*, and a predaceous coccinellid, *Rodolia cardinalis* (vedalia beetle). Stocks of both were sent to Los Angeles to be reared and released onto scale-infested trees enclosed in tents on J. W. Wolfskill's Los Angeles farm. From there, they spread to orchard trees nearby. People came from all over the state with little boxes to collect the beetles and take them home with them. With the assistance of citrus growers and the Los Angeles County Board of Horticultural Commissioners, the beetles were soon established throughout the county. One year later, shipments of citrus from Los Angeles County went from seven hundred to two thousand railroad cars, the citrus industry was saved, and, best of all, $500 remained of the $2,000 originally allocated for Koebele's trip to Australia. Koebele received a gold watch and his wife a pair of diamond earrings from the grateful growers.

Today, even home gardeners can send for mail-order ladybugs for release in their own backyards. Aspects of the life cycle of certain species, however, make them a little less than reliable as garden defenders. Many coccinellids are migratory and fly long distances to reach a site to overwinter, usually in large aggregations. *Hippodamia convergens,* the convergent lady beetle, is one such species. In California, first-generation adults follow prevailing westerly winds and head for the mountains in spring, spending the dry winter months in diapause in the high country. They fly back to the valleys the next February or March, when the weather warms up, taking advantage of northeasterly winds generated by seasonal high-pressure systems.

What all this shuttling back and forth has to do with the price of corn in Iowa is that many people who sell ladybugs for home gardeners collect them while they're aggregated in huge numbers and sluggish— that is, from mountain populations in diapause. They're kept in cold storage until someone back east orders a few dozen and releases them in the backyard. Once warmed up, these beetles, totally unaware of their change of venue, are likely to do what comes naturally—head for the hills (no doubt to the delight of the resident aphids). Releasing them late in the day into a well-watered and well-mulched garden in relatively small groups (two or three per spot) will increase the probability that they'll settle in and start to feed the next morning and decrease the chances that the ladybirds will fly the coop.

MANTISPIDS

If any group of insects could pass for an April Fool's joke, certainly the mantispids could. The mantispids are the original humbugs. They belong to the order Neuroptera, home to such insect oddities as the hellgrammites, snakeflies, antlions, dustywings, and spongillaflies. Like all good neuropterans, mantispids have two pairs of membranous wings crisscrossed by a network of nervelike veins (hence, the name Neuroptera, from the Greek, "nerve wing"). From that point, the superficial resemblance to the rest of their relations ends. Mantispids, or false mantids, are so named because they bear an uncanny resemblance to a praying mantis, an insect to which they are only remotely related. Their two front legs are greatly enlarged, equipped with spines, and are folded at rest in a beatific pose. Credibility is stretched, however, by the fact that mantispids are rarely more than an inch in length and the praying mantids one is most accustomed to seeing are rarely less than twice that size.

Mantispids: "A fly in your glass? I'm so sorry, sir, I'll replace it with a spider right away!"

Like the praying mantis, mantispids are predaceous, but even their diet sounds incredibly improbable. Members of the subfamily Mantispinae feed exclusively on spider eggs. Since spider eggs are not exactly available at every local supermarket, mantispids have developed a number of rather bizarre ways of locating them. Adult mantispids lay clusters of whitish eggs on short stalks attached to foliage. The newly hatched larva is extremely active, albeit tiny; a first instar *Mantispa uhleri* is less than a millimeter in length. There are three options for the larva at this point. While some species actively run around in search of spiders, some literally sit back on their tails and wait for spiders to come to them. Others seek out and penetrate egg sacs directly, bypassing the middleman (or middle-arachnid). When a spider is available, the larvae hop on and wait for the presumably female spider to lay eggs (mantispids unfortunate enough to land on a male spider aren't entirely out of luck; they may possibly transfer to a female during mating, particularly in species in which the female spider eats her mate after the act). While waiting, *Mantispa uhleri* often enter a spider's book lung (the breathing apparatus) to snack on spider blood as a sort of hors d'oeuvre. When the spider molts to adulthood, the mantispid leaves the book lung and waits on the pedicel (the spider's waist) until eggs are laid. The mantispid enters the egg sac before the female spider can complete spinning the silken protective case. Once in the egg sac, the mantispid begins to eat in earnest and undergoes three molts. Second and third instar larvae, unlike the active, athletic first instar, are grublike and sluggish. After two to three weeks, depending on the species, the mantispid spins a cocoon inside the egg case and emerges as an adult one to two weeks later. Frederick Brauer deserves the credit for figuring out the basics of mantispid biology. In 1852, he first described the egg and first instar of *Mantispa styriaca* on vegetation. It took him seventeen years to find the remaining instars in spider egg sacs.

There are fewer than three hundred species of mantispids worldwide. Of the approximately ten species in North America, the most abundant is the one least likely to be recognized as a mantispid, *Climaciella brunnea*. Unlike most mantispids, this species has wings boldly patterned with brown and for all the world looks like *Polistes*, a paper wasp. Not only do they look like wasps, they act like wasps. They fly during the day, visit flowers, and even hang out with local wasp aggregations. Among insects it would seem that mantispids either suffer from an acute identity crisis or a peculiar sense of humor.

MILKWEED BUGS

Large milkweed bugs aren't necessarily found on large milkweeds; actually, they can be found on milkweeds of all sizes. Entomologists call *Oncopeltus fasciatus* the large milkweed bug to distinguish it from *Lygaeus kalmi*, the so-called small milkweed bug. There aren't too many obvious differences between the large and small milkweed bugs aside from size. Both species are in the family Lygaeidae, and, like most lygaeids, use their piercing-sucking mouthparts to feed on the seeds and pods of species in the Asclepidaceae, the milkweed family. Both species are black and red or orange in color, although there are subtle differences in pattern. The large milkweed bug has three continuous black bands running across its body, one across the thorax, one across the wings, and one across the abdomen; in contrast, in the small milkweed bug, the band across the wings is broken in the middle. Even the size difference between large and small milkweed bugs isn't that dramatic—only a few millimeters separate the largest large milkweed bug from the smallest small milkweed bug.

The two species have more than just physical characteristics in common, too. For example, they share the same taste, both literally and figuratively. Not only do they share the same preference for foodplants, they share the same taste *with* their foodplants. Both large and small

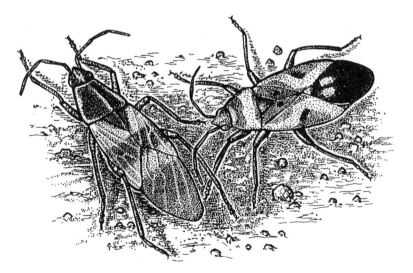

Milkweed bugs: "Looks like everybody's wearing warning colors this season."

milkweed bugs ingest toxic chemicals, called cardiac glycosides, from their hostplants and store them in special cuticle-lined chambers along the edges of the thorax and abdomen. The cardiac glycosides in their dorsolateral spaces are present in concentrations up to one hundred times greater than they occur in the plants, and a single *O. fasciatus* adult can contain as much as one hundred micrograms of cardiac glycoside in its body.

Cardiac glycosides owe their name to their ability to cause cardiac problems, such as heartbeat arrhythmias, in vertebrates that consume them. Usually, vertebrates run into them when they ill-advisedly attempt to consume the foliage of milkweeds, which is rich in the compounds. Heart arrhythmia is only one of a veritable panoply of distressing consequences of ingesting milkweed foliage. Charles Millspaugh, in his book *American Medicinal Plants* ([1898] 1974), warns would-be milkweed gourmets of "pain and weight in the pit of the stomach; soreness and colic, followed by flatulence; soft foetid stools, preceded by rumbling in the bowels; dry, hard, hacking cough, with painful respiration; sharp, shooting pains, especially between the ribs and about the heart, aggravated by deep inspiration and by motion of the arms" and, last but not least, "darting, shooting pains in the extremities, followed by a sense of languor and debility"—not a reaction likely to lead to requests for seconds. Needless to say, milkweeds are scrupulously avoided not only by humans but by discriminating vertebrate herbivores everywhere.

Ingesting milkweed sap, with its load of cardiac glycosides, however, appears to have absolutely no ill effects on milkweed bugs, either large or small. Moreover, they don't even appear to expend any metabolic energy transporting and storing the cardiac glycosides they ingest. Not only does ingesting cardiac glycosides not harm the bugs, it brings them the added benefit of protecting them from their own enemies. By storing cardiac glycosides essentially in the form in which they are found in the plants, milkweed bugs acquire all the noxious properties of the plants they eat. Granted, while milkweed bugs may be at no risk from attack by vertebrate herbivores, they are potential targets for vertebrate predators, who are likely to react just as negatively to cardiac glycosides in their food as are their herbivorous kin. Moreover, cardiac glycosides have definitely adverse effects even on invertebrate predators. Praying mantids that grab and bite large milkweed bugs drop them almost immediately and begin frantic grooming behavior. If they happen to bite off more than they can chew, they actually vomit. After a few such encounters, they leave milkweed bugs alone and seek out more appetizing prey.

The chemical resemblance to their foodplants is probably the reason behind the physical resemblance between large and small milkweed bugs. In general, poisonous insects advertise their distastefulness by flaunting bright warning colors. Just as an orange and black sign on the highway indicates a road hazard ahead, an orange and black insect indicates a culinary hazard ahead.

Although it would seem that cardiac glycosides are all a bug needs to eat in peace, *Oncopeltus fasciatus* leaves nothing to chance. Just in case it gets snatched by a hard-hearted predator unaffected by cardiac glycosides, it has a backup defense system up its sleeve—or, more accurately, up its thorax. *O. fasciatus* manufactures its own noxious compounds, consisting mostly of unsaturated aldehydes. On the first and last segments of the thorax, *O. fasciatus* has glands that produce and store these volatile and reactive compounds. The two sets of glands actually differ in their aldehyde content and composition—for that matter, aldehyde production differs between the sexes, and between nymphal and adult bugs. All together, it's a sure bet that *O. fasciatus*, despite its flashy appearance, epitomizes bad taste for the predators that encounter it.

Because it has so few predator problems, the life of a milkweed bug is a leisurely one. Eggs laid directly on the milkweed plants hatch in about four days, and the hatching nymphs take about a month to go through five molts to adulthood. Once they reach adulthood, milkweed bugs don't reach sexual maturity for another five to twelve days. In some parts of its range, sexual maturity can be delayed even longer, as adults undergo migratory flights to warmer climates—the insect is rarely found above the fortieth parallel and is so averse to cold conditions that in the northern part of its range it migrates south before winter sets in.

O. fasciatus does have one very unlikely enemy. *Lygaeus kalmi*, the small milkweed bug, has been reported to kill and feed on its larger relative. This behavior, especially for a herbivore, is quite puzzling but for one fact—chemically, milkweed bugs are very much like milkweed plants. It's therefore not very surprising that on occasion it may be difficult for an insect to distinguish the dinner from the diner.

MINUTE PIRATE BUGS

There's nothing noticeably nautical about minute pirate bugs except possibly for the fact that they frequent the amber waves of grain. Minute pirate bugs, insects in the family Anthocoridae, are indeed bugs in the strict sense, that is, members of the order Hemiptera, characterized by a partially thickened, partially membranous wing (hence, "Hemiptera" or "half-wing") and piercing-sucking mouthparts in the form of a beak. Like most bugs, the minute pirate bugs are equipped with such a beak, which they tuck between their front legs when not in use.

When it is in use, the beak efficiently punctures and sucks out the juices from the soft, fragile bodies of a variety of insect prey. Minute pirate bugs are limited in menu not by their appetite but by their size. Even the largest North American representative, perhaps inappropriately dubbed *Orius minutus* (from "minute"), reaches a length of only 2 to 2.4 millimeters, less than $1/10$ of an inch for those not up on metric conversions. The most common representative of the family,

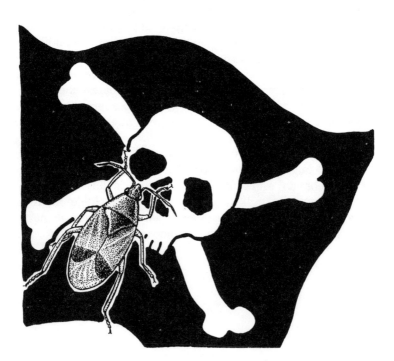

Minute pirate bugs

Orius insidiosus, is known as the false chinch bug, since it bears a superficial resemblance to the chinch bug, *Blissus leucopteris,* a seasonal pest of grains. Like chinch bugs, *Orius insidiosus* is black, with wings that are yellowish at the base and tipped by a black triangular area. Savants, however, can distinguish quickly on the basis of size; chinch bugs, at $^{14}/_{100}$ of an inch, are enormous by comparison. The two species can also be distinguished by habit—*Orius insidiosus* is the one eating and *Blissus leucopteris* is the one being eaten.

Orius insidiosus is also sometimes called the insidious flower bug since it is partial to sitting on flowers to await unsuspecting insect passersby. It's not especially particular as to where it sits; it's been recorded on over seventy-five crop plants, including corn, soybeans, alfalfa, walnuts, melons, cassavas, and mushrooms. Nor is it particular as to what it eats; it has been observed eating caterpillars, beetle grubs, thrips, mites, aphids, springtails, leafhoppers, lace bugs, whiteflies, scales, plant bugs, flies, and innumerable sorts of insect eggs. It doesn't stalk, track, or lure its prey. It mostly stumbles into it, a ploy that is greatly complemented by a broad diet.

Since it feeds on such a tremendous number of economically important pests, the insidious flower bug is an important biological control agent in corn, soybean, and alfalfa. Most people, however, are less than appreciative because *Orius insidiosus* has the irritating habit of biting humans. It's entirely unintentional. People walking through fields dislodge them from their perches and from force of habit the insidious flower bug inserts its beak to sample a prospective meal. *Orius insidiosus* is probably as repelled by the taste as humans are at the sensation, but that's small consolation for those who are bitten.

MOURNING CLOAKS

The mourning cloak butterfly, *Nyphalis antiopa*, is about the only one more anxious for spring to begin than you or I. Every spring, the mourning cloak is almost invariably the first butterfly to make an appearance. It's not just in America either that it's heralded as a harbinger—the mourning cloak's among the most cosmopolitan of butterflies and is even reported to appear every spring in Siberia. Exactly when it makes its first appearance depends on the locality. As Edward Hulme, British author of *Butterflies of the Countryside, Figured and Described*, remarked in 1903, "The go-aheadism of the Americans would appear to extend even to their Lepidoptera. Packard, an American entomologist of repute, affirms that *antiopa* appears in the spring before the snow is off the ground."

Nymphalis antiopa is capable of putting in such an early appearance because, unlike most butterflies, it overwinters as an adult hibernating amid fallen leaves and branches. The mourning cloak owes its rather funereal name not to any morbid interests of its own but rather to the velvety crepelike consistency of its dark purplish brown wings. It is, name notwithstanding, a rather gaily colored butterfly (and in fact is known in England as the Camberwell beauty or the grand surprise). The two-inch wings are edged on either side with pale blue spots next to a wide yellow margin.

Mourning cloaks

The more prosaically minded call *Nymphalis antiopa* the spiny elm caterpillar because, aptly enough, the spiny caterpillars have a fondness for elm, although they obligingly feed on poplar and willow as well. Full grown, the caterpillar can measure up to two inches in length. The rows of branched spines running the length of the body are characteristic of the family Nymphalidae (the brush-footed butterflies), the family to which *Nymphalis antiopa* belongs. Along with a row of spines is a row of red spots on a black background, which is finely peppered with tiny white dots. From the moment they hatch, mourning cloak caterpillars stick close together. They line up side by side, heads aligned along the edge of the leaf, and they eat communally with a discipline that would put a military academy to shame. When disturbed, the whole aggregation collectively rears up on back legs and shakes menacingly, which, if not terrifying, is at least bizarre enough to give a predator second thoughts.

By getting such an early start on things, *N. antiopa* can lay eggs not only in the spring but also in late summer. The females lays eggs in compact clusters around twigs of choice. The eggs are not your average run-of-the-mill egg-shaped eggs. They're highly ornate, with complex ridges and sculpturing ornamenting the surface. Moreover, they're not just ovoids, they're variously septahedral or octahedral (seven or eight sided). Try putting those in your Easter basket this year and see what your neighbors will say.

QUESTION MARKS AND COMMAS

As graduates across the country come out in May to accept diplomas certifying they have mastered the fundamentals of reading, writing, and arithmetic, at least two butterflies are coming out for whom punctuation is a daily habit. The question mark, *Polygonia interrogationis*, and the comma, *Polygonia comma*, are nymphalid butterflies who would find themselves at home in almost any sentence. When not punctuating, the question mark entertains itself feeding on tree sap, fermented fruit, dead animals, or dung. It owes its name to the conspicuous silvery question mark adorning the underside of its otherwise grayish drab hind wing. Like other species in the genus *Polygonia*, the question mark's wings are irregular in outline (or "many angled," as the Latin would have you believe).

Question marks can be found ranging north to Canada, west to the Rockies and south to the Gulf Coast. They migrate to the southern part of their range for the winter and fly north to breed in spring, generally arriving by Memorial Day or so. The first order of business is mating. Males set up territories, perching on tree trunks or other suitable substrates, sally forth to chase out other male question marks who happen

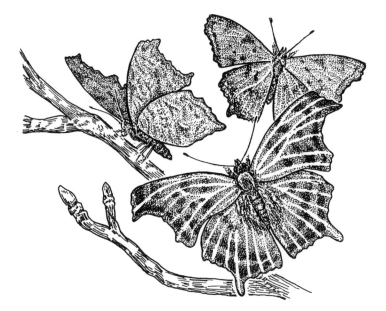

Question marks and commas: "You guys think you've got all the angles figured."

82

by, and wait for a willing female to pop the question, as it were. After mating, females seek out plants for egglaying. Their egglaying is restricted to a brief period, about an hour and a half starting at noon. The rest of the day is spent hitting the rotting fruit or animal dung or just resting on the ground in wet areas. Unlike most butterflies, the question mark is less than precise about where it lays its eggs (perhaps the result of excessive indulgence in fermented fruit) and the eggs often end up on nonedible plant species.

Caterpillar tastes range from low-lying herbs such as nettle to trees like elm and hackberry. The caterpillars are reddish brown to black, with irregular red or yellow longitudinal lines. Like all anglewing caterpillars, they're profusely equipped with branched spines, including an antlerlike pair on the head. Even the larvae are punctuated after a fashion, with eight metallic silver "periods" along their backs. After larval development is complete, the caterpillar pupates. The pupa, about ⅞ inch in length, is camouflage-colored brownish gray with olive drab mottling and can easily be mistaken for a withered leaf. Butterflies emerge for a second round of mating, egglaying, and feasting on fermented fruit in the north, and for a third, fourth, or even fifth time in the southern part of the range.

Not surprisingly, a close relative of the question mark is the comma, *Polygonia comma*. This species is similar in appearance to the question mark, rust brown with black notches on the upperside of the wings, but with a silvery comma on the underside rather than a question mark. Its life cycle and behavior are very similar to those of the question mark but there are a few notable exceptions. First of all, it's a little more discriminating in its taste. Indulging in another collegiate pastime, the comma can often be found at the "hop" or, rather, the "hops." Among its favorite food plant is *Humulus*, or hops, and among the grammatically unlettered the comma is called the hop merchant. Other choice food plants are members of the Urticaceae, or nettle family, and American elm. The caterpillars are extremely variable and can be any color from black to green to white. Like the question mark, the caterpillars are spiny; even the pupae of the comma are well endowed with spiny projections.

Both the question mark and the comma are members of the family Nymphalidae, the brush-footed butterflies. The key family characteristic is that in the adults the first pair of legs is greatly reduced and is used not for walking but for "tasting" leaf surfaces. Despite the alteration in function, the modified front legs are still equipped with a tarsal claw at the tip, as well it grammatically should be—after all, independent "claws" usually follow a comma.

SPRING AZURES

Only an entomologist would look forward to the first weeks of spring as a great time to get the blues. Actually, the blues are butterflies in the family Lycaenidae, otherwise known as the gossamer-winged butterflies. Like most lycaenids, blues are small as butterflies go, rarely exceeding an inch or so in wingspan; as the name implies, they're generally (but not always) blue on the upperside, and white or brown on the underside. One of the earliest species to appear in the spring is the spring azure, *Celastrina ladon*. The spring azure is on the wing as soon as weather permits, as early as March in Illinois and January in Mississippi.

Not ones to waste any time, spring azures emerge from their overwintering pupal stage and almost immediately begin the business of courtship and mating. Males are on patrol from about midafternoon to dusk. When not in hot pursuit, they can be found aggregating in all-male groups called puddle clubs on moist soil along streams and roadsides, sharing one for the road with the boys. Females emerge and

Spring azures: "Just once I'd like to see some peonies in bloom."

mate their first day out; the next morning they get a late start on the morning and lay eggs from 10:30 or so till dusk. A few stalwart individuals survive to oviposit for another day or two, but for most spring azures, spring fever and life in general rarely last longer than a couple of days.

Depending on locality, there may be one or two generations a year. The choice of foodplant is determined at least in part by the season. First-generation butterflies lay their pea-green, turban-shaped eggs in and among the flower buds of dogwood and wild cherry, and second-generation individuals oviposit on viburnum, staghorn sumac, dogwood, and New Jersey tea. Other hosts include meadowsweet, blueberry, wingstem, black snakeroot, and bittersweet (or *Celastrus*, from which derives the generic name *Celastrina*).

The growing larvae feed avidly on the buds and developing flowers of their hostplants; they vary in color from greenish yellow to pink, with a dark stripe along the back and oblique greenish stripes along the sides. They're seldom bothered by predators or parasites, largely due to the company they keep. The larvae possess a protrusible gland on the seventh abdominal segment, from which exudes a sweet clear fluid that drives ants to distraction. Ants congregate around spring azure larvae and single-mindedly lap up the secretion; they're so enamored of the substance that they take personally anything that threatens to cut off their supply and fiercely defend the caterpillar from enemies. On the eighth abdominal segment is a pair of openings from which can be everted a membranous tube equipped at the tip with slender tentacles. The function of these organs is unknown but it's likely that they produce chemicals to attract ants from a long distance to signal that chow's on.

Spring azures range from the Maritime Provinces of Canada west to Alaska and the Pacific Coast, and south throughout the United States all the way down to the mountains of Central America. Over their range, they are among the most variable of butterflies. There are, for example, no fewer than three forms of the spring brood, all with different patterns on both the upper and lower surfaces of the wings. "Lucia" has brown margins and a brown central patch, "marginata" has only the brown margins, and "violacea" has no brown markings at all. The second brood form, "neglecta," has considerable expanses of white scaling on both sexes and black markings on the female forewing. Once considered only a form of the spring azure, the dusky blue, which resembles the "violacea" form, is now recognized to be a separate species—demonstrating that it's never really been easy to tell who's really "true blue."

THRIPS

Anyone who has spent any amount of time outdoors admiring or inspecting flowers has undoubtedly seen thrips—slender, elongate, and tiny insects rarely more than 1 millimeter (1/25 of an inch) in length. But anyone who claims to have seen a single thrip is mistaken. It's not that thrips only travel in throngs—although population densities of some species can reach enormous levels. In one study, for example, the average number of *Thrips imaginis* per rose flower was in excess of fifteen hundred. It's not that thrips are so small that they can only be distinguished by the naked eye when they assemble in large numbers—although there are species that, at body lengths less than 0.5 millimeter (1/50 of an inch), certainly challenge the myopic. It's just that, for peculiar etymological, not entomological, reasons, the singular form of "thrips" is "thrips." Like several other animal names ("deer" and "fish" come to mind), the word "thrips" doesn't change even though the population size does. The name derives from a Greek word for "wood worm," a fact that may make etymological sense but isn't completely entomologically comprehensible, since thrips are neither wormlike nor particularly closely associated with wood.

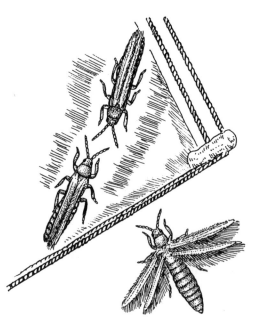

Thrips: "Those two can slug it out if they want, but I'm a lover, myself."

Their name is hardly the only peculiar thing about thrips. In fact, just about everything about thrips is peculiar. For one thing, thrips wings are unique in the insect world. The vast majority of insects have wings constructed of thin cuticular membranes stretched across a framework of strutlike veins. Some thrips have no wings at all; those that do have two pairs of wings that are either veinless or at most have one or two veins. There's no cuticular membrane, either. Instead, the wings consist of long fringes. These fringes are the feature to which thrips owe their ordinal name, Thysanoptera—from the Greek for "fringe wings." The fringes are thought to facilitate flight for these minute creatures. Large flying animals don't have to deal with the viscosity of air creating drag as they fly. Thrips are so small that moving through air for them is like swimming in a fluid. The fringes may cut down on air resistance and reduce drag. In addition, the absence of thick, rodlike veins on the trailing edge of the wing probably cuts down on drag as the wings are brought forward on their return stroke.

The wing design must be effective, because, despite being collectively the world's smallest flying animals, thrips do manage to fly substantial distances. Some species even undertake mass migratory flights, and individuals have been collected in airplane traps at elevations in excess of ten thousand feet.

The mouthparts of thrips are no less unique than their wings. The most striking thing about thrips mouthparts is that they are asymmetrical. The mouthparts of thrips are contained inside a cone-shaped sheath (which gives most thrips a definite conehead appearance). There are three piercing structures—a pair of maxillary stylets, and a single heavily sclerotized mandibular stylet. The right mandibular stylet is for all intents and purposes nonexistent.

The disadvantages of asymmetrical mouthparts are abundantly apparent to anyone who, for example, has had wisdom teeth removed on only one side (or, for that matter, has tried to cut paper with scissors with a tip missing or to pick up noodles with a spaghetti fork missing tines). The system seems to work well for the thrips, though, since as a group they feed on a staggering variety of items. They use the asymmetrical stylets not to chew but to pierce, tear, and rasp; they then can lap up the contents of the cells or tissues they rupture. Plant-feeding thrips feed variously on foliage, fruits, flowers, buds, twigs, and even pollen grains. Some are such voracious feeders that they are serious plant pests; the flower thrips, *Frankliniella tritici*, name notwithstanding, feeds on foliage as well as flowers of grasses, herbs, shrubs, and trees. There are also predaceous thrips that rip and tear the flesh of fellow arthropods, and fungivorous thrips that use their asymmetrical mouthparts to puncture spores and mangle mycelia of molds and fungi.

Even the growth and development of thrips is peculiar. Most insects are either holometabolous (that is, undergo a dramatic metamorphosis during a generally quiescent pupal phase) or hemimetabolous (that is, undergo a gradual development accompanied by external progressive development of the wings). When it comes to development, thrips are neither fish nor fowl, as it were. The first two instars start out ordinarily enough, as active youngsters. But at the next molt, most thrips enter a stage that is nonfeeding and quiescent. After still another molt, they enter a second nonfeeding quiescent stage (sometimes, as is the case for true holometabolous pupae, ensconced in a cocoon). While the nonfeeding stages are strongly reminiscent of holometabolous development, the fact that these nonfeeding stages undergo progressive external wing develoment is more reminiscent of the hemimetabolous hoi polloi. These complicated arrangements have not made thrips life difficult, but they have certainly made life difficult for entomologists keen on classifying insects into neat, tidy groups.

Since everything else about thrips is so peculiar, it's no surprise to discover that the sex lives of thrips are on the odd side as well. Some thrips are parthenogenetic and produce all-female offspring without benefit of males. The rest of the thrips are haplodiploid: females can produce male offspring from unfertilized eggs and female offspring from fertilized eggs. These arrangements make for some remarkably skewed sex ratios. That there are some species in which males have ceased to exist is perhaps more comprehensible when the courtship activities of thrips are examined closely. In several species of fungus-feeding thrips, males engage in elaborate fights over egglaying females and the patch of fungus in which they communally deposit their eggs into a large mass. In most animals that engage in such combat, the fights are largely ceremonial, with a lot of ritualized behavior, a clear victor, and a loser who slinks off to look for a lesser opponent. In the case of tiny *Hoplothrips karnyi*, a bit over a tenth of an inch in length, the fights are to the finish. Males have specially modified spurs on their enlarged and thickened front legs. These spurs are used to stab and slash at opponents. Aside from hand-to-hand (or femur-to-femur) combat, they engage in below-the-waist blows as well, pummeling each other with their abdomens. About half of these encounters end with the death of one of the combatants. In the face of these odds, not all males even try to fight. These pacifists are lovers, not fighters, sneaking around the colony and mating with females when they move off the egg mass to munch on mycelia nearby. Males that do guard females and engage in combat, however, appear to mate more often and with more success—at a price. Clearly, when it comes to mating for *H. karnyi*, there's no holds barred and let the thrips fall where they may.

References

Blum, M. 1980. *Chemical Defenses of Arthropods.* New York: Academic Press.

Bristowe, W. S. 1949. The distribution of harvestmen (Phalangida) in Great Britain and Ireland, with notes on their names, enemies, and food. *J. Anim. Ecol.* 18:100–114.

———. 1976. *The World of Spiders.* London: Collins Clear-Type Press.

Crespi, B. J. 1988. Risks and benefits of lethal male fighting in the colonial, polygynous thrips *Hoplothrips karnyi* (Insecta: Thysanoptera). *Behav. Ecol. Sociobiol.* 22:293–301.

Edgar, A. L. 1971. Studies on the biology and ecology of Michigan Phalangida (Opiliones). *Misc. Publ. Mus. Zool. University of Michigan* No. 144:1–64.

Elgar, M. A., and D. R. Nash. 1985. Sexual cannibalism in the garden spider *Araneus diadematus. Anim. Behav.* 36:1511–17.

Exell, A. W. 1989. *The History of the Ladybird with Some Diversions on This and That.* Warwickshire: Peter I. Drinkwater.

Feir, D. 1974. *Oncopeltus fasciatus:* a research animal. *Ann. Rev. Ent.* 19:81–96.

Foelix, R. F. 1982. *Biology of Spiders.* Cambridge, Mass.: Harvard University Press.

Hagen, K. S. 1962. Biology and ecology of predaceous Coccinellidae. *Ann Rev. Ent.* 7:289–326.

Hathaway, B. 1962. *The Age of Criticism: The Late Renaissance in Italy.* Westport, Conn.: Greenwood Press.

Hook, N. S. 1958. *Spiders for Profit.* Illustrated Library of the Natural Sciences, E. M. Weyer, ed., vol. 4, 2731–42. New York: Simon and Schuster.

Hulme, F. E. 1903. *Butterflies of the Countryside, Figured and Described.* London: Hutchinson and Co.

Lewis, T. 1973. *Thrips: Their Biology, Ecology, and Economic Importance.* New York: Academic Press.

Millspaugh, C. [1898] 1974. *American Medicinal Plants.* New York: Dover Publications.

Redborg, K. E., and E. G. MacLeod. 1985. The developmental ecology of *Mantispa uhleri* Banks (Neuroptera: Mantispidae). *Illinois Biological Monographs,* 53.

Sauer, D., and D. Feir. 1972. Field observations of predation on the large milkweed bug, *Oncopeltus fasciatus. Env. Ent.* 1:268.

Savory, T. H. 1928. *The Biology of Spiders.* New York: Macmillan.

Smith, K. V. G. 1988. *A Manual of Forensic Entomology.* Ithaca, N.Y.: Cornell University Press.

Chapter 4

Bushwhackers

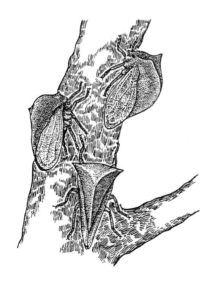

Bagworms

Bronze birch borers

Cankerworms

Elm bark beetles

Fall webworms

Oystershell scale insects

Pine sawyers

Pine webworms

Treehoppers

Walkingsticks

Willow leaf beetles

BAGWORMS

The concept of the mobile home is classic and is nowhere better exemplified than by the bagworm, *Thyridopteryx ephemeraeformis*. That the bagworm is even an insect, much less a moth in the family Psychidae, is not immediately apparent to the casual observer. The male bagworm moth pulls no surprises—with its black body, clear wings spanning an inch (2.5 centimeters) or so, and prominent feathery antennae, it is a fairly typical male moth. The female is another story altogether. The female bagworm is characterized by an astonishing diminution of body parts: she lacks antennae and wings altogether and possesses only the most rudimentary eyes, legs, and mouthparts. The soft, unsclerotized abdomen is firmly encased in the pupal skin, which in turn is inserted into a spindle-shaped silk-lined sack bedecked with bits of foliage, twigs, or bark. The bagworm bag is not exactly the last word in comfort; it's fairly formfitting, and the female has to dangle upside down inside the sack, with only her sclerotized head and thorax protruding through the posterior opening.

The life of a female bagworm is less than enviable, too. She is essentially a sackful of eggs—hundreds crowd both thorax and abdomen—and her sole function in life is to attract the more mobile male bagworm moth. This she does by producing a pheromone, a sexual

Bagworms: "Does this thing come with a zipper?"

scent that males can detect over considerable distances, purportedly a mile or more. Once the male arrives, the bag proves a formidable obstacle to consummating courtship—his abdomen must penetrate the entire length of the bag in order to reach the female genitalia. It's an arduous task and some males never do manage to find what they're looking for. Some fly off in frustration; the less fortunate frequently die of exhaustion, still clinging to the bag.

After fertilization, the females lay eggs inside their own pupal cases. As the case fills with eggs, the female's body shrinks accordingly, and after about seven days and six hundred to twelve hundred eggs, the spent female drops out of the bag to the ground to die. As a parting gesture, the fine hairs that break off her abdomen during her maneuvering remain behind as a protective blanket for her eggs.

Swaddled in hair, pupal case, and bag, the yellowish eggs, only a millimeter in length, pass the winter in comparative security. In late spring to early summer, the eggs hatch and the secure winter haven becomes a prison. The tiny caterpillars must work their way out of the tangle of hairs, twigs, and silk to reach the outside world. The process can take a day or more. Once out, even before they take their first meal, the caterpillars go about building their own pint-sized versions of bags. Without a bag, the bagworm caterpillar is utterly defenseless. The bag not only provides a physical defense against predators—the bagworm can withdraw completely into its bag and even pull the posterior opening shut with a silk drawstring—it is also a disguise. The bags resemble nothing so much as tiny mobile pinecones, of little interest to insectivorous birds and other enemies. Bagworms divested of their bags almost invariably fall prey to predators or to the elements.

Larvae feed day and night, adding fragments of leaves to the front margins of the sacks. As they grow, bags increase in length from ¼ to 2½ inches (0.6 to 6.4 centimeters) within approximately 90 days after hatching. They eat practically any species of deciduous or evergreen tree—according to one authority, they feed on 128 different plants. Their extraordinarily catholic tastes are tempered by regional preferences. In the East, they are partial to juniper and eastern redcedar; in the Midwest, their taste runs to hardwoods, such as black locust, sycamore, and maple; and in the Southwest they thrive on cypress, willow, and cedar. When they are small, they border on comical, feeding on leaf surfaces with the tiny "pinecones" pointing contrarily upward. Feeding damage by young larvae is a characteristic brown spotting, the result of damage to the upper epidermis of the leaf. When they are larger, their feeding begins in earnest. Larger caterpillars are so voracious that they can strip a tree completely of foliage—leaves of deciduous trees are reduced to nothing but veins and petioles. Trees that aren't killed outright are left stripped and ragged, almost worthless as shade or ornamental trees. Problems are exacerbated by the fact that populations tend to build up on single trees, due to the limited mobility of the caterpillars, and these trees bear the brunt of the onslaught.

There are, however, chinks in the leafy armor of the seemingly invincible bagworm. While birds and other predators are fooled or deterred by the bags, various species of parasitic wasps (which lay their eggs inside or on the body of their hosts) actively seek out the bags. Three species are fairly effective in reducing bagworm populations— *Allocota thyridopteryx, Pimpla (Itoplectis) inquisitor,* and *P. conquisitor* (names seemingly designed to strike fear in bagworm hearts). Several of these parasitic wasps overwinter in the bags and can be found nesting comfortably in bagworm debris for the duration of winter. This habit of sleeping surrounded by the remains of one's dinner adds new dimensions to the concept of the "brown-bag" lunch.

BRONZE BIRCH BORERS

One of the more boring topics for conversation every spring is *Agrilus anxius*, otherwise known as the bronze birch borer. This species is a member of the family Buprestidae, the flatheaded wood borers, a group of about seven hundred American insects that as larvae bore into all manner of things, including trees, bushes, fungus, buildings, and even lead cable. In the case of the bronze birch borer, the menu of choice is, as the name implies, the wood of birch trees, although cottonwood, poplar, alder, and aspen are never scorned. Adults are hard to miss—about a half-inch in length, blackish green in color with a bronze metallic sheen, and the flat head that characterizes the entire family. The adults are fairly innocuous in their feeding habits, nibbling on leaves of birch and alder. Females lay eggs starting in May and continuing on through June.

The boring begins when the eggs hatch ten to eleven days later. *Agrilus anxius* larvae are dirty white in color, generally tapered in shape, and legless (and in fact have been compared favorably with a horseshoe

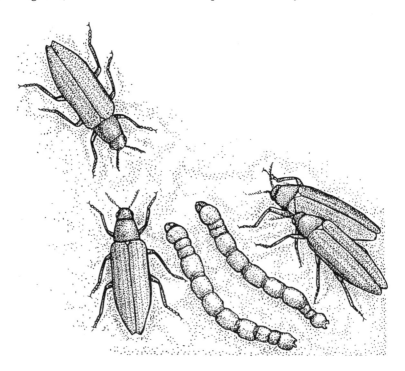

Bronze birch borers: "Sorry, I'll have to inspect your right wing before you can join the Bronze Birch Borer Society."

nail in appearance, although, at home relaxing, the larvae more closely approximate a bent horseshoe nail). The larvae bore into the cambium, the thin layer of woody tissue that produces phloem to the outside and xylem to the inside. Xylem conducts sap up from the soil and phloem channels food and nutrients down from the leaves. By excavating a complex series of tunnels against the grain and cutting the vascular channels, the larvae effectively starve the tree. The legless larvae use a pair of tiny sharp forklike projections on their tails to grab their excrement and pack it into an out-of-the-way end of their tunnel home to keep it clean.

These galleries are impressive engineering feats, some in excess of four feet long. Larvae may continue tunneling under the bark for up to two years, depending on location and weather. Under the best of circumstances, they spend the winter in hibernation, complete development, pupate in early spring, and emerge in May to mate and lay eggs.

As far as birch trees are concerned with respect to *Agrilus anxius*, the bite is worst for their bark. The feeding tunnels that girdle the trunk or branch produce characteristic swellings. Damaged trees have yellowing leaves and missing foliage on upper limbs. In fairness to the bronze birch borer, it appears that the insect can survive only in birch trees that are in a weakened condition in the first place, such as trees damaged by other insects or birches reaching the end of their fifty- to sixty-year life span. The problem with this approach from the human perspective is that people tend to plant trees, such as white birch, as ornamentals well outside their natural range, so even in a well-tended garden, fertilized and mulched with loving care, birch trees are under stress pining for the fjords (or pining for the pines) of northern Canada. Throughout its range, from Canada into the northern United States west to Colorado and Idaho, the bronze birch borer is most pestiferous in the southern extremities.

Controlling bronze birch borer is a matter of good timing, specifically applying insecticide just as borers are hatching and beginning to bore. Controlling an insect that lives under bark, however, is a difficult proposition. Well beneath the bark, ensconced in the cambium, the bronze birch borer is safe from virtually all its enemies, content, no doubt, with the thought, "there's no place like phloem."

CANKERWORMS

Humpty Dumpty may have had a great fall, but it doesn't compare to the sorts of falls *Alsophila pometaria*, the fall cankerworm, is accustomed to. It doesn't wait till spring, like most self-respecting moths, to emerge and begin laying eggs. Fall cankerworms get a jump (or rather a crawl) on everyone else by emerging from their subterranean pupal chambers in mid-November. As soon as the leaves and the temperatures drop, the fall cankerworm perversely begins the business of laying eggs rather than hibernating for the winter. Female fall cankerworms are atypical not only in habit but also in appearance. Unlike most other moths, noted above all else for their scaly wings (from which comes the name of the order Lepidoptera—"scaly wing"), female fall cankerworms are wingless and at first glance resemble a hefty grayish spider more than a typical moth.

The flightless female crawls up the nearest tree trunk (usually the same tree she grew up on as a caterpillar) and lays about one hundred

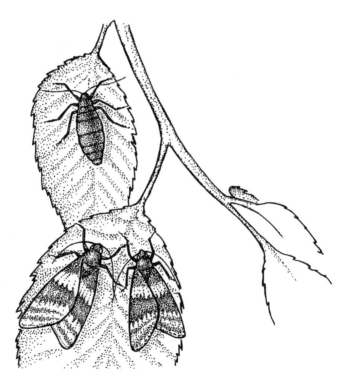

Cankerworms: "I'd leave her alone, Fred—she's one sore canker right now."

eggs in tight clusters around twigs, from mid-November through New Year's. According to one account, the eggs resemble little flower pots. The eggs are situated such that the hatching larvae won't have to travel very far to start stripping leaves the moment they begin to bud out in April or May the following spring.

The spring cankerworm, *Paleacrita vernata*, isn't quite as early a riser as its close relative the fall cankerworm. It stays snug in its pupa underground through January and doesn't begin crawling up tree trunks and laying eggs until February or March, months not normally associated with balminess throughout the moth's range from Nova Scotia west to Manitoba and south to the Carolinas and Texas. The eggs of the spring cankerworm, also laid in tight clusters of a hundred or so, are more spindle-shaped than those of fall cankerworms and are generally found in bark crevices of larger limbs. The moths are harder to distinguish. The wingless females of both species are grayish with a double row of red spines across each abdominal segment, but female spring cankerworms have a dark stripe down their backs. The winged males are even more similar; both species are grayish brown with two transverse white bands across the forewings. Distinguishing between them is most easily done by calendar; in November, it's likely to be a fall cankerworm, and in March odds are good it's a spring cankerworm.

When the weather warms up and the trees leaf out, the eggs of both species hatch and the caterpillars begin to eat buds and leaves with a passion. They eat leaves down to the midrib and can easily defoliate a tree. If they run out of food, they each simply release a thin silk thread and parachute down to a lower branch or a neighboring tree. They're not particularly discriminating and eagerly defoliate elm, aspen, apple, oaks, ash, maple, linden, cherry, hickory, or whatever else is in the neighborhood. Caterpillars of both species are inchworms or loopers; missing the full complement of prolegs or false legs on the abdominal segments, they crawl in typical inchworm fashion. Fall cankerworms have three pairs of prolegs, one pair of which is reduced in size and useless, and spring cankerworms have only two pairs. When the caterpillars have made short work of the foliage, anywhere from four to five weeks after hatching, they spin silk threads down to the ground to pupate and wait for cold weather to set in.

The onset of cold weather puts female fall cankerworms in the mood for motherhood but not in the mood for sex. Fall cankerworm females for the most part forgo courtship and romance—they are perfectly capable of laying fertile eggs without benefit of male genes. Although they can occasionally be seen mating, on most of those rare occasions none of the male's genetic material ever gets incorporated into the eggs, making him, no doubt, the "fall guy" in this autumnal tryst.

ELM BARK BEETLES

In recent years European imports have caused problems in a number of American industries; one European import, which arrived in Boston in 1904, still has an impact in almost every state in the Union. The year 1904 was when entomologists believe that *Scolytus multistriatus*, the smaller European elm bark beetle, was accidentally introduced into the United States, possibly in Carpathian elm logs imported for furniture veneer. Now, elm trees in this country were no strangers to elm bark beetles; *Hylurgopinus rufipes*, the native elm bark beetle, had routinely infested elm trees across America for centuries. The European elm bark beetle in fact is remarkably similar in habits and appearance to the native American species. Both species are small (about an eighth to a tenth of an inch in length), chunky, and round-shouldered in profile. The adult version of the European elm bark beetle is a dark reddish brown while the adult American elm bark beetle is a dark brown to black in color; however, the eggs, larvae, and pupae of the two species are so similar even experts are hard-pressed to tell them apart. Both species live by making extensive tunnels or galleries in the inner bark of elm and occasionally basswood trees. Larvae spend the

Elm bark beetles: "Now, be careful over at the neighbors'—no telling what they might have brought back from Europe with them."

100

winter at the ends of their tunnels (although the native species occasionally overwinters as an adult under bark).

In the spring, after pupation, adults emerge and begin to feed on the bark of twigs, generally concentrating in the crotches. When females are ready to lay eggs, they find weak or injured elm trees and tunnel out a brood chamber through the cambium. Here one difference between the two species appears. European elm bark beetles tunnel as adults *with* the grain to lay eggs and feed as larvae on the cambium *across* the grain; native elm bark beetles tunnel as adults *across* the grain to lay eggs and feed as larvae *with* the grain. (This may be the entomological equivalent, one supposes, of holding one's dinner fork right-handed in America and left-handed in Europe.) Females deposit from eighty to over one hundred eggs on each gallery. Larvae develop in a few weeks and by mid-August are adults ready to mate and lay more eggs.

The European elm bark beetle is so similar to the native elm bark beetle that its arrival probably wouldn't even have been noticed except for one thing: it didn't come alone. Covering the bodies of the imported beetles were spores of *Ceratocystis ulmi*, a fungus known as Dutch elm disease. Not only do the beetles carry the fungal spores, but, by burrowing deep into the tree, they effectively inoculate each tree, providing the fungus access to vulnerable tree tissue. Dutch elm disease is a debilitating disease in European elms, but in American elms it's fatal. Shortly after the arrival of the European elm bark beetle, elm trees began to die. Leaves wilted, shriveled, and then dropped off; twigs curled and the inner bark turned brown. As the European elm bark beetle population grew, the elm tree population crashed. The first trees died in the Northeast in 1930; by 1974 elms in forty-five of forty-eight continental states were affected. Some trees die gradually over a period of years, but if the fungus produces fruiting bodies and spores enter the vascular system, a tree can die in just a matter of weeks.

Control of Dutch elm disease is a community-level project. The beetles are often the first target for elimination; while they themselves can't kill trees, the fungus can't get a foothold (or a hyphal-hold) on the tree without their assistance. Beetles can be lured into traps baited with all sorts of enticing odors (such as female pheromones and essence of dead elm) and then destroyed. Dead, dying, or diseased trees should be removed and burned. While all of these measures may help to check the spread of the disease, nothing can bring back the millions of elms that have died in the relatively short time since *Scolytus multistriatus* slipped past immigration and adopted America as its homeland. All across the country, *S. multistriatus* continues to change Elm Streets and Elmwood Avenues into misnomers.

FALL WEBWORMS

The fall webworm is one of relatively few insect pests that have traveled from America elsewhere instead of vice versa (the vice versas include European cabbageworm, European cornborer, European earwig, European pigeon bug, European red mite, European horse-biting louse, and European elm scale, the German cockroach, and the Oriental cockroach, Oriental fruit fly, and Oriental fruit moth). While it's not much of a pest in its hometown, its taste for mulberry leaves has wreaked considerable havoc with the Asian silk industry since the source of silk, *Bombyx mori*, the Japanese silk moth, will eat nothing else.

As an adult, *Hyphantria cunea* is a satiny white moth with a wingspan of 2 to 2½ inches, an orange abdomen, and a few black spots scattered haphazardly on both front and hind wings. Adults lay a mass of eggs, from four hundred to nine hundred a day, on the undersides of leaves in late spring and early summer (name notwithstanding). The female isn't particular as to which tree she chooses; her offspring are fully capable of devouring the foliage of over a hundred different tree species, including maples, alders, birches, hickories, dogwoods, beeches, walnuts, tulip poplars, apples, cherries, oaks, poplars, willows, and just about any other species you could think of (except, for some reason, for evergreens). In a pinch, they can happily grow and develop on shrubs, weeds, and wildflowers as well. After the eggs hatch, the tiny larvae spin large silken webs on the tips of branches.

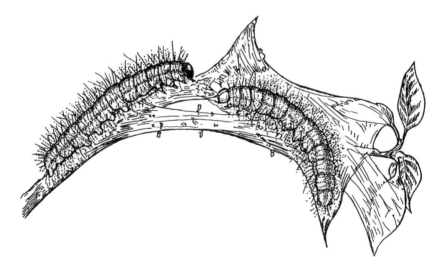

Fall webworms: "You redheads are so temperamental!"

The location of these webs is in part a reflection of the fact that *H. cunea* is a sun-loving type. Caterpillars prefer leaves in the upper and outer parts of the crown and pitch their tents in the most exposed branches. Webs appear to spring up overnight with good reason since the caterpillars do most of their webspinning in the wee hours. Another tent-making species, the Eastern tent caterpillar, *Malacosoma americanum*, prefers to web the inner forks and dark recesses of cherry and other rosaceous trees. Another difference between the caterpillars is that the Eastern tent caterpillar never eats at home, preferring to travel outside the web to feed. The fall webworm, in contrast, makes a regular habit out of eating in bed.

Like most of its relatives in the family Arctiidae (the woollybear a case in point), fall webworms are very hairy. They are covered with fine yellow-to-brown hairs, interspersed with long white hairs attached to orange and black tubercles. After four to six weeks and five to six molts, the full-grown caterpillars, an inch or more in length, give up the communal life to wander around in search of a place to hibernate. They spin cocoons under bark or in leaf litter under trees and wait out the cold winter months.

The larvae of the fall webworm have attracted considerable attention from entomologists because they come in two varieties. Most caterpillars in the northern United States have black heads and most in the south have red heads; in Kentucky and Louisiana, both forms can be found living side by side. The difference is more than just head color. The redheaded type is much more particular as to the type of tree on which it feeds and in areas of overlap manages only one generation per year to the blackheaded's two. The question is more than just academic—only the blackheaded variety seems to like mulberry and only the blackheaded variety has been found in Japan, eastern Europe, and western Asia. Even in the People's Republic of China, only the blackheaded types are found—despite the fact that the *red*headed one would probably better suit the political climate there.

OYSTERSHELL SCALE INSECTS

Lepidosaphes ulmi, the oystershell scale, may well be the original "scale model." Unlike its namesake, the oystershell scale is a landlocked insect that at maturity happens to bear an uncanny resemblance to a tiny oyster no larger than ⅛ inch in length. *Lepidosaphes ulmi* manufactures its shell from waxy secretions produced by glands near the tip of its abdomen. Like real oyster shells, it's usually gray to brown in color.

During the winter months, the only thing to be found under the shell are eggs, 40 to 150 packed under each shell thoughtfully provided by the mother, whose shriveled body can be found in the anterior end of the shell. The shell affords excellent protection against the elements, enemies, and even insecticides. Come spring, when trees begin to blossom, the eggs hatch, and the first-stage nymphs, called crawlers, busily set about finding a place to poke their proboscesand start sucking sap. Oystershell scale are hardly discriminating eaters; they feed on almost one hundred different tree species in many different families. A few favorites include apple, pear, plum, raspberry, grape, walnut, ash, lilac,

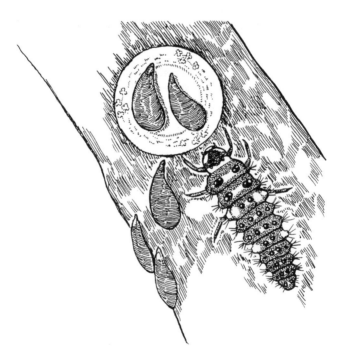

Oystershell scale insects: "Mmmm . . . oysters on the half shell."

willow, elm, poplar, maple, dogwood, rose, and peony. Once they settle, the crawlers molt and in the process lose their legs, antennae, and anal filaments, losses that enhance their resemblance to oysters and reduce their resemblance to the standard model insect. Breeding will tell, though, and by the final molt, in mid-July to mid-August, at least the males regain antennae, legs, and tail, and, for the first time, acquire wings.

All these restored appendages aid the male in accomplishing his prime directive—to find and fertilize females. The task is less than challenging inasmuch as females are completely sedentary and never leave the spot where they settle in as crawlers. After mating, the female begins to lay eggs underneath her shell, gradually shrinking in size to accommodate them until she eventually dies of exhaustion, boredom, or whatever.

An infestation of oystershell scale is bad news as far as trees are concerned. A heavily infested tree can be literally covered with scales; the bark cracks and peels, and leaves become stunted and yellow due to the continual drain of sap. *Lepidosaphes ulmi*, however, is not without its own problems. Without legs or wings for most of its life, oystershell scale can't exactly outrun its enemies and as a result is a favorite appetizer on the half shell for many parasitic eulophid wasps and predaceous ladybugs and mites. Unfortunately for *Lepidosaphes ulmi*, these insect gourmets don't restrict their activities to months with "r's" in them.

PINE SAWYERS

If it's true that "little strokes fell great oaks," then it's also true that even smaller strokes can fell a mighty pine tree. The hatchetmen in the case of pines in recent years are cerambycid beetles in the genus *Monochamus*. As is the case for most of the twenty thousand members of the family Cerambycidae worldwide, *Monochamus* larvae bore through and eat the wood of live, dead, or dying trees. *Monochamus* engages in this activity so enthusiastically that the sounds made by mandibles grinding through wood is distinctly audible, earning it the common name "sawyer." *Monochamus titillator*, the southern pine sawyer, has a distinct predilection for pine trees. The adults, brown in color mottled with fine gray or black hairs, feed on the needles or young branches. Males and females are easily distinguished by virtue of the fact that the antennae of the male are about four times the total length of its body (which is why cerambycids are known as long-horned beetles, a name that is clearly not an entomological overstatement).

Once mated, females find a dead or dying pine tree, chew shallow depressions in the bark, and lay eggs there. The cylindrical white,

Pine sawyers: "What? I thought *you* brought the gas can!"

virtually legless grubs hatch one to two weeks later and begin to feed under the bark. About midway between grubhood and adulthood (in one or two months), the larvae tunnel straight toward the central heartwood, turning sharply before reaching it, to construct a characteristic U-shaped burrow that terminates not very far from where they started. After more chewing, the grubs construct a round chamber in which to pupate during the following spring. Adults emerge in late spring through early fall by chewing a nice round quarter-inch exit hole through the relatively thin layer of wood separating them from the world outside.

Pine sawyers are of some economic importance due to their habit of colonizing recently felled trees before they can be hauled away to the mill. But in recent years, the reputation of the pine sawyer has considerably worsened because of its practice of aiding and abetting a known felon (that is, a plant pathogen), a nematode known as *Bursaphelenctus xylophilus*. This plant-parasitic nematode, first recognized in 1979 in Missouri, is responsible for the sudden, heartrending death of pine trees throughout much of eastern North America. Within a matter of weeks after infection, pine trees progress from evergreen to gray to yellow to ever-dead. The nematodes, only $\frac{1}{30}$ inch in length at maturity, feed on the thin-walled cells that line the resin canals of pines. They mate, lay eggs, and produce juveniles. The young are so anxious to grow that they molt once in the egg before they even eat, twice more while feeding as larvae, and reach adulthood in a breathtaking four days. Disruption of the resin canal system stops resin flows and cuts off the water transport system of the tree. A tree can't last too long without water and, as a result, quickly expires.

Once a tree dies, it's no longer of interest to the nematode, which shuts down reproduction. The second-stage juveniles molt not into a feeding stage but into a dark-colored dispersal stage, bereft of feeding stylets with which to pierce cells and resistant to whatever kinds of stress nematodes are likely to encounter. These larvae can lie in wait for up to three years. What they're waiting for is a visit from a pine sawyer looking for a nice dead tree in which to lay its eggs. The nematodes, having waited this long, wait until the beetle grubs have just about finished their life cycle. When beetle larvae construct a pupation chamber, the dispersal-stage nematodes surround the pupating beetle and molt into yet another stage, the dauer-larva. These can immediately work their way into the body of a newly molted adult beetle, generally gaining access through the spiracles (air holes) and gathering in the tracheae, or respiratory passages. As beetles travel to mate and lay eggs, they carry from tree to tree as many as ninety thousand nematodes per beetle. These nematodes enter the tree through feeding wounds made by the beetle, starting the deadly cycle anew.

Fortunately, pine trees vary in their susceptibility to pine wilt nematodes and most native species are relatively resistant. Among the most sensitive is Scots pine and, unfortunately, Scots pines are widely planted as windbreak, landscape, and especially Christmas trees. The disease is always fatal in Scots pine and as a result the tree is threatened whenever *Monochamus titillator* is found. Although it's now known as the pine sawyer beetle, it may someday be known as the grub who stole Christmas.

PINE WEBWORMS

If small ornaments appear in your pine trees in mid-summer, it doesn't mean that it's Christmas in July. Right about that time of year, many caterpillars begin festooning Christmas trees—much to the detriment of the trees and to the consternation of Christmas tree growers. What could pass for tinsel but for the season is the pine webworm, *Tetralopha robustella*, a moth in the family Pyralidae. When the twelve days of Christmas are but a dim memory, pine webworms begin their dirty work. Moths begin to emerge in the off-season in June, with stragglers following through July and into August. After mating, the females lay from one to twenty eggs in a single row along the edges of pine needles. The young larvae that hatch a few days later amble about the needles, spinning silk threads as they go. They then begin to tunnel inside the pine needles, eating their way through until they grow so large that they no longer fit inside a single needle. After mining their own business, as it were, they change their ways and adopt a colonial lifestyle, with up to eighty caterpillars in a nest. The nests aren't really material for a Good Housekeeping Seal of Approval. They're built of silk and dead needles, interspersed with brown oblong fecal pellets. Depending

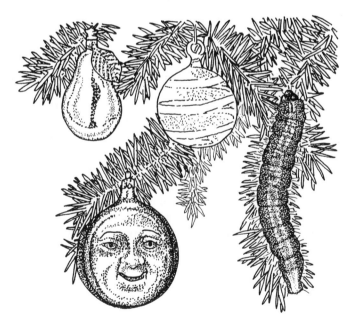

Pine webworms

on the size of the colony, the nests range from two to six inches in length. The larvae themselves aren't exactly award winners either—full grown at about ½ inch, they are muddy yellow in color with dark brown stripes running the length of the body. The full-grown larvae either crawl or drop out of their nests in late fall, dig into the ground to spin a cocoon, and pupate.

Although the pine webworm sleeps through the Christmas holidays, the damage it causes is a major problem for commercial growers of Christmas trees. Complicating the problem is the insects' catholic tastes in the Christmas tree department. In the Northeast, they nest in pitch, red, Scots, Virginia, and mugho pine; in the Southeast, they feast on slash, shortleaf, longleaf, and loblolly pine; and in the Midwest they make merry on jack, red, Scots, and eastern white pine.

The pine tube moth, *Argyrotaenia pinatubana*, is a small tortricid moth more discriminating in terms of its taste for pines. It also webs together pine needles with silk, but it does so only on eastern white pine, *Pinus strobus*. It's not only more particular about the company it eats, it's particular about the company it keeps. Unlike the pine webworm, the pine tube moth leads a solitary life, each caterpillar spinning together from five to twenty needles into a neat little web in which it resides, feeding on tips of needles. Adult moths emerge in early May to lay eggs on the needles. By July, *Argyrotaenia pinatubana* is working on a second generation. All this needle nibbling causes the needles to discolor and turn brown, and, while pine web moths don't kill the tree, they can at least put a damper on Christmas spirit.

The Zimmerman pine moth, *Dioryctria zimmermanni*, a dark-gray mottled moth in the family Pyralidae, has its own ideas about decorating Christmas trees. The dark-colored striped caterpillars feed on bark, twigs, or cones instead of on needles. They bore into the terminal shoot of Scots, Austrian, Japanese, and black pine, as well as a host of other pine species; the damaged twigs then exude pitch, which, mingled with sawdustlike excrement, marks the entrance hole. When damaged in this manner, twigs generally die at points beyond the site of injury, and the dead "flag" remaining is a dead giveaway of Zimmerman pine moth infestation. The blackheaded dark-colored larvae are at their peak in the Northeast and Midwest in July.

The pine webworm is not to be confused with the pine false webworm, *Acantholyda erythrocephala*. The pine false webworm also spends Christmas underground and emerges as an adult, lays eggs, and starts feeding on pine needles as early as May and June. Like the real pine webworms, pine false webworms live in silken nests in large groups. They cut off the needles at the base and pull them into the web with them to feed. The mature larvae are basically shaped like caterpillars and are even colored in the Christmas spirit with reddish stripes on a greenish gray background. But be forewarned—the pine false webworm isn't even a real caterpillar. *Acantholyda erythrocephala* is a sawfly—a member of the order Hymenoptera—so its closest relations aren't moths and butterflies at all but rather are bees, ants, and wasps.

None of the Christmas tree pests are active around Christmas time—they all pass the winter in a state of arrested development either in the soil or safely ensconced in silk on the tree. The damage they do, however, is of sufficient magnitude to concern homeowners who plant pine as an ornamental and to people who grow Christmas trees commercially. While there is no denying the appeal of a real live tree at Christmas, one advantage of the artificial trees, then, is that they are guaranteed free of insect damage. If anyone tries to tell you he's got insects in his artificial Christmas tree, you can be sure, like Scrooge, that it's a humbug.

TREEHOPPERS

People generally celebrate Arbor Day by going out and planting a tree or two, but for certain members of the family Membracidae the holiday is just another excuse to take a tree to lunch. Membracids, otherwise known as treehoppers, are sap-sucking bugs (in the order Homoptera) who spend all or part of their lives up a tree. Their most distinguishing feature is the enlarged process projecting from the first thoracic segment. Depending on the species, this horn takes on all manner of dimensions. *Enchenopa binotata*, the two-spotted treehopper, is fairly conservative by treehopper standards. Its horn is only half the length of its body and projects forward over its head. Since the two-spotted treehopper is only about ¼ inch long and dark brown in color, the overall effect is that it resembles a thorn. To add to the effect, adults are gregarious and line up in rows single file along the length of a twig.

Female two-spotted treehoppers lay eggs in late summer through fall. The female uses her ovipositor like a Ginsu knife to cut a slit through tree bark; she then lays six to twelve eggs on either side to

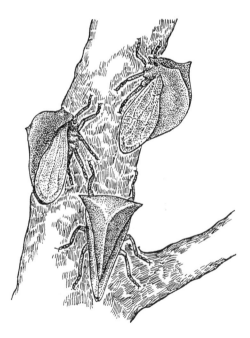

Treehoppers: "Oh give me a home, where the treehoppers roam . . ."

leave a characteristic double-crescent scar in the bark. Through the winter the scar isn't obvious because the female thoughtfully provides blown-in insulation in the form of a frothy white secretion over the eggs. This froth keeps the eggs safe and warm until early May through June, at which point the eggs hatch and the nymphs begin to suck sap from the growing tips and twigs. The nymphs, unlike the spotted adults, are solid black and spiny. They stick to young growth because their mouthparts are not strong enough to penetrate thicker bark and more mature foliage. After about five weeks and six molts, they mature into adults to complete the cycle.

Enchenopa binotata is hardly promiscuous with respect to its selection of tree species. It rather selectively frequents black walnut, black locust, butternut, viburnum, redbud, and bittersweet. To make things etymologically confusing, this treehopper is also found on the *hop*-tree (*Ptelea trifoliata*).

Its name notwithstanding, the buffalo treehopper, *Stictocephala bubalus*, spends comparatively little time in trees. While these insects do spend the entire winter as eggs under the bark of an enormous variety of trees, including maple, elm, hawthorn, cherry, poplar, locust, and ash, as soon as they hatch in late spring, the spiny green nymphs immediately bail out and abandon their arboreal existence for a life on the ground, where they feed on a number of weeds and grasses. As adults, in late August, buffalo treehoppers return to the trees to lay their eggs and die.

Just as the tree part of its name is a bit misleading, the hopper part isn't exactly diagnostic either. While buffalo treehoppers can and do hop, occasionally up to several feet, most of their time is spent crawling. When they are disturbed on their branches, their most common reaction is simply to shift around to the other side of the twig and resolutely carry through their imitation of a thorn. The buffalo part of the name refers to the humplike pronotum. It's tipped with two horns and overall it's a credible impression of the flipside of an Indian head nickel. It's unlikely that anyone other than a human thinks that there is a resemblance to a buffalo (to hungry birds, the buffalo treehopper is just another thorn) but, given its namesake, it's somehow less surprising that the buffalo treehopper leaves the trees where it's born to end up at home on the range.

WALKINGSTICKS

If there's one thing you can say about walkingsticks, it's that they certainly live up to their name. Of the 2,500-plus species in the world, the majority resemble the twigs, sticks, and even occasionally the leaves of the plants they feed on. Unfortunately, at least from the point of view of entomologists, walkingsticks don't resemble very closely any other insect currently residing on planet Earth. As a result, there's a bit of confusion as to where they belong in the grand scheme of things. They've been placed in the Dictyoptera, along with cockroaches and mantids; some people feel they'd be more comfortable included with crickets, grasshoppers, and other Orthoptera; and still others throw their hands up in despair and place walkingsticks all by themselves in their own order, called either Phasmatodea or Cheleutoptera.

Almost everyone familiar with walkingsticks is familiar with their often uncanny mimicry of dead twigs or leaves; walkingsticks, however, have quite a few other "shtiks" up their sleeves. If a predator sees through the twig act and makes a move to capture the walking-

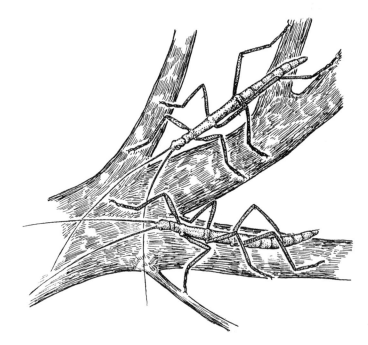

Walkingsticks: "For the last time, no, I don't want to see your impression of a willow branch!"

stick, some walkingsticks begin a peculiar side-to-side rocking motion by randomly flexing their legs. This behavior, known as quaking, can go on (if uninterrupted) for a half hour or more. If quaking doesn't inspire a predator to move on to less peculiar dinner fare, some walkingsticks drop down to the ground and play dead. Others, instead of dropping down, leap up, often opening their wings to display a startling flash of color in an otherwise drab insect. A few other species make sounds, either by rubbing their wings together or (in the case of one species from Sri Lanka) by rubbing their antennae together, producing what one author described as "a feeble sound like water dripping rapidly but regularly onto an umbrella." Perhaps this prompts gullible predators into heading for the nearest storm cellar.

Still other walkingsticks forestall attack by taking the offensive. At least a dozen species produce repulsive substances from glands in the prothorax; one secretion if sprayed in a human eye can cause pain and inflammation for two days. There are even walkingsticks that can use the spines on their third pair of legs to draw blood. If all of these ruses fail and a walkingstick gets grabbed, it still has one more ace to play—nymphs of many species can autotomize a leg. In other words, if you grab a leg of a walkingstick, it will walk away and leave you holding just a severed leg for all of your efforts. Within a couple of weeks, the walkingstick simply acquires a new leg at the next molt (which is really getting a leg up on your enemies).

When not outmaneuvering their enemies, walkingsticks lead a quiet life. It's been estimated that nymphs spend up to 95 percent of their time just resting. Presumably the remaining time is spent in leisurely fashion, nibbling at the foliage of trees and shrubs. Adults are a bit busier than the nymphs, having to deal with the responsibilities of mating and laying eggs (although some species dispense with the former and lay eggs parthenogenetically, or asexually). Oviposition behavior runs the gamut from carefully depositing eggs with a gluelike substance on the appropriate hostplant, to digging a hole and burying them, to casually dropping them to the ground, to recklessly catapulting them from the end of the abdomen over distances of fifteen to twenty feet. Mating is a relatively straightforward affair, with the male climbing onto the female's back and snaking his abdomen around to her underside to lock into her genitalia. The actual mating process doesn't take very long but males of some species remain mounted on the female's back for weeks or even months while the female lays its eggs—demonstrating a commitment that can only be called walkingstick-to-itiveness.

WILLOW LEAF BEETLES

If you ever wondered what makes weeping willows so lachrymose, it may have something to do with the fact that no fewer than a half dozen species of beetles make their living eating leaves of weeping willow and related trees. Defoliating willows is a family affair among the willow leaf beetles; eggs, larvae, and pupae are all found on willow leaves. Both adult and larval stages eat nothing but willows, cottonwoods, poplars, aspens, and other trees and shrubs in the family Salicaceae. Adult beetles mate in the spring and females lay large clusters of yellow-orange eggs on the undersides of leaves. After a short time, the eggs hatch and the grublike larvae set about skeletonizing the leaves. As they grow, their mouthparts grow with them, and when the larvae reach their final instar they can damage leaves just like their parents do, stripping away all leaf tissue but the midrib and veins. In as little as a week, the larvae complete development and pupate on the willow leaves. Adults emerge in about another week and the whole process starts in again, as many as five times through before cold weather set in. When willow leaves fall, come winter, so do the adult beetles—onto the ground, where they hide under leaf litter until the weather warms up and the willow leafs out the next spring.

Willow leaf beetles are all in the family Chrysomelidae and share

Willow leaf beetles: "The doctor said to take two and call him in the morning."

more than a few family resemblances in appearance and habits. The largest, *Chrysomela scripta*, the cottonwood leaf beetle, reaches ⅓ inch in length. It's greenish to reddish yellow in color and its elytra or wing covers are marked with black irregularly shaped spots. The willow leaf beetle, *Chrysomela interrupta*, reaches about ³⁄₁₀ inch in length. It's metallic green or yellow, with seven black spots that on occasion run into each other to form a band across its midsection. *Chrysomela lapponica*, the poplar leaf beetle, is similar in size and shape to the willow leaf beetle, although marked more heavily with black (it's restricted in distribution to the Northwest). The aspen leaf beetle, *C. crotchii*, is black with brown wing covers and does most of its defoliating in western Canada.

One additional member of the weeping willow fan club came all the way from overseas to feed on its favorite plant. *Plagiodera versicolor*, the imported willow leaf beetle, is only ⅛ inch in length and is shiny metallic blue in color. Like the other willow leaf beetle larvae, the larva of the imported willow leaf beetle is a shiny black grublike creature equipped with paired glands on the thorax. The same sorts of glands, in fact, show up in other willow leaf beetle species in Europe. When disturbed, the larvae secrete a milky white fluid from these glands. This fluid contains salicylaldehyde, a chemical that is not only bad tasting, it's bad for you, too (it uncouples mitochondrial oxidative phosphorylation, a process living cells have to do to stay alive). Needless to say, predators getting a mouthful of salicylaldehyde think twice about eating willow leaf beetle larvae.

The willow leaf beetles are not, however, to be commended for their chemical ingenuity. They are totally dependent upon willow leaves for their ability to manufacture salicylaldehyde. Many willow species contain salicin, a chemical that the leaf beetles store and then convert to salicylaldehyde internally. When beetles feed on a willow tree low in salicin, they're more likely to be picked off by predators, and in general willow leaf beetles avoid feeding on willow species that don't make salicin. The more salicin a willow tree produces, the more likely it is to be damaged by willow leaf beetles. The irony of the situation, from the willow viewpoint, is that salicin is a very toxic compound to most other organisms. Chemically, salicin is closely related to acetylsalicylic acid—otherwise known as aspirin. Unfortunately, as far as the willow leaf beetles go, salicin has only turned out to be a headache for the weeping willow.

References

Bedford, G. O. 1978. Biology and ecology of the Phasmatodea. *Ann. Rev. Ent.* 23:125–49.

Johnson, W. T., and H. L. Lyon. 1976. *Insects that Feed on Trees and Shrubs.* Ithaca: Cornell University Press.

Malek, R. B., M. C. Shurtleff, J. E. Appleby, and J. K. Bouseman. 1984. Pine wilt disease. *Report on Plant Diseases.* Illinois Cooperative Extension Service 1104.

Malek, R. B., and J. E. Appleby. 1984. Epidemiology of pine wilt in Illinois. *Plant Disease* 68:180–85.

Rowell–Rahier, M. 1984. The presence or absence of phenolglycosides in *Salix* (Salicaceae) leaves and the level of dietary specialization of some of their herbivorous insects. *Oecol.* 62:26–30.

Smiley, J. T., J. M. Horn, and N. E. Ronk. 1985. Ecological effects of salicin at three trophic levels: new problems from old adaptations. *Science.* 229:465–69.

Smith, R. L. 1986. Walkingsticks—masters of disguise. *Animal Kingdom* 89:18–21.

Chapter 5

Sodbusters

ANT-GUEST ROVE BEETLES

One of the hazards of owning beachfront property is that, come summer, uninvited guests are apt to turn up at your door and stay to socialize for longer than you dreamed possible. For the social insects, especially ants and termites, uninvited guests are a problem of considerably greater magnitude. Take lomechusine staphylinids, for example. Lomechusines are members of the Staphylinidae, or rove beetles, a very large family of beetles (over twenty-six thousand species at last count). Rove beetles are generally recognizable by their flattened elongate shape and their very distinctive front wings (so short that they reach only as far as the third abdominal segment, leaving the remainder of the abdomen exposed to the elements). In such a large family, one would expect to find a diversity of lifestyles, and lomechusines are among the rove beetles that choose to live as permanent residents of ant nests.

At first glance, an ant nest hardly seems like a hospitable place to live, what with thousands of easily agitated worker ants armed with stingers and venom. Lomechusine staphylinids, however, have mastered the art of misrepresentation to the envy of even the slickest salesman. Ant behavior in general is strictly regulated by chemicals—alarm, recruitment to food, trail following, grooming, exchange of food particles, and recognition of nestmates are all behaviors elicited by a particular chemical signal. Lomechusines have effectively cracked the chemical code, as it were, of their unwilling hosts, ants in the genus *Formica*. The beetles have two sets of tufted yellowish hairs, one at

Ant-guest rove beetles: "Sure, I'd like to get high! Do you have the stuff on you?"

the tip of the abdomen and the other along the sides of the abdomen (some species, for good measure, have glands on their leg joints as well). When a beetle approaches an ant nest, workers come out to see what's going on. At first contact, the beetle lifts its abdomen to present the tufted glands at the tip, which contain substances that are not only tasty from the ant's perspective but mind-altering. These appeasement glands produce substances that completely eliminate any aggressive behavior on the part of the ants. After the ants have nibbled on the appeasement glands, they move onto the so-called adoption glands on the abdomen, which produce substances that act in the same way as the substances produced by ant grubs. Their maternal instincts activated, the ants then carry the beetle into the colony and care for it as they would their own child, feeding it whenever the beetle solicits attention and even carrying it away from danger when the colony is threatened. Meanwhile, the beetle is free to wander throughout the colony, consuming ant eggs and grubs whenever the mood strikes. Moreover, the beetle lays its eggs in the ant colony, and the larvae, equipped with adoption glands like their parents, continue to manipulate the benighted ants, who magnanimously feed and groom them as they systematically slaughter the ants' own offspring. The beetle larvae actually receive more food, more care, and more attention than do ant grubs in the same nest, who have to worry not only about competing for the ant workers' attention for a few scraps of food but also about avoiding the mandibles of their roommates.

On observing this peculiar behavior, the great ant biologist William Morton Wheeler (1910) remarked, "Were we to behave in an analogous manner, we should live in a truly Alice-in-Wonderland society. We should delight in keeping porcupines, alligators, lobsters, etc., in our homes and insisting on their sitting down to table with us and feed them so solicitously with spoon victuals that our children would either perish of neglect or grow up as hopeless rachitics." Life for lomechusines is not without its risks, however. The ants continue to care for the beetle grubs when they pupate, burying them in soil as they do their own pupae. However, once an ant grub spins a cocoon and pupates, the ants dig it up and move it into a nice, dry pupation chamber. The ants also carefully dig up the buried beetle pupae and move them into the pupation chamber, which is instant death for the moisture-loving beetles, who don't spin cocoons and can't tolerate the dry conditions of the pupation chamber. The only lomechusines that survive to adulthood are the ones the ant workers overlook when they begin their excavations. But don't waste sympathy on the lomechusines— they've made their bed, so it's not all that surprising they have a little trouble lying in it from time to time.

BEROTHIDS

Next time you have a termite problem, instead of calling Terminix, you might try calling *Lomamyia latipennis*; although the name doesn't bring a glimmer of recognition even to most entomologists' eyes, it lives in infamy in the world of termites. *Lomamyia latipennis*, which doesn't come equipped with a common name, is a member of the Berothidae, a very obscure family in the order Neuroptera (a pretty obscure order in and of itself). Thus, *Lomamyia* includes among its close relatives such insectan eccentrics as dustywings, lacewings, antlions, mantispids, and snakeflies. The berothids are easy to distinguish from other neuropterans by the presence of a hook midway around the outer edge of the membranous forewing.

Adult *Lomamyia* are fairly innocuous from the termite perspective; if they feed at all, it's on honeydew or nectar, neither of which is of much concern to termites. However, female *Lomamyia* lay their stalked egg clusters on logs, stumps, or trees infested with termites (especially subterranean termites in the genus *Reticulotermes*). The tiny newly hatched first instar larvae crawl down the stalk supporting their egg cluster and scurry across the surface of the wood, seeking out cracks and crevices that will lead them to the termites within.

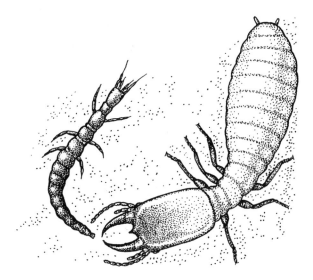

Berothids: "I'm warning you, I've got gas!"

At first glance it seems exceedingly unlikely that a newly hatched *Lomamyia* could wreak much havoc in a termite colony. First of all, termites are about twenty-five times heavier; *Lomamyia* pits its 0.07 milligrams against a termite's 2.5 milligrams. Secondly, while adult termites come equipped with a tough, hardened, armorlike outer skeleton, first instar *Lomamyia* larvae are pale, slender, and soft-bodied. But, like David in his confrontation with Goliath, *Lomamyia* has something better than brute strength to fall back on. A first instar larva confronted with a termite maneuvers around until the tip of its abdomen is pointed at the termite's head; it then waves its tail back and forth under the termite's nose (or the place where a nose would be if insects had noses). In about one to three minutes, the termite collapses, paralyzed. After waiting another minute or so, the berothid moves in to feed at its leisure, which it can afford to do, since the termite remains motionless and paralyzed for up to three hours, whereupon it expires whether it's eaten or not.

After two to three weeks of gassing and guzzling termites, *Lomamyia* molts. Second instar larvae are C-shaped and completely inactive, either suspended on a strand of silk or prone on the substrate; they don't walk, they don't run, they don't feed, they don't pass "Go" and collect two hundred dollars. This lifestyle gets old quickly, so after only three days of literally hanging around with nothing to do, *Lomamyia* molts again and as a third instar resumes its termite-eating ways. The larger third instar larvae can gas up to six termites at once. After about three weeks, the larva, having had its fill of termites, spins a dense white silken cocoon, suspended in place by a scaffolding of coarser silk and camouflaged with bits of bark, mud, wood splinters, and other debris. After about a month, the adult berothid, still enclosed in its pupal skin, chews a hole through one end of its cocoon and crawls out to molt.

Scientists are at a loss to explain why termites don't attack and kill *Lomamyia* while they're totally helpless either as second instar larvae or as prepupae in their cocoons. For that matter, they can't explain why the poisonous gas released by the berothid has absolutely no effect on flies, bark lice, wasps, or the other berothids that may share a log with a termite colony; the entomological profession has yet to design such a highly species-specific insecticide. But *Lomamyia*'s greatest technical accomplishment, perhaps, is this—it has developed a way to get gas *before* it eats, rather than *after*.

CARROT RUST FLIES

Many miners measure the value of their work in terms of the number of carats they collect; *Psila rosae*, however, is one miner that *eats* the "carrots" it finds. *Psila rosae*, otherwise known as the carrot rust fly, spends its formative instars tunneling through the roots and crowns of carrots, parsnips, celery, and other related plants in the family Umbelliferae (all of which share a characteristic umbrella-shaped flowerhead). The larvae are legless, headless maggots that are yellowish brown to dark brown in color and less than a third of an inch in length when fully grown. Their assault on the umbellifer family begins each spring when female flies emerge from overwintering pupation sites around the base of plants near where the root crown pokes through the soil. The hatching maggots burrow into the crown and gradually work their way deep into the root. The first and early second instar larvae stay mainly in the fibrous lateral parts of the root, whereas older second instar and third instar larvae take a different "route," as it were, and confine their feeding to the main tap root. Areas where the maggots feed turn a rusty red color; hence the name "carrot rust fly." The roots aren't the only place, however, where carrot rust flies change the color

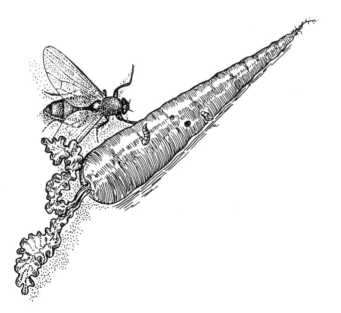

Carrot rust flies: "What do you mean, carrots are good for my eyes? Maggots don't *have* eyes!"

scheme. The extensive damage they cause to the water transport system in the roots causes the upper parts of the plants to wilt and turn yellow.

Carrot rust flies concentrate most of their root-mining efforts north of the fortieth parallel; in the northern extremes of their range they can be found from British Columbia to Newfoundland to Europe (whence they came originally) and in the southern part of their range from Colorado eastward to Maryland. Adults are tiny flies about 3/20 inch in length, with a shiny blue-back to blue-green body, yellow legs, and a few yellow hairs scattered here and there. Adults can frequently be found resting on vegetation in the shade.

If *Psila rosae* restricted its activity to resting in the shade, it would be of considerably less interest to entomologists, farmers, and gardeners, but its unerring ability to find and lay eggs on carrots makes it a major threat to those who hold carrots near and dear. Female carrot rust flies are able to find their hosts by virtue of a highly sophisticated chemical detection system. Receptors in their antennae respond selectively to a group of volatile plant odor components called propenylbenzenes; the flies can detect one particular compound, trans-asarone, at concentrations of 500 attograms per milliliter (that's 0.0000000000000005 of a gram, for those not up on tiny numbers). They are also sensitive to other volatile plant chemicals and orient selectively to unique combinations of chemicals characteristic of their hostplants. These volatile chemicals are used by the fly to orient from a long distance, up to several miles away. Once the female arrives at the plant, she checks for the presence of two more types of carrot chemicals, by walking up and down on the leaf surface. If all the right chemicals are in the right places, she'll finally lay eggs.

Curiously, once carrot rust fly eggs hatch, the maggots in the soil use almost entirely different chemical cues for finding their hostplants. Probably the most important cue to which carrot rust fly maggots orient is plain carbon dioxide, a universal product of root respiration. Although some researchers feel that the maggots can respond to highly specific host chemicals like their parents do, the larvae are nowhere nearly as sensitive to as many compounds at such low concentrations; in other words, the chemical messages broadcast by carrots may be rated "R"—that is, not suitable for "miners."

126

HONEY ANTS

In human society, gorging yourself at the dinner table to the point of bursting has never been considered an act of altruistic behavior toward one's fellow human beings. In certain ant societies, however, gorging to the point of immobility is indeed an act of altruism. This behavior has arisen on at least three continents. In western North America, members of the genus *Myrmecocystus* engage exuberantly in the practice. Called honey ants, *Myrmecocystus* worker ants gather the sweet secretions of certain galls on oak trees and carry the nectar back to the colony in their crops, the region of the digestive tract between the esophagus and midgut. Once back underground in the nest, they take their load to another group of workers, generally the largest in the nest. The sole job of these workers is to store the nectar in their crops. So totally dedicated are they to this task that their abdomens swell to enormous size and grapelike dimensions with stored nectar. These aptly named repletes are so engorged that they can barely move and as a result literally do nothing but hang around, dangling in clusters from the roof of the nest. If for some reason they're dislodged and fall

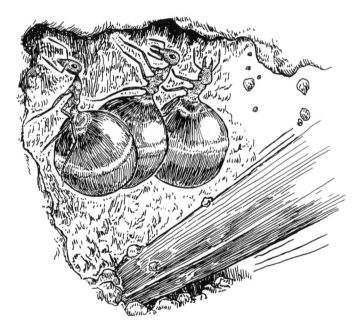

Honey ants: "Look out! Here it comes again!"

to the floor of the nest, they can't even right themselves, much less return to their roost, without the help of a few of their more slender nestmates. The abdomen of a replete is so stretched that the nectar inside is actually visible through the thin membranes connecting the abdominal segments; moreover, all of their other abdominal organs, including such useful items as midgut, intestine, and rectum, are forced backward and downward to accommodate the nectar supply.

This honey hoarding, however, hardly counts as gluttony. Repletes come equipped with a heavily muscled valve-and-filter system between the crop and the midgut, called a proventriculus. The valve ensures that only a very small amount of nectar passes into the midgut of the replete, to satisfy its nutritional needs. The remainder of the nectar sits in the replete's crop just as a jar of honey sits on a shelf in your house. When times are tough in the ant colony, workers head for the repletes and touch them with their antennae, whereupon the replete regurgitates and releases a droplet of nectar, which is then happily licked up and swallowed by the hungry worker. On this un-antlike passivity and forbearance, Wheeler (1910) was moved to remark: "Those who, in anthropomorphic mood, are wont to extol the fervid industry and extraordinary feats of muscular endurance in ants, should not overlook the beatific patience and self-sacrifice displayed by the replete . . . as it hangs from the rafters of its nest, month in, month out—for years perhaps—a reservoir of temperamental as well as liquid sweetness."

Honey ant nests are, as ant nests go, very deep and extensive. One investigator excavated a colony in Arizona with the help of professional grave diggers and managed to follow 16¼ feet of nest galleries until they uncovered the queen in the royal chamber. One possible reason for burrowing so deeply is that honey ant colonies are at risk from any wandering predator with a sweet tooth or fang. On all three continents where it is found, the honey ant's major enemy is the notorious human being. In the days before Twinkies, obtaining a sugar fix was a challenging problem. Honey ant colonies, which can contain as many as 1,500 repletes, provided a tolerable solution. One calculation puts the return-on-investment at 960 honey ants per pound of honey Troy weight, 1,166 for avoirdupois.

In Australia, honey ants in the genus *Melophorus* (which translates to mean "honey carrier") are greatly prized by the Aborigines (who call them *yarrumpa*). According to McKeown (1936), it's the woman's job to find the colonies and dig them up:

> The nests of the Honey Ant are dug up by the women with a speed which is astonishing. The hard ground round the entrance to the nest is loosened with the point of a digging stick and the loose earth is then scooped out with the hand or a small bowl, the woman alternately breaking up the soil,

and throwing it behind her, until a hole is dug large enough to contain her body; she goes on digging deeper and deeper, until she may reach a depth of six feet or even more. Sir Baldwin Spencer says: "In parts of the scrub, where the ants live . . . acre after acre of hard sandy soil is seen to have been dug out, simply by the picks of the women in search of the insect, until the place has the appearance of a deserted mining field where diggers have for long been at work 'prospecting.' "

For those in search of something sweet, however, the "gold" is measured in calories instead of carats and is no less valuable for that.

ROUND FUNGUS BEETLES

Insects have adopted some unusual diets to be sure and eating slime molds has to rank right up there among the most unusual. Slime molds owe their less-than-endearing name to their less-than-endearing appearance. The slime molds, placed by bewildered biologists in their own phylum (the Myxomycetes or Mycetozoa), straddle the fine line between animal and vegetable (or to be more specific, between protozoa and fungi). Like fungi, slime molds reproduce by forming spores and obtain nourishment by absorbing nutrients from decayed plant material or nonliving soil matter. But they resemble protozoans or one-celled animals by virtue of their ability to take in solid food particles by engulfing them and by virtue of their remarkable ability to crawl along a substrate.

The most conspicuous life stage of a slime mold consists of a naked mass of protoplasm with many nuclei. This unappetizing arrangement is called a plasmodium. Plasmodia can be any of a number of gay colors—red, violet, yellow, and so on—but they're always slimy. When ready to reproduce, the plasmodium produces spore cases, or spor-

Round fungus beetles: "So round, so firm, so fully packed, that's my gal!"

angia. Depending on the species, these spore cases can be colorful or colorless, stalked or unstalked, round or ovoid. Inside the spore cases are spores, which germinate to form a single-celled myxamoeba. Two myxamoeba fuse to form a zygote, an amoebalike creature that flows among and engulfs bacteria by surrounding them with protoplasm. A number of these zygotes can get together and lose all their integrity to form the large, wandering plasmodial form. Plasmodia typically (and understandably) lead a concealed existence for most of their lives, secreting themselves under bark or dead leaves, slithering out to face the world only to release their spores and reproduce. The entire process of development, from spore to fruiting plasmodium, can take as little as twenty-four to forty-eight hours or as long as two years.

While this lifestyle may not sound appetizing to you or me, it's just the sort of thing certain insects really get into. Not just one or two species but species from at least six families of beetles make their living feeding occasionally or even exclusively on slime molds. The entire family Sphindidae eats nothing but (which is a good reason to decline any invitation to a sphindid family gathering). Most slime-mold-feeding insects are relatives of fungus feeders and some have remarkable adaptations for their unusual diet. In the genus *Agathidium* (family Leiodidae), beetles have little brushes on their mouthparts for raking in spores and minute teeth on their mandibles for crushing the hard outer wall of the spores. More advanced *Agathidium* eat just the softer, juicier plasmodia. Since chasing down a crawling mass of protoplasm doesn't require great predatory skills, some of the *Agathidium* species lack wings and some have greatly reduced, possibly even nonfunctional, eyes.

One bizarre characteristic of many slime-mold-feeding beetles is their great contractile skill. When disturbed (by heaven knows what), they roll into a tight little ball (whence the common name "round fungus beetle," for these very uncommon insects). This behavior may be due to the fact that associating with slime molds means hanging out in tiny cracks and crevices, where one doesn't have many options for escape when confronted by an enemy. Since the beetles' bodies are usually covered with spores, rolling up into a motionless ball may simply be an attempt to look as unappetizing to their enemies as the slime molds they eat.

For *Agathidium*, slime molds are the be-all and end-all of existence. Curiously, slime molds, if they feel anything, may feel the same way about their consumers. Although round fungus beetles do eat slime molds, they also have special spore-bearing pits in their guts and may actually carry viable spores to new habitats. By ingesting spores in one place and defecating them some time later in another place, beetles can carry slime molds over far greater distances than if the molds had to depend exclusively on their own tedious mode of locomotion. If this sort of association seems like a singular aberration, think again: there are over six hundred species in the genus *Agathidium* alone, all passionately devoted to slime molds. That's about as many species as there are birds in the United States. Ornithologists, however, need not worry—watching beetles eat slime molds will never replace birdwatching as a national pastime.

SANGUINARY ANTS

Abraham Lincoln notwithstanding, slavery remains a "peculiar institution" today in ant societies all over the world, even in the purported Land of the Free and Home of the Brave. Perhaps best known of the slavemaking ants is *Formica sanguinea*, the so-called sanguinary ant of Europe. Sanguinary ants are not so much out for blood as they are out for larvae and pupae of *Formica fusca*, the silky ant, and its relatives. What makes slave owning so reprehensible even among the sanguinary ants is that the species is perfectly capable of functioning as a free society; workers are capable of doing everything a worker ant is ever called upon to do during its life. Indeed, the proportion of free societies among *F. sanguinea* populations ranges from an unenlightened 2 percent to a positively abolitionist 98 percent.

Generally, when sanguinary ants go on a slave raid, they choose a conveniently located neighboring *Formica fusca* colony—not a difficult task since *F. fusca* and its close relatives are among the commonest ants in the north temperate zone and their compact mound nests are familiar sights in fields, forests, hills, and dales. According to Wheeler

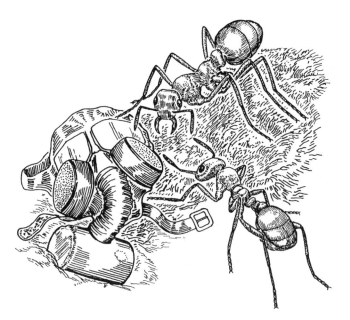

Sanguinary ants: "We found it when we raided their Defense Department research laboratory."

(1910), raids typically take place in July or August, after *Formica fusca* colonies have swarmed and left behind only workers, the queen, and the children. Raids can take place either in the morning or in the afternoon, and particularly aggressive populations can manage two raids in succession before calling it a day. The slavemaking workers leave the nest in an open phalanx, up to three or more feet across. As the phalanx approaches the nest, the first detachments to arrive surround the nest and await the arrival of the main army. The *Formica fusca* under attack adopt one of two strategies—either they gear up to defend their nests to the death or they grab the larvae and pupae and try to break through the sanguinary line to safety. Presented with the opportunity, sanguinary ants grab the children away from the fleeing workers and then turn around to invade the nest, pillaging pupae in brood chambers and robbing nurseries. They attack and kill the slave species only if they encounter resistance. Afterward, the ants under attack struggle back to their devastated colony and attempt to piece together a semblance of a social life.

Considering the outrages to which slave-species are subjected, it's curious to see that they offer so little resistance to their would-be masters. Sanguinary ants are not appreciably larger than silky ants—both run about ⅕ to ¼ inch in length. Slavemaking species, however, have an unfair advantage; they resort to chemical warfare. Ant societies are almost completely dominated by chemicals. Chemicals indicate to an ant when to fight, when to mate, when to eat, even when to bury the dead. Sanguinary ants take ruthless advantage of this chemical dependency when they enter the nest of the species to be enslaved. As they enter, they release enormous amounts of low molecular weight volatile chemicals called acetates. These chemicals, known as propaganda substances, mask the alarm and attack signals emitted by the colony being invaded. Receiving no instructions from higher-ups or fellow workers, the bulk of the colony stands idly by in confusion as the babies in their charge are spirited away.

When the captured larvae and pupae develop into adults, they face a life of slavery in their new home in the nest of the sanguinary ants, feeding them, foraging for them, and raising their offspring in subterranean servitude. For silky ants, then, the Underground Railway leads not to freedom but to something else altogether.

SCORPIONS

It's not at all surprising that Halloween, a holiday dedicated to glorifying all the dangerous things that creep along in darkness, should fall, astrologically speaking, under the sign of Scorpio, the scorpion. Scorpions rightly belong in the category of "things that go bump in the night." Virtually all scorpions adhere strictly to a nocturnal lifestyle. It's easiest to define a scorpion by starting at the tail end. Perhaps the most distinctive characteristic of the order Scorpionida is the long five-segmented tail topped off with a bulbous sac and a mean-looking sting. Were it not for the sting, scorpions would be pretty unremarkable as arthropods go. Like other members of the class Arachnida, they walk with eight legs, breathe with book lungs, and consume their prey (mostly insects, spiders, and millipedes, although larger species won't turn down a small rodent if the opportunity presents itself) by sucking out body fluids through their chelicerae, or jaws. Unlike spiders, which inject venom into their prey through the chelicerae, scorpions use the sting at the end of the tail to paralyze their prey. On either side of their jaws is a leglike pedipalp, the last two segments of which form crablike chelae, or pincers. While the chelae grasp the prey in a death grip, the long tail whips forward over the scorpion's body and sinks in, often repeatedly. All of this grasping, coiling, and thrusting would

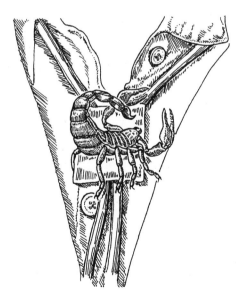

Scorpions

be academic were it not for the fact that scorpions protect themselves from their real or imagined enemies in the same way. Thus, when the woodpiles, rocks, debris, or loose boards they're hiding under during the day are disturbed by blundering humans, they're likely to respond in the only way they know how.

Scorpion venoms vary widely in their toxicity; of the forty or so species known to occur in the United States (primarily throughout the South and Southwest), only two are considered to be dangerous to humans. Both belong to the genus *Centruroides; C. sculpturatus* is confined to Arizona, and *C. suffusus*, the Durango scorpion, occurs sporadically throughout the Southwest. Among the symptoms of scorpion sting is a burning sensation at the site of injection with little or no swelling. Shortly thereafter, the reaction begins in earnest—convulsions, ataxia (uncoordinated movements), drooling, muscle twitches, slurred speech, abdominal cramps, and respiratory difficulties. Usually, recovery occurs within forty-eight hours, but, for children under five, heart patients, or people stung numerous times on the face or neck, death may ensue.

Despite the fact that Halloween is under the sign of Scorpio, scorpions aren't likely to be out trick-or-treating on October 31. Generally, they're active only when nighttime temperatures are above seventy-seven degrees Fahrenheit, so during the winter they keep a low profile. Come spring, when temperatures rise, a young scorpion's thoughts turn to romance. Scorpion courtship is very elaborate, involving a complicated dance routine in which males clasp their partner's chelae and commence a series of do-si-dos that can last for hours. At the appropriate moment the male drops a sperm packet, called a spermatophore, on the ground and positions the female so that she can pick it up with her genital opening. Instead of laying eggs, female scorpions give birth to living young, who scramble onto her back and ride piggyback at least until their first molt. Once molted, they leave their mother and, after six more molts in about twelve months, are ready to assume the tasks and responsibilities of adult scorpions.

Sting notwithstanding, scorpions are a favorite food item for grasshoppers, mice, snakes, lizards, and some birds. Their major source of mortality is probably the souvenir industry. In regions where their population densities are high, scorpion hunting is a popular and profitable pastime involving little or no expense. Scorpions are easily spotted at night simply by shining an ultraviolet or black light; their fluorescent glow can be detected from several feet away. Literally thousands of scorpions have ended up encased in acrylic to serve as string ties, paper weights, or bookends. Humans would probably figure prominently, then, in scorpion-style Halloween stories.

SEXTON BEETLES

In human society, burial of the dead is generally a somber occasion, during which eulogies are said and fond farewells are bid; in sexton beetle society, however, burial of the dead marks the beginning of a beautiful friendship. Sexton or burying beetles are species in the genus *Nicrophorus*. Like other members of the family Silphidae, they feed on dead and decaying animals, but, unlike their relatives, they respectfully bury their food before they begin to consume it. Burying beetles as a rule are shiny black, as suits members of the funerary profession, and are equipped, in the words of the French naturalist Jean Henri Fabre (1911), with a "double, scalloped scarf of vermilion," across their elytra, or wing covers. The six or seven species in North America range in size from a little over ½ inch to 1½ inches in length. Their small size relative to the objects they bury—rodents, snakes, birds and the like—makes their undertaking, as it were, all the more impressive.

Actually, burial of a carcass is a joint project, involving two beetles, usually a male and a female. Both male and female adult beetles arrive at and stake out a carcass. Although Fabre observed, "to this carrion, ripened by the sun, the insect will not fail to hasten from the various points of the horizon, so accomplished is he in detecting such a deli-

Sexton beetles: "A mouse, maybe, Bob, but a *moose?*"

137

cacy," scientists, as they are wont to do, demonstrated that the reality of the situation is not quite so remarkable; indeed, it appears that most carrion is discovered by random wandering. Odor detection occurs only within ten to twenty feet from the carrion. The beetles' short-range olfactory prowess, however, is really quite remarkable. They are particularly sensitive to odors of decomposition and can detect skatole, a breakdown product of protein, at concentrations of 0.00009 percent (about nine parts per ten million). Once a beetle claims a body, he or she aggressively defends it from preemption by any other beetles of the same sex. Once a likable member of the opposite sex shows up, however, work begins in earnest, with no time off for hearts and flowers. The basic burial protocol for both sexes is that one beetle lies on its back under the carcass and uses its legs as levers to shift it into position. Periodically, the beetle turns right-side up and digs down into the ground to clear a path. The pair may work together maneuvering and digging or may spell each other, taking turns lifting and digging. Eventually, the carcass moves underground, ensconced in a chamber about one inch below the surface. Once underground, the carcass is stripped of fur, rolled into a ball, and treated with both oral and anal secretions, which are thought to act as meat preservatives. All of this activity makes males amorous, and copulation romantically occurs as the carcass is being readied. Unlike most male insects, sexton beetle husbands don't abandon their mates once the deed is done; rather, they stay around to aid in child care.

The process of preparing a carcass stimulates egg development in female sexton beetles, who build a short passageway above the burial chamber and lay eggs in the side wall. Once the larvae hatch, they are summoned to the dinner table by their parents, who make sounds by rubbing a plectrum, on the inside surface of the forewing, against a series of ridges on the abdomen. They also make sounds when mating, so, unlike their clerical namesakes, they ring their chimes for other than religious reasons. Larvae feed from a pool of partly digested regurgitated material thoughtfully provided by their parents. As they grow larger and stronger, the larvae can feed directly from the carrion. When they are finally ready to pupate, their parents construct a horizontal tunnel for them and then depart, their parental responsibilities at an end.

If all this seems a bit unbelievable, be consoled by the fact that even entomologists have had a hard time believing that an inch-long beetle could move and bury an object weighing upward of four ounces. One author, C. F. Selous, in a 1911 paper on the "so-called carrion-feeding Coleoptera," wrote that he was "by no means convinced that the 'burying' of the carcase [sic] is due only to the Necrophori or that it is a purposeful act. The burial of a carcase is partly apparent and partly real." He continues to attribute the disappearance of the carcass to the liberation of gases generated by decomposition and death of underlying vegetation due to exposure to "deleterious juices." It would be interesting to know if sexton beetles were by no means convinced of the credentials of one C. F. Selous as an entomologist.

Sexton beetles are not the only underground gourmets interested in buried culinary treasures. Carrion flies are perhaps the biggest problem sexton beetles face once they've located a body. As the beetles bury their prey, flies attracted to the decomposing body lay innumerable eggs on the carcass; left to hatch, these eggs would produce maggots that would make short work of the carcass and leave the larval sexton beetles without a morsel to sustain themselves. To that end, *Nicrophorus* is everywhere accompanied in its travels by *Poecilochirus necrophori*, a tiny mite that lives only on the bodies of burying beetles. The mites leave the body of the beetle as the carrion is prepared for burial and they feed on the eggs and hatching larvae of the carrion flies. They reboard the beetles when they leave the underground chamber to seek out newly dead life forms. Carrion flies who plan to crash a funeral, then, would be well advised to find out who else might be attending, or the funeral they attend may very well be their own.

SNOW SCORPIONFLIES

Every four years, a day is added to the end of February; this leap day evens out discrepancies in the calendar system. But for *Boreus brumalis,* every day in February is a leap day. *B. brumalis* is known by some as a snow scorpionfly, and by others as a snowflea. The former is the more descriptive name, since *Boreus brumalis* and the other twelve or thirteen members of the family Boreidae all belong to the order Mecoptera, the scorpionflies. The order in turn owes its name to a related family, the Panorpidae, male members of which have a large recurved genital capsule reminiscent of the sting of a scorpion—but the panorpids are a different story. While boreids don't share impressive male genital equipment with the panorpids, they do have the characteristic elongated chewing mouthparts that give them a sort of horsefaced appearance.

Boreids are called *snow*fleas because they are calendar-shifted from the majority of insectkind. Adult boreids are active from late November through mid-March. The dingy brown to black insects, slightly over $\frac{1}{10}$ inch at the outset, have thin straplike wings that are useless for flying. As a consequence, they move around and among snowdrifts by hopping, occasionally six inches or more at a shot. If you're inclined to stand around in the snow in temperatures barely above freezing,

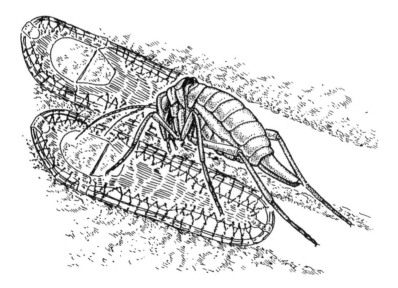

Snow scorpionflies

you may spot *Boreus brumalis* nibbling on its favorite food, moss. Even the larvae develop on moss. Females either lay eggs directly onto moss or bury their very long ovipositors deep into the soil. Either way, they adopt a relatively unusual vertical position for the proceedings.

Eggs hatch in anywhere from eight days to six weeks, depending on temperatures. The larva is vaguely grublike, with the requisite six walking legs on the thorax. Some species have caterpillar-like prolegs on the abdomen. Nobody knows exactly how many times they molt, but they're ready for pupation by mid-August to September and burrow down into the sod to find a moist spot to pass the time. The pupa is actually almost as mobile as the larva, wiggling up and down in its sod chamber when disturbed. Adults emerge again in November and December. The life cycle is thought to take at least two years.

Very little of the life cycle of snow scorpionflies has been studied, with one conspicuous exception. The mating behavior has been documented in excruciatingly fine detail. This reflects not so much the sorry state of entomologists' minds but rather the uniqueness of the whole business in boreids. Mating takes place basically all winter. Males initiate courtship by firmly grasping the female with his claspers. He'll start with any body part—femur, tibia, tarsus, or even antenna. If she acquiesces, he then grabs her body with his tonglike wings and hauls her up onto his back, where he moves his tail along her abdomen until he finds her genital opening. Once he inserts his genitalia, he lets loose with his wings. Then the female boreid does two unusual things, at least as far as insect sex practices are concerned. First, she inserts her genitalia into the male (in a process called reciprocal intromission) and then she rocks backward until she's vertical, perpendicular to her mate, to form an "L." She next falls into a cataleptic state, legs and antennae folded, for the next one to twelve hours and rides around on the male, who runs, hops, climbs, eats, and otherwise goes about his business undisturbed (an "L" of a way to travel, as it were).

Mating in the Boreidae is unusual, then, in many respects. First of all, it takes place in the dead of winter; second, the female faces the male's back, and third, reciprocal intromission takes place. Probably the most unusual aspect of this whole operation is that the *successful* male snow scorpionfly is the one who gives the "cold shoulder" to a prospective mate.

TARANTULAS

Well-informed people can congratulate themselves for recognizing that a tarantula is not an insect. Insects, after all, have three body segments and three pairs of legs. With only two body segments (albeit big ones) and with four pairs of legs, a tarantula can safely be classified as a spider by those in the know. There's only one problem, however, and that is that tarantulas aren't exactly spiders, either. While it's true that tarantulas are card-carrying lifetime members of the class Arachnida and even of the order Araneida, just like spiders, that's as close as they get to what arachnologists like to consider as spiders. Tarantulas are sufficiently unlike the average run-of-the-mill spiders that they are not placed in the suborder Araneomorphae, along with "true" spiders, but rather in their own suborder, the Mygalomorphae.

The differences are, to say the least, somewhat esoteric and involve getting closer to a tarantula that the average person cares to do. The main difference between mygalomorphs and true spiders (you'll be happy to hear) is in how their fangs work. The large, two-segmented jaws, or chelicerae, of the mygalomorphs are aligned parallel to the

Tarantulas: "I don't suppose you'd consider artificial insemination . . ."

long axis of the body and move in a vertical plane. Peer into the face of a cobweb spider or black widow and you'll notice immediately that the jaws of true spiders are held perpendicular to the body and move in a horizontal plane. The mygalomorph arrangement is called more primitive than the spider's (although, one imagines, not to a mygalomorph's face). Whatever its evolutionary status, the mygalomorph arrangement is certainly more cumbersome. Among other things, a tarantula must elevate its body off the ground in order to drive its fangs into its prey.

There are about 1,500 species of tarantulas (that's 120,000 legs) worldwide, about 30 of which can be found in North America. The largest spiders in the world are tarantulas (although tarantulas are not necessarily large); one bird spider from the Amazon has a leg span of about ten inches and a body weight approaching a quarter of a pound. A far more reliable trait than body size is hairiness: practically all tarantulas are noticeably hirsute. In fact, the Spanish name for members of the family Theraphosidae (what we call tarantulas) is *arañas peludas*, or "hairy spiders." The Spanish name is actually more accurate than is "tarantula," a name that, technically speaking, belongs to *Lycosa tarentula*, a wolf spider from Europe.

Tarantulas are also known as bird spiders, not because some species are larger than birds (which is nonetheless true) but because some species do on occasion eat birds (to be fair, they feed mostly on nestlings). This behavior was first reported by Maria Sibylla Merian in 1705, but no one believed it until H. W. Bates corroborated her story in 1863. Although the larger species of theraphosids can feed on birds, small mammals, and reptiles, the smaller, homegrown varieties like *Brachypelma emilia*, the Mexican redleg, make do with insect fare. All tarantulas spring on their prey, strike them with their fangs, inject venom and other substances that reduce the innards of the struggling victim to liquefied pulp, and then suck up the contents. Since tarantulas are so large and strong, relative to their prey, they rely more on brute strength, rather than powerful venom, to subdue their suppers.

While bird-eating tarantulas can climb trees, most species content themselves with a down-to-earth existence, constructing burrows in the ground lined with silk webbing. No fly-by-nights (indeed, no fly-at-all), tarantulas can occupy a single burrow for their entire lifetime, which, for females, is upward of twenty years. Sexual maturity takes up to eight to ten years to reach. A male interested in mating spins a small silken sheet, or sperm web, upon which he deposits sperm; he then inserts the tips of the two leglike appendages on either side of his mouth, the pedipalps, into the sperm and withdraws it into the pedipalps. Male tarantula genitalia never come in contact with female genitalia; instead, a male tarantula uses his pedipalps as marital aids. He has a few other tricks as well; when he approaches a female, he grabs her fangs with mating hooks, structures underneath his front legs, thus preventing her from snacking on him during sex. He raises her upward, inserts his sperm-laden palps, injects the sperm, and then swiftly releases her and removes himself from the premises, lest she confuse him with dinner. After mating, a female spins a silken sheet in her burrow and places her eggs on the sheet. After spinning a top-sheet for the eggs, she stitches the whole arrangement together into a little sac and stands guard over her eggs, even bringing the bundle out of the burrow up into the sunshine on warm days to incubate, until the spiderlings hatch and disperse.

Tarantulas, though much feared and despised, are in reality quite beneficial from a human perspective. They consume, for example, vast quantities of destructive insects every year. What's more, indigenous peoples in Thailand, Annam, Burma, and Cambodia eat spiders regularly and consider them quite a delicacy. Eating tarantulas may actually be a good idea, even for Americans; after all, with eight juicy legs, just about everybody could get a drumstick at Thanksgiving.

WEBSPINNERS

When a woman is expecting, she may feel the urge to knit a pair of little baby booties; embiopterans that are expecting feel the urge to weave instead of knit and don't even have to go to the notions store to buy their thread. Embiopterans are among the more obscure insects of the world. Mostly tropical, a few species have settled in the southern part of the United States, where they're easily overlooked, since they rarely exceed four to seven millimeters (¼ inch) in length. Their most distinctive feature is undoubtedly the basal segment of their front legs. This segment is enlarged and contains silk glands and spinning hairs. Embiopterans construct extensive silken galleries under or on bark, in debris, on plants, or in cracks in the soil, and thus are know in common parlance as webspinners.

Webspinners of all ages, even newly hatched ones, can spin silk. Like emperors in old China, embiopterans are swaddled in silk starting on the day they're born. The always wingless females prepare for the arrival and the pitter-patter of lots of little feet by doing what they do best—spinning silk. *Clothoda urichi,* a species found only in Trinidad,

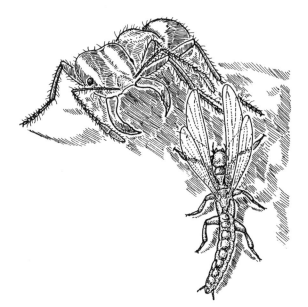

Webspinners: "Of course I'm a spineless coward! I'm an invertebrate, for crying out loud!"

145

has been extensively studied (by an entomologist who knows how to pick a study site). The copper-brown females, just over ½ inch in length (1.6 centimeters), construct silken sheets by waving their front legs back and forth, casting out multiple strands of silk at the same time. Up to two dozen females or more share a silken gallery. Unlike the vast majority of insects, webspinners don't feel that their parental responsibilities end at egglaying. Each female lays a cluster of eggs, covers it with a layer of macerated wood, silk, and fecal pellets, and positions herself over the eggs till they hatch, a process that can take up to six weeks. Maternal devotion even extends to standing guard over the newly hatched nymphs as well. Females remain with their offspring for up to ten weeks, about half the time the young need to reach sexual maturity (just about the time they reach adolescence and start asking for the keys to the car). Females continue to spin silk (and in fact pick up the pace) once their eggs have hatched. While they don't feed their offspring, as do conscientious mammalian mothers, they are devoted enough to change their diapers—they pick up fecal pellets and silk them into the walls of the gallery, out of harm's way.

What is it that webspinners face that's so dangerous that their mothers have to supervise their wonder years to ensure a future supply of webspinners? Basically, just about anything poses a threat to a webspinner. They eat moss, lichen, dead grass, and decaying debris, so they're not equipped with sharp claws, spines, teeth, or poison glands to snare prey or defend themselves. About the best they can manage when threatened is to feign death or run away, usually backward. In fact, so well equipped are webspinners for backing out of a dangerous situation that the wings of the males can actually flex backward up and over their heads. Their only defense against the cold, cruel outside world is their silk blanket. While some predators like fire ants cut their way through the silk, the majority simply walk directly overhead, blissfully unaware that dinner lives just underfoot, all wrapped and ready for takeout. Even for predators that know enough to cut through the silk, the process takes a sufficiently long time for everybody underneath to run away, backward, forward, or whichever-ward. Faced with a maze of crisscrossing threads, many predators just give up and wander off in search of easier pickings. Thus, the Ethiopian proverb "When spider webs unite, they can stop a lion" applies to six-legged webspinners as well as eight-legged ones.

References

Abbott, C. E. 1927. Experimental data on the olfactory sense of Coleoptera, with special reference to the Necrophori. *Ann. Ent. Soc. Amer.* 20:207–16.

Browning, J. G. 1981. *Tarantulas.* Neptune City, N.J.: T. F. H. Publ.

Brushwein, J. 1987. Observations on *Lomamyia longicollis* (Neuroptera: Berothidae) in South Carolina. *Journal of the Kansas Ent. Soc.* 60:150–52.

Byers, G. W., and R. Thornhill. 1983. Biology of the Mecoptera. *Ann. Rev. Ent.* 28:203–28.

Carpenter, F. M. 1931. The Biology of the Mecoptera. *Psyche* (Mar.):41–55.

Cooper, K. W. 1940. The genital anatomy and mating behavior of *Boreus brumalis* Fitch (Mecoptera). *Am. Midl. Nat.* 23:354–67.

———. 1974. Sexual biology, chromosomes, development, life histories, and parasites of *Boreus,* especially of *B. notoperates.* A Southern California *Boreus* II. (Mecoptera: Boreidae). *Psyche* (March):84–120.

Edgerly, J. J. 1987. Maternal behavior of a webspinner (Order Embiidina). *Ecol. Ent.* 12:1–11.

———. 1988. Maternal behavior of a webspinner (Order Embiidina): mother-nymph associations. *Ecol. Ent.* 13:263–72.

Fabre, J. H. 1911. *The Wonders of Instinct: Chapters in the Psychology of Insects.* London: T. Fisher Unwin.

Foelix, R. *The Biology of Spiders.* Cambridge, Mass.: Harvard University Press.

Holldobler, B. 1971. Communication between ants and their guests. *Sci. Am.* 220 (Mar.): 86–93.

Johnson, J. B., and K. Hagen. 1981. A neuropterous larva uses an allomone to attack termites. *Nature* 289:506–7.

Kistner, D. 1979. Social and evolutionary significance of social insect symbionts. In *Social Insects,* ed. H. R. Hermann, 340–414. New York: Academic Press.

McCook, H. C. 1882. *The Honey Ants of the Garden of the Gods and the Occident Ants of the American Plains.* Philadelphia: J. B. Lippincott.

McKeown, M. D. 1936. *Insect Wonders of Australia.* Sydney: Angus and Robertson.

Milne, L. J., and M. Milne. 1976. The social behavior of burying beetles. *Sci. Am.* 235:84–89.

Scott, M. P., and J. F. Traniello. 1987. Behavioral cues trigger ovarian development in the burying beetle *Nicrophorus tomentosus. J. Insect Physiol.* 33:693–96.

Selous, C. F. 1911. A preliminary note on the so-called carrion-feeding Coleoptera. *Ent. Monthly Mag.* 47:86–89.

Shubeck, P. P. 1968. Orientation of carrion beetles to carrion: random or nonrandom? *N.Y. Ent. Soc.* 76:253–65.

Springett, B. P. 1968. Aspects of the relationship between burying beetles, *Necrophorus* spp. and the mite, *Poecilochirus necrophori* Vitz. *J. Anim. Ecol.* 37:417–24.

Tauber, C. A., and M. Tauber. 1968. *Lomamyia latipennis* (Neuroptera: Berothidae) Life history and larval description. *Can. Ent.* 100:623–29.

Wheeler, Q. D. 1984. Associations of beetles with slime molds; Ecological patterns in the Anisotomini (Leiodidae). *Bull. Ent. Soc. Amer.* 30:14–18.

Wheeler, W. M. 1910. *The Ants.* New York: Columbia University Press.

Wilson, E. O. 1971. *The Insect Societies.* Cambridge, Mass.: Harvard University Press.

Chapter **6**

Aerialists

BELLA MOTHS

They say the way to a man's heart is through his stomach, but for bella moths the route is just a tad more circuitous. Bella moths, otherwise known as *Utetheisa bella* and *U. ornatrix*, are members of the moth family Arctiidae. They are, however, far from typical members of the family. Whereas most arctiid moths are boldly patterned with spots or swatches in some combination of black, orange, or white (earning them the common name tiger moths), *Utetheisa bella* is much more subtle in color—the hind wings are sort of a pastel pink bordered with black and the front wings pale pinkish orange delicately dotted with rows of small black spots edged with white (hence *bella*, or beautiful). The larvae, too, are out of step in terms of fashionable apparel. Whereas most larval arctiids are covered neck to tail (if caterpillars can be said to have necks) in thick fur (earning them the common name woollybears), the immature stages of *Utetheisa bella* have only a few sparse, scraggly hairs on each segment.

Bella moths: "Take my word for it, Gloria, it really isn't size that counts!"

It's not just in appearance that bella moths break with family traditions. As far as eating habits go, bella moths show unusual taste and discretion. The majority of caterpillars in the family Arctiidae are notorious for their lack of fussiness. *Isia isabella*, for example, the banded woollybear, is known to feed on over one hundred different species of plants. *Diacrisia virginica*, the yellow woollybear, may lay claim to an even more varied menu. By contrast, the bella moth caterpillar feeds on only a single plant—*Crotalaria*, or rattlebox, a plant in the bean family that grows throughout the southeastern United States. In fact, this insect connoisseur feeds not on rattlebox in general but just on the tender flowers and seeds.

Actually, this fanatic devotion to one plant pays off in the long run. Rattlebox is one of very few plants that can manufacture a class of chemicals called pyrrolizidine alkaloids. Normally deadly toxic to most insects, bella moth caterpillars thrive on the stuff. In fact, the alkaloids are even feeding stimulants. *Utetheisa bella* not only can tolerate these alkaloids, they can store them in their bodies to use as protection against their own predators (one possible reason they've lost the thick fur coat of their cousins—they're unappetizing enough without it). The extremely bitter alkaloids make bella moths so unpalatable that even spiders will cut them out of a web rather than touch them (much less eat them).

This love affair with pyrrolizidine alkaloids isn't left behind when the caterpillar pupates in a silken cocoon among the leaf litter and emerges as an adult, ready to leave childish foodplants behind forever. Male bella moths use the pyrrolizidine alkaloids they've stored up during their larval days in a very grown-up way—they convert them into aphrodisiacs. Like most moth species, the female bella moth produces a sex attractant or pheromone to bring males close for mating. As is true for most female moth pheromones, the principal components of the pheromones are long-chain unsaturated hydrocarbons. Once they're in the neighborhood, however, male bella moths enter into the act. Upon maturity, the male moth converts the pyrrolizidine alkaloids into a substance called hydroxydanaidol. When he approaches a calling female, the male bella everts a peculiar pair of organs, called coremata, from the tip of his abdomen. These organs, which look like dandelion seed heads, are loaded with hydroxydanaidol, and he thrusts them directly at the head of a female, after which she lifts her wings as a signal of acceptance and the affair is consummated. Males whose coremata have been experimentally removed don't stand a chance at winning over a female.

Interestingly, an Asian relative of *Utetheisa*, *Creatonotos*, isn't quite as single-minded as far as food goes; as a larva, it feeds on a variety of plants. But family habits die hard, and the males still depend on pyrrolizidine alkaloids to make it in the adult world. If a larva consumes plants containing pyrrolizidine alkaloid, his coremata will be substantially larger as an adult. The more alkaloids, the bigger and fancier the glands, which can end up amounting to 10 to 14 percent of the total weight of the male and exceed in length the entire span of the moth's body when they are inflated. The larger the gland, the more pheromone produced, the more attractive the male is to the female. Love and sex for *Creatonotos*, then, can be summed up with the pithy phrase, "You are what you eat."

BUCK MOTHS

Hunters know, as fall progresses and the leaves begin to turn color and fall from the trees, that buck season is close at hand. Entomologists know, however, that buck *moth* season is close at hand. The buck moth, *Hemileuca maia*, is so named because it is most abundant right around buck season, late September through October, depending on locality. The buck moth is unusual in that, not only does it fly so late in the year that most other self-respecting moths have long since put up for winter, it also flies, in very unmothlike fashion, during the day. It's hard to mistake for any other moth (and not just because it's usually the only moth around). The adults are brown- or black-bodied, with a conspicuous red tuft attached to the tip of the abdomen. The wings are brownish and almost scaleless, with a broad white stripe running down the middle of both front and hind wings. Like other members in the family Saturniidae, male buck moths have long, conspicuous, feathery antennae. With a wing span of two to three inches, the buck moth is large as moths go, but it's one of the smallest saturniids (whose

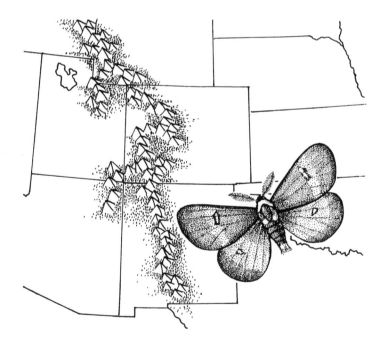

Buck moths: "Obviously, 'Go West' doesn't apply here."

ranks include the five-inch cecropia and the four-inch luna and who are otherwise known as the "giant silk moths").

Buck moths mate in late fall, after which females lay clusters of forty to two hundred eggs in rings around twigs of their favorite foodplants, usually oak or willow. The eggs hatch in April or May, at which point the caterpillars begin to feed furiously. The caterpillars are as hard to mistake as are their parents. They're brownish black with yellow spots and are equipped with hundreds of stinging hairs arising from knobby protrusions along their entire length, which, at maturity, can exceed 2½ inches. To make the effect even more dramatic, the larvae are communal, with every individual from an egg cluster hanging around in family groups until just before pupation.

There are several theories to account for this family togetherness, overall very atypical for insects. Early in the season, aggregation may help caterpillars keep warm, an important consideration for cold-blooded animals anxious for an early start in spring. In addition, while the stinging hairs of each caterpillar help protect it from most enemies, the stinging hairs of several dozen caterpillars assembled in one place could deter even the most persistent predator.

After five molts, the larvae fall off the tree and pupate in the ground, unlike the other giant silk moths, who spin cocoons in trees. While a few remain underground and emerge the following year, the majority emerge in fall the same year, just about the time hunters begin to stock up on buckshot. The buck moth can be found as far north as Nova Scotia and Maine, as far south as Florida, and west to Colorado and New Mexico. In the West, two closely related species are common: the range caterpillar, which feeds on grasses, and the Nevada buck moth, which feeds on willow and poplar. *Hemileuca maia*, however, is never, ever found west of the Rockies—so residents of the Far West know that the buck moth stops there.

BUMBLE BEES

The energy crisis of the 1970s led a reluctant American automobile industry to design vehicles with greater fuel efficiency. Energy crises and fuel efficiency are daily concerns for bumble bees. For insects in general, flying is about the only time-effective method for traveling long distances; while six legs are useful for traveling, they don't cover a lot of ground when each is only a fraction of an inch long. Flying does not come cheap, however—it requires tremendous amounts of energy. Among other things, small animals have to contend with the viscosity or friction of the air through which they fly, a force with which large flying animals (or gas-powered manmade vehicles) need not reckon.

Aerodynamicists use a value called the Reynolds number to express the ratio between the inertial force of a moving object (its mass times its acceleration) and the resistance it encounters due to changes in the medium through which it travels (the viscous force, the friction and pressure generated by a body passing through a medium). For large

Bumble bees

animals, Reynolds numbers are high and, accordingly, viscous forces are small. For insects, however, they're formidable. For example, a hang glider traveling at a speed of ten meters per second has a Reynolds number of about a million; a dirigible traveling at the same speed has a Reynolds number of about one hundred million. In contrast, an insect traveling at the same speed has a Reynolds number on the order of about one thousand—so it has to contend with viscous forces 100,000 times those faced by a dirigible.

The seemingly overwhelming physical forces with which flying insects must contend may be at least partly responsible for a popular misconception that has acquired a remarkably robust scientific reputation—that is, the notion that bumble bees are theoretically incapable of flying. This notion was popularized in the mid-1930s, possibly by a Swiss professor with impeccable credentials in physics—an association with Ludwig Prantl, founder of the field of aerodynamics, and a well-deserved reputation for excellence in supersonic gas dynamics. After a few quick calculations prompted by casual conversation, this professor allegedly pronounced that bumble bees should not be flying.

This pronouncement did not lead to any action on the part of the Federal Aviation Administration to ground all bumble bees, nor did it lead to a massive erosion of bumble bee confidence worldwide. Evidently, aerodynamicists may know their math and physics, but they have a few things to learn about insect anatomy. The insect wing, for example, is not as simple as these early investigators assumed. If a bumble bee wing was indeed a flat plate, as was assumed in the legendary calculations, then Reynolds forces would tend to cause such turbulence that, no matter how frantically they flapped, the bees could never get off the ground. However, the bumble bee wing (like most insect wings) is anything but a flat plate. It is indeed mostly a thin, tough membrane, but it is crisscrossed by a series of hollow veins and struts, so it is quite three-dimensional in cross section. In fact, in cross section it resembles an airplane wing—a smooth airfoil—far more than it does a flat plate. Stalling is thus not such a problem.

What is far more of a problem than physics is physiology—how to provide the flight muscles with enough fuel to power the wings (which, in bees, beat at two hundred times a second, or more). Basic insect anatomy is a help; the tracheal system, for example, delivers oxygen directly to the rapidly metabolizing flight muscles at speeds 300,000 times faster than it could be delivered in a fluid-based system. But bumble bees have incorporated a few energy-saving devices into their design. For one thing, the wings rotate at the base (like a canoe paddle) so that less energy is required to draw them forward. Bees are also relatively unusual among insects in that they can generate their own body heat, to make sure their flight muscles are warm enough to function at maximum efficiency. They accomplish this feat both by shivering and by deregulating several biochemical reactions so that they run simultaneously, releasing heat. Having a thorax covered with fuzz (a hallmark of the family Apidae) helps to insulate the flight engine.

At least partly due to their built-in engine block heaters, bumble bees can fly in places that are otherwise inhospitable to cold-blooded insect life. Bumble bees can be found on the wing from the Arctic Circle to Tierra del Fuego and from sea level to high mountaintops. About the only places where they are not found in any numbers are Australia and sub-Sahara Africa, where desert conditions can lead to serious overheating problems.

The main fuel for bumble bee flight is floral nectar, which consists mostly of water but is rich in simple sugars such as fructose, glucose, and sucrose. It also contains a few complex carbohydrates and a smattering of amino acids and water-soluble vitamins (including—no pun intended—the B vitamins). Nectar is generally found only in small quantities in flower parts—bees obtain sufficient quantities for their needs by visiting tremendous numbers of flowers (covering a great distance) over the course of a day. Nectar is lapped up by the proboscis, a tonguelike subset of mouthparts. The length of the tongue determines at least in part the sorts of flowers that are visited; long-tongued bumble bees can insert their proboscis into deep corollas and extract nectar that is inaccessible to most shorter-tongued flower visitors. Some short-tongued bumble bees compensate for their anatomy by using their mandibles or chewing mouthparts to cut a hole in the base of the flower and lapping up their fill (an approach akin to that used by Alexander the Great when confronted with the Gordian knot).

Aside from fueling their own flight engines, bumble bees also have to expend energy to keep hearth and home together. Queen bumble bees mate in the fall and spend the winter lying low, often in an underground hibernaculum, saving their strength for the taxing months ahead. Come spring, the queen seeks out a place to set up a nest on or under ground—often choosing an abandoned nest of a mouse or chipmunk. After lining it with plant fibers, she secretes wax from glands on her abdomen and molds a "honeypot." After a few quick trips to flowers, she fills up her crop (a distensible "stomach" used for transporting food from field to nest) and returns home, regurgitating the nectar into the honeypot. While she is visiting flowers, she also starts collecting pollen. Pollen, rich in protein, is a necessity for raising strong, healthy larvae. Like honey bees, she gathers pollen grains by grooming them off her hairs and onto a smooth pollen basket on her hind legs. Back at the nest, she scrapes off the pollen and pats it into the honey pot, either in a mass or in a wax pocket off to the side. She then lays about eight to twelve eggs and sits with them until they hatch, keeping them warm with her furry body.

After the eggs hatch, the female single-handedly (or six-leggedly) cares for her brood, bringing back nectar and pollen when the need arises; in some species, this involves forcing her way through the wax cap covering the developing brood. In the middle of the two- to three-week development period, another honeypot is constructed and more eggs are laid. The queen assists her offspring in chewing their way out of both their cocoons and their wax chambers; her young daughters, after a day or two in the nest getting prepared, then assist her in raising her new brood. Tasks for the young females, who are sterile and cannot lay their own eggs, include foraging for nectar and pollen and refashioning their old cocoons into new honeypots or pollen storage containers.

Bumble bee colonies can build up over the season from only a single founder to two or three hundred individuals. Maintaining such an enterprise requires major inputs of energy and material—on a typical day in midsummer, this means some two thousand trips by foragers, who bring in up to twenty grams of pollen and forty-five grams of sugar for the colony. Bumble bee colonies, unlike honey bee colonies, last only for a single season in temperate regions. As fall approaches, larvae are fed almost continuously and develop into reproductive adults—males and new queens. After mating, the males die and it is only the fertilized queens who live to see another year.

Because of their enormous energy demands, bumble bees are particular about the sorts of flowers they visit—generally they prefer the ones that, understandably, contain large amounts of nectar that other flower-visiting insect species aren't going to pilfer. As a result, there are many plants that have come to depend on bumble bees for pollination—moving pollen grains from one individual to the waiting stigma on another individual, thereby effecting fertilization. At least one hundred species of plants, some of great economic importance, are pollinated exclusively by bumble bees. This service provided by bumble bees was even remarked upon by Charles Darwin, who contended that, among other plants, red clover depended on bumble bees. Critics disputed his assertion and Darwin accordingly published a report of a number of carefully controlled experiments demonstrating incontrovertibly the necessity of bumble bees for successful clover seed production. Darwin in fact considered bumble bees to be patriotic British citizens, part of a lengthy chain that led to the greatness of the British Empire. Curiously, this chain began with spinster ladies. Darwin argued (with at least the tip of his tongue in his cheek) that old spinster ladies keep cats for companions; these cats hunt and kill rodents, which would otherwise destroy bumble bee nests; these bumble bees proceed to pollinate red clover, which is used to feed cattle; these cattle give up their lives to provide beef to the Royal Navy; which ensures the strength and dominion of British civilization throughout the world. These bees demand no payment for their patriotic service to the Empire; perhaps it is in recognition of their unassuming toil that the British at times refer to them as "humble bees."

BUMBLEBEE HAWK MOTHS

Sometimes, staying in one place can really get you somewhere. Take the hummingbird hawk moths, for example. Hummingbird hawk moths are species in the family Sphingidae that are among the few insects capable of hovering flight. Like hummingbirds, hummingbird hawk moths hover around open flowers and use their long, strawlike prosbosces for sucking up nectar. Hawk moths in the genus *Hemaris* are among the hovering sphingids, although physically they look a lot more like bumble bees than hummingbirds. *Hemaris* species are striped black and yellow like a bumble bee, are hairy like a bumble bee, and are about the same size as a large bumble bee. In very unmothlike fashion, they even have membranous wings like bumble bees; although they start adult life with scaly wings, the wing scales fall off when they set off on their first flight. Not surprisingly, these insects are known as the bumblebee hawk moths.

Hovering is energetically an extravagant way to travel. It's been estimated that hovering insects (or birds) require three times more energy to hover than they need to fly. Hovering works for both hawk moths and hummingbirds because it allows them to visit more flowers

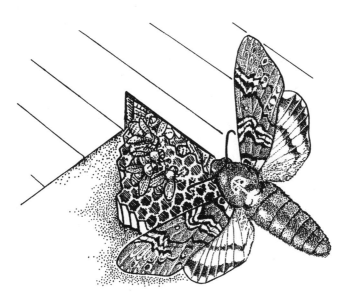

Bumblebee hawk moths: "Ah! Comb, sweet comb!"

in a given amount of time than they could possibly manage by flying and alighting. For example, *Hemaris* can visit as many as fifty *Kalmia* flowers in a patch in a minute; in the same amount of time, a bumble bee, with a reputation for being "busy," can only manage twenty flowers a minute.

Hawk moths, like hummingbirds, visit flowers to consume nectar. Although as a larva *Hemaris* consumes foliage of such plants as honeysuckle or snowberry, it can't store enough calories to sustain itself through adulthood. While hummingbirds can use sugars directly to power their flight muscles, *Hemaris* and other hawk moths must convert sugars first into lipids, which are then used for fuel for the powerful wing muscles. Since some energy is lost in chemically converting nectar into usable flight fuel, hawk moths in particular have to visit nectar-rich flowers. A hawk moth weighing six grams needs to consume about six milligrams of sugar per minute (about equivalent to a 125-pound person consuming two ounces of sugar—an eighth of a cup—every minute). Flowers frequently visited by hummingbird hawk moths include milkweeds, *Kalmia*, jewelweed, and *Epilobium*.

The flowers favored by hummingbird hawk moths often benefit from the visit. In addition to carrying off nectar, hawk moths can inadvertently carry pollen along with them on their hairy bodies as they travel from flower to flower. Frequent visits to different flowers of the same species can mean pollination for the plant providing nectar to the hawk moths. Many plants are apparently pollinated exclusively by hawk moths. These flowers tend to have nectar concealed in long floral spurs, accessible only by pollinators with long, thin tongues. Charles Darwin, upon finding an orchid with a spur twenty-five centimeters (ten inches) long, remarked with assurance that someone would someday find a moth with a proboscis ten inches long. Several years later, when the hawk moth was found and described, it was named *Xanthopan morganii* var. *praedicta* in honor of Darwin's prescience.

Hovering certainly takes its toll. Hawk moths have to warm up their flight muscles to temperatures of thirty-five degrees Centigrade or more in order for them to flap their wings fast enough to generate and maintain lift—not an easy proposition for hawk moths that are actually heavier than some hummingbirds. Some sphingids have devised ways to conserve energy. *Hemaris* can rest its front legs on flowers as it hovers and feeds, cutting down on the weight that its wings must support. By far the most creative energy savings must be practiced by *Acherontia atropos*, the European death's head moth, and its relatives. Like *Hemaris*, *Acherontia* species have black-and-yellow-striped abdomens. Unlike bumble bee moths, however, they have proper mothlike scale-covered wings and a thorax covered with scales in a pattern that looks for all the world like a skull and crossbones. Death's head moths don't bother hovering; for that matter, they don't even bother visiting flowers for nectar. Even if they were inclined to take nectar from flowers, they would have a hard time of it, because, unlike the vast majority of sphingids, they have rather puny probosces.

What they do instead is hang around the entrances to honey bee hives. At opportune moments, they force their way into the hive and use their short, stout probosces to siphon off honey from the comb. As they enter the hive, they often emit a series of squeaks, which may mimic the sound of a queen bee as she prepares a hive for swarming. Not all bees fall for the ruse, however. According to one account, a colony defended itself by erecting barriers of propolis, or bee resin, to keep out the intruders. Security is a high priority, since one death's head moth, with a wingspan of four inches or more, can do a lot of damage once inside a hive. It's likely that bees on guard at hive entryways watch for them—like a hawk.

CHIRONOMID MIDGES

If you've ever thanked your lucky stars for surviving a trip through a swarm of bloodthirsty mosquitoes, you might be better off thanking insect taxonomy instead. Not everything that looks like a mosquito actually is a mosquito. Many swarming flies can live out happy and fulfilling lives without ever tasting human or any other kind of blood. Probably the prize for "most frequently mistaken for a mosquito" goes to the chironomids, or midges. To the learned eye, midges don't really look a whole lot like mosquitoes. Unlike mosquitoes, the mouthparts are short and not at all suited for piercing skin, the last segment of the thorax has a deep groove that is absent in biting flies, and the head is uncharacteristically flattened from behind. Granted, these distinctions may be less than obvious to the less than interested public at large, so midges get a great deal of undeserved bad press.

As insects go, chironomid midges are incredibly innocuous. They begin life as a gelatinous mass of eggs deposited in any of a variety of aquatic habitats, including arctic lakes or hot springs, running water or stagnant pools, freshwater streams or marine tidepools. Once the eggs hatch, the larvae—wormlike, legless creatures with peglike projections just behind the head and just above the nether end—make

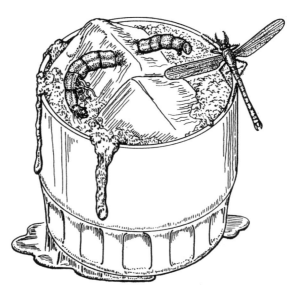

Chironomid midges: Alaskan cocktail

164

their appearance. Several species, called bloodworms, are bright red; they live in the airless ooze of stagnant lakes and owe their red color to hemoglobin, the same oxygen-carrying pigment that is found in human blood. Depending on the species, the larvae either swim freely or build silk-lined cases out of mud, sand, or whatever else they can find. Most chironomid larvae feed on any stray bits and pieces of organic matter that come their way, although members of one entire subfamily, the Tanypodinae, are predaceous on aquatic invertebrates. *Microtendipes pedellus* actually goes fishing, in a way. It spreads a thin line of salivary secretion out from its case and then reels it in, consuming whatever is attached to the sticky line.

By far, the largest part of the life cycle of most chironomids is spent underwater, but they only attract human attention for the brief period they spend as adults. Emergence from the underwater pupa is very rapid, requiring only ten to thirty seconds to a few minutes at most. In any given area, emergence is more or less synchronous, so literally thousands appear at once as if on cue. Immediately after emergence, midges fly to a resting site to recover from the stresses of metamorphosis and to size up their situation. The males then proceed to form a swarm. In most species, males form large, stationary aggregations suspended in air over some distinctive environmental marker. At times, these aggregations hum with the sound of simultaneous wingbeats. Characteristically, swarms form at twilight or in the early morning hours, although some species swarm during daylight instead. Swarming serves no function other than to promote mating. According to one author, "there appears to be little doubt that the main function of the swarm is to bring the sexes together." Once females orient to the swarm, the whole thing is somewhat anticlimactic. Mating takes only a few seconds and in some cases is completed even before the couple reaches the ground. Once mated, females go off to oviposit, to complete the life cycle.

There are over five thousand species of midges worldwide and they probably have the widest distribution of any insect group. There are species ranging from the hottest tropics to the coldest polar regions; two species actually live in Antarctica. Not surprisingly, living in Antarctica or Alaska has necessitated rather impressive adaptations. Many of these polar midges are actually capable of freezing solid throughout the winter and defrosting come spring. In view of this remarkable ability, perhaps the name "fridge" is more appropriate than "midge."

HARVESTERS

While it's true that entomologists, faced with the prospect of coming up with over a million names for described species of insects, must run into problems now and then, it nonetheless seems a little peculiar to name a butterfly after a ruthless Roman tyrant. *Feniseca tarquinius* is an attractive little butterfly with angled orange and black forewings spanning a distance of a little over an inch. A member of the family Lycaenidae (the gossamer-winged butterflies), the species was named by Fabricius over two hundred years ago—*Feniseca* meaning "mower" or "harvester" and *tarquinius* for Lucius Tarquinius Superbus, Etruscan emperor of Rome in the sixth century B.C. Tarquinius murdered his predecessor and ruled despotically for twenty-four years. The epithet "superbus" means "haughty or cruel."

When Fabricius named the harvester, as it's popularly called, nothing was known of its life cycle, so it's remarkable how apt the name really is. *Feniseca tarquinius* is no ordinary butterfly. Throughout its range, from Nova Scotia south to Florida and west to Minnesota through Texas, it is a common sight flitting through the woods, especially along streams, rivers, marshes, and swamps. Males in particular like to perch on sunlit leaves high up off the ground. It's not so much appearance or habits that set harvesters apart from the butterfly hoi polloi—rather, it's their diet. The harvester's proboscis is shorter in length in pro-

Harvesters: "Forget the vegetables!"

portion to its body than in any other butterfly. Instead of delicately probing flowers to sip nectar, the harvester sucks up honeydew (the excrement of aphids) and occasionally urine and animal droppings along forest paths or roadsides.

Odd tastes are not strictly the province of adult harvesters. The caterpillars were the first butterfly larvae discovered eating other insects. Instead of inoffensively nibbling on leaves, harvester caterpillars systematically devour colonies of woolly aphids, usually *Pemphigus* and *Schizoneura*, who are minding their own business sucking the sap of trees and shrubs such as alder, witch hazel, wild currants, and beech. The female butterfly carefully lays a single egg on a branch in the midst of a woolly aphid colony and the newly hatched larva spins a protective web around itself. Thus protected, the larva is free to attack the aphids from underneath. "Harvester" is thus not an inappropriate designation for a carnivorous caterpillar that systematically mows down its helpless, soft-bodied prey.

Typically, the caterpillars, which are greenish brown with long white hairs, bury themselves in among the dead aphids; the long hairs projecting outward from between the body segments catch and accumulate bits of debris and waxy material from the bodies of the victims. Harvester caterpillars develop astonishingly rapidly for caterpillars—they require only three molts (instead of the customary five or six) and only a week to ten days to reach the pupal stage. Their rapid development may be due to their high-protein, all-meat diet.

Harvesters are not, however, completely invincible. The caterpillars must contend with ants who feed on the honeydew of aphids and act as their pugnacious bodyguards, attacking any and all potential predators. Pupation is also a perilous time, when a harvester must sit and motionlessly metamorphose. But even during its pupal stage, the harvester is unusual. The pupae of most butterflies are cryptic, tending toward nondescript greens and browns designed to blend in with foliage to avoid detection. The pupa of *Feniseca tarquinius*, however, looks on close inspection like the head of a monkey in miniature. Considering that the pupa is only about a third of an inch in length, *F. tarquinius* is apparently banking on the inability of certain predators with poor binocular vision, like most insectivorous birds, to distinguish between a large object far away and a small object close up. From a distance, the pupa is said to resemble a bird dropping rather than a monkey head, which, from the perspective of a hungry bird, is a more horrible prospect than even a bird-eating monkey.

There is one small problem with the idea that a monkey face protects against bird predation. Such a theory works fine in Africa and India, where the closest relatives of *F. tarquinius* all live; in North America, however, there are no native monkeys. Birds, then, should by rights have no fear of primate faces suddenly appearing amidst the foliage. Granted, there are South American monkeys that migrating birds from North America might encounter, but by all accounts *F. tarquinius* pupae resemble Old World anthropoid apes rather than New World monkeys. About the only primate predictably found in North America is *Homo sapiens*, the human, who has been hanging around North America since the Pleistocene. The possibility has been raised that harvester pupae are mimics not of monkey faces but actually human faces, humans possibly being the most frightening and dangerous species ever to appear on earth. Any Roman subject of the fearsome Emperor Tarquinius would probably be inclined to agree.

LUNA MOTHS

For those who consider insects uniformly disgusting and otherwise lacking in redeeming aesthetic value, consider C. V. Riley's 1876 description of *Actias luna*, the luna moth: "Whichever . . . moths may carry off the palm of beauty in the eyes of different persons, no one will hesitate for a moment to accord to *Luna*, our queen of the night, entire supremacy in grace, elegance and chasteness. No other North American insect can win this distinction from her, the delicate green, relieved by the eye-spots and by the broad purple-brown or lilaceous anterior border, the soft downy hair of the body, and above all the graceful prolongation of the hind wings . . . are first to attract the eye." Granted, Riley was an entomologist, and an eccentric one to boot (given on occasions to carrying his enthusiasm for insects over to eating grasshoppers), but the opinion he expressed is representative of many non-entomological types as well.

The luna moth is one of several North American members of the family Saturniidae, the giant silk moths. With a wingspan of 3 to 3½

Luna moths: "No, I *wouldn't* call this a banquet fit for a queen!"

inches, it's midsize as far as North American saturniids go. The luna is unique among the North American saturniids in that it possesses greatly elongated tails on its hind wings. Its pale green color is also distinctive. Topping it all off is a magnificent pair of feathery antennae with which the male detects the pheromone or sexual attractant of the female. They fly at night (hence "Luna," or "moon") and mate among the trees in the hours after midnight.

The subtle style and elegance of the adult moth is entirely lacking in the caterpillar. The larva is large and plump, greenish in color with yellow lateral stripes and orange knoblike protrusions arising from vermilion red spots along the length of its body. Females lay eggs in small clusters on twigs of walnut, hickory, beech, birch, sweetgum, persimmon, black cherry, and other trees. After the eggs hatch, for the next six to eight weeks the caterpillars devote themselves to eating. A newly hatched caterpillar weighs $\frac{1}{20}$ gram; within ten days it weighs $\frac{1}{2}$ gram, 10 times its original weight. By the time it's ready to spin a cocoon and pupate, it weighs 207 grams, or 4,140 times its original weight. This translates into about 120 tree leaves consumed, or $\frac{3}{4}$ pound. In other words, it eats 86,000 times its own weight to complete development. It's not altogether surprising, then, that the adult moths don't have to eat at all; in fact, they totally lack functional mouthparts.

After the caterpillar completes development, it draws several leaves together with silk and spins a cocoon. The cocoon is whitish to brownish in color, dense and tough, and after the leaves fall it can be found on the forest floor, where it remains until the moth emerges in late April or early May. In some areas, there are two generations a year, with a second emergence in July. It may seem like a crazy way to make a living, but that's what makes a luna tick.

SALLOWS AND PINIONS

Connoisseurs with a sweet tooth probably know that warm, sunny spring days followed by clear cold nights make the sap flow in sugar maple trees. With a spile and a bucket in the right place, you can collect enough to boil down and make your own maple syrup. Sunny spring days and clear cold nights bring out another sort of connoisseur with a taste for sugar—the sort with six legs and a long coiled "sweet tongue" in place of a "sweet tooth." In the family Noctuidae, the largest in the Lepidoptera, there's a tribe of free thinkers who buck the trend and spend winter and spring feeding, mating, and reproducing, and spend summer and fall in sound slumber. These winter moths in the tribe Lithophanini have a remarkable ability to function at low temperatures (which, thanks to their chosen calendar, they are called upon to use quite frequently). At twenty-eight degrees Fahrenheit, when most of their relatives have safely shut down most major body functions to survive, winter moths are out and about. Most spend the winter sheltered under fallen leaves, head tucked up against their hairy thorax and antennae neatly folded under the wings. Their dense covering of hair no doubt provides insulation against winter's more bitter blasts.

Winter moths are forced to leave their shelters intermittently even

Sallows and pinions: "I can't imagine where Junior disappeared to. Didn't you hire the neighbor's kid to watch him?"

during the coldest part of winter in order to seek moisture; cold air holds very little moisture and winter moths are in greater danger of desiccation than they are of freezing. When temperatures finally soar to a balmy thirty-six to forty-two degrees Fahrenheit or so, moths take wing in search of one of their life's greatest pleasures—sugar. These moths feed avidly on sap flows, honeydew, or any other substance with a substantial amount of sugar. Why these moths in particular are so enamored of sugar has given rise to some heavy speculation. One current theory is that these relatively heavy-bodied, small-winged moths need a lot of energy to warm up their thoracic muscles to beat their wings with sufficient force and frequency to get up off the ground—and, as any athlete can tell you, sugar is a quick energy fix.

Insect collectors in the nineteenth century discovered this propensity for sweets among winter moths quite accidentally. One legend has it that Henry Doubleday of Epping, England, noticed moths attracted to an empty sugar hogshead tossed into the yard behind his shop and came up with the idea of baiting moths with a sugar solution (although after he died his friend James English claimed *he* came up with the idea while Doubleday was in France).

An extraordinary need for fuel, particularly at low temperatures, may account for the fact that the larvae of winter moths, which hatch from eggs in early spring, engage right away in the very uncaterpillar-like behavior of eating flesh. In his book *Talking of Moths* (1943), P. B. M. Allan cited a fellow entomologist's description of a species of sword-grass caterpillar (*Calocampa exoleta*) as "not only a cannibal but a double-dyed villain who thirsted for the blood of his own brethren." (Allan himself described another species, the dun bar, as "a foul fiend of a larva, a savage that will raven raw beef—nay even cold mutton. . . . By whatever standards one judges him he is an outcast, a bloodthirsty beast, a verminous rat . . . [who] will kill for the lust of killing.")

When not munching down on friends and family, winter moths eat a variety of more traditional fare, including buds, foliage, and fruits of a variety of trees, shrubs, and herbs. Probably the most conspicuous of the lithophanine moths are the sallows (species in the genus *Eupsilia*), who, name notwithstanding, range in color from brown to reddish to even yellow (in the case of *Pyreferra hesperidago*, the mustard sallow). Sallow larvae are mottled red-brown or greenish, with a black shield behind the head and a hump at the tail end; they feed on the foliage of cherries, oaks, and maples. Their association with maples makes them conspicuous at maple-syrup time, when adults drown by the hundreds in the buckets filled with sweet aromatic sap. Another group of winter moths, closely related to sallows, that routinely fall victim to bucket and spile are the pinions, or species in the genus

Lithophane. Like the sallows, the pinions are heavy-bodied, hairy, shortwinged moths that come in a variety of colors. To distinguish among them, well-trained eyes must microscopically examine the hairs, scales, tufts, and genitalia. Even when you've gone to all the trouble needed to separate the many species, all you really have when you're done is a difference of "a pinion . . . ."

STALK-EYED FLIES

Nowhere in the animal kingdom is the expression "beauty is in the eye of the beholder" more true than it is for the stalk-eyed flies of tropical Asia and Africa. Stalk-eyed flies, which belong to the family Diopsidae, are relatives of Drosophilidae, or "fruit flies," and, like their relatives, feed on molds, yeasts, and bacteria growing mostly on fallen leaves. The more or less featureless maggots live immersed in decaying vegetation, feeding on microbes and other such nondescript fare for about three weeks, at which point they pupate and emerge as adults; adults are sexually mature and females begin laying the first of the two thousand or more eggs they can lay over their twelve-month lifetime after about ten days. The adults are slender-bodied, long-legged flies, rarely over a centimeter (½ inch) in length, which would be completely unremarkable but for the fact that their eyes are located not in normal insectan fashion on either side of the head but rather on the ends of enormously elongated stalks (hence the common name, stalk-eyed flies). Male *Cyrtodiopsis whitei*, a southeast Asian rainforest species, have a body length of about eight millimeters and an eyespan of eleven millimeters, so at their widest, these basically slender flies are wider than they are long. The eyes and supporting structures account for a whopping 12.5 percent of the total body weight of the fly.

The drawbacks to having eyes projecting outward more than a body length's distance are obvious. Even if diopsids never have to deal with

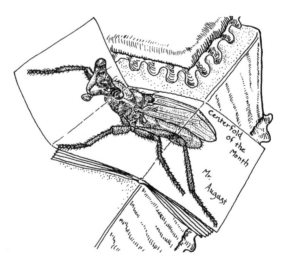

Stalk-eyed flies

revolving doors, they still have to balance their enormous appendages whenever they move. Actually, that's the beauty of it—diopsids use their eyes to great advantage. When disturbed, the flies gather their long legs up underneath their bodies and jump off their resting surface. The eyestalks create so much air resistance that they function as parachutes and allow the flies to float gently to the forest floor. Moreover, the placement of the eyes at such a distance confers upon diopsids remarkably acute nearfield vision. The diopsids have about the finest spatial resolution known among insects, with a divergence angle of less than one degree. The field of vision for each eye is so wide that the two fields overlap extensively, giving diopsids binocular vision in nearly any direction. About the only things they can't see well, due to the placement of the eyes, is their own body, so narcissism must be completely unknown among the stalk-eyed flies. Whatever the disadvantages, stalk-eyed flies can certainly see better than other insects of comparable body length—thirty times farther than a lacewing and ten to twenty times farther than a blow fly (the latter being no slouch among insects in the "field of vision," as it were).

Exactly what diopsids are using their remarkable visual organs to see was something of a mystery until the observation was made that in most species only the males are so remarkably endowed. While female diopsids do indeed have eyestalks, they barely measure up to even a single body length in dimension. They also have fewer ommatidia, or facets—a paltry fourteen hundred, compared to up to twenty-seven hundred in a large male. So what diopsids are looking at is primarily other diopsids. Male diopsids do not merely engage in idle girl-watching, however. Males use their eyes mostly to size up their competition. From dusk to dawn, males stake out territories on threadlike plant structures dangling above the ground. Generally, an overnight gathering consists of one large male and several females. The large male spends his time patrolling the thread, looking for interloping males. If one is encountered, the two begin to fight in ritualized fashion; each spreads out his front legs parallel to the eyestalks and rises up on his back legs. This posture is accentuated by sideways shaking, beating on the substrate with the abdomen, and occasional wing flapping. The victor in these bouts is almost invariably the one with the widest eyes; his competition, unable to see eye to eye, must depart in ignominious defeat.

This is not to say that only other male diopsids appreciate an eyespan. Females also prefer males with the widest eyes—scientific study reveals a positive correlation between eyespan and the number of successful matings. A female diopsid, then, is easily swayed once a suitor "gives her the eye."

WEDGE-SHAPED BEETLES

Anyone who has ever traveled anywhere by plane is familiar with the discomforts of air travel—confining seats, bland food, and tedious air traffic delays among them. But these inconveniences pale by comparison with the problems faced by rhipiphorid beetles when they fly. Most insects become airborne under their own power; adult rhipiphorid beetles are no exception. These tiny, wedge-shaped beetles (known, appropriately enough, by the common name "wedge-shaped beetles") are generally equipped, as are most self-respecting beetles, with a set of hardened front wings (called elytra) and a pair of eminently flight-worthy hind wings. In late summer, female *Rhipiphorus* lay eggs on the flowerheads of goldenrods and other late-blooming wildflowers. The hatching first instar larva, called a triungulin, measures a mere 0.5 millimeters ($\frac{1}{50}$ of an inch) in length. It bears little resemblance to its parents; overall, it's shaped like a flattened inverted triangle, with a suction-cup-like structure on the tail end and a pair of large, curved, heavily sclerotized mandibles at the head end. The six long slender legs are tipped by leaf-shaped suction devices called pulvilli.

Wedge-shaped beetles

176

The tiny, wingless triungulin waits patiently for a male sweat bee (a member of the family Halictidae) to visit the flowerhead on which it rests. While the bee is engaged in obtaining refreshment, the triungulin climbs aboard and clamps onto the body hairs of the bee with its powerful jaws. When the bee takes off, the triungulin takes off with him.

According to the triungulin itinerary, the male bee is just a commuter line to take the triungulin to its main flight. Male halictids, aside from visiting goldenrod flowers and picking up passengers, are busy around this time of year searching for females with which to mate. When a male halictid successfully copulates with a female (a process lasting 5½ minutes or more), the triungulin unclenches its jaws and scrambles onto the body of the female bee, at first grasping any convenient hair or appendage but eventually settling in on the ventral or undersurface of the hind wings—a connection more difficult to make than anything that even O'Hare Airport has to offer.

The triungulin spends the next eight to ten months clinging, with the aid of its suckerlike tail and feet, to the wings of its halictid host. This is, to say the least, a rough trip. For one thing, there's no meal service on this flight; the triungulin does not eat for the duration of its stay on board the bee. And the flight is bumpy beyond belief. Attached to the wing, which beats at a frequency of about 150 Hz, the triungulin is subjected to centripetal accelerations of about 180 g. In addition, the triungulin must cope with aerodynamic drag forces of seven times its own weight (the equivalent of an accelerative force of 7 g). In order to prevent itself from being tossed out into the void, the triungulin must exert an estimated suction of 1,146 kg/m² for each pulvillus and anal sucker (a force actually greater than the theoretical maximum at one atmosphere). Yet another hazard faced by the triungulin is the halictid bee herself, whose grooming and scraping can threaten to dislodge any triungulin straying from the comparative security of the hind-wing undersurface, a spot difficult for the average bee to reach.

In late spring and early summer, the triungulin finally arrives at its desired destination—the underground burrows of the halictid bee. Female halictids excavate a series of underground tunnels, which are equipped with an egg and a mass of pollen and nectar. Under normal circumstances, the hatching grub consumes the provision mass left behind by its mother. A halictid larva sharing its burrow with a rhipiphorid triungulin, however, gets eaten itself.

Once a rhipiphorid arrives in a burrow, larval life becomes far less of a challenge. In the security of the underground burrow, it is free to feed at its leisure on the hapless halictid grub. Like the vast majority of rhipiphorids, it spends at least part of its larval life inside the body

177

of its host; as it grows, however, it chews its way out and lives as an ectoparasite, draped like a collar around the thorax of the bee grub. During the course of its larval development, its morphology reflects its less demanding lifestyle; while first instar triungulins are active, fast-running, slender creatures, third instar larvae are bloated, legless grubs equipped with a number of grotesque lobes of flesh protruding at odd angles. After pupation, the emerging beetle flies off under its own power, in pursuit of pollen and a place to lay its eggs. For the rest of its life, the rhipiphorid is a pilot rather than a passenger, facing few of the stresses and strains of its first forays into the skies.

Not all rhipiphorids engage in aerobatic adventures during their formative stages. *Ripidius pectinicornis,* for example, is an internal parasite of *Blattella germanica,* the German cockroach. It was first described from cockroaches on shipboard in 1808. Females scatter their eggs apparently randomly on the ground and triungulins wait patiently for a cockroach to walk by (which, depending on the neighborhood, may not be much of a wait). Once a host is located, the triungulin boards and burrows inside, never departing until it's ready to pupate. Despite the fact that German cockroaches do possess fully functional wings, they are loathe to leave the ground except in instances of dire emergency. Thus, *R. pectinicornis* is resolutely earthbound until it acquires its own wings—from its perspective, under its own power is "the only way to fly."

YUCCA MOTHS

Unless you know where to look, yucca moths—species in the genus *Tegeticula*—are easy to miss. Not only are they nocturnal, as are so many other moths, they're also small (with a wingspan of barely an inch or so) and not particularly distinctively marked (most species in the genus are pure white, with few if any markings on the wing). Thus, they are not exactly a familiar sight to most Americans, despite the fact that they range from Ontario west to California.

Where to look to find a yucca moth is wherever yuccas are flowering; *Tegeticula* species feed exclusively on the developing seeds of yucca plants. The three species of *Tegeticula* vary in their devotion to yuccas. Whereas two species feed only on a single *Yucca* species, one species appears to be able to feed on almost all of the forty or so yucca species in North America.

Like most plants, in order to produce seeds, yuccas need to be pollinated; also like many plants, firmly rooted in the ground and unable to carry out courtship and mating on their own, yuccas depend on insects to carry pollen (containing sperm cells) to a receptive ovary (containing the egg cells). In late spring, the yuccas produce a single flowering stalk, often containing over a thousand individual flowers. The flowers open in succession, from the bottom of the stalk to the top of the stalk, over a period of several weeks, although each individual flower stays open and available to pollinators only for a few days.

Firm believers in the adage "if you want a job done well, do it yourself," yucca moths assure themselves of an abundant supply of

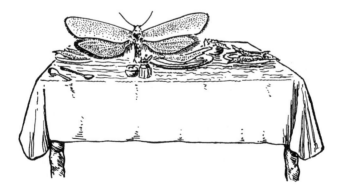

Yucca moths: "Yucca, yucca, yucca, every day the same old thing . . . I'd kill for a burger right about now."

yucca seeds by serving as the exclusive pollinator of yucca flowers. In late spring, coincident with the flowering of yuccas, yucca moths emerge from the soil, where they overwinter as pupae, and fly directly to an open yucca flower. Mating occurs right in the yucca flower. After mating, the female yucca moth doesn't waste time on a honeymoon—she immediately gets to the business of pollination. She walks up the stamens of the flower in which she mated until she reaches the anthers, the pollen-bearing structures at the tip of the stamens. There, she collects pollen and packs it into little balls, which she carries in long tentacle-like projections of her maxillary palps. Once she's all packed, she flies directly to another yucca flower and inserts her sharp, pointed ovipositor into the ovary of the flower. After laying a few eggs, she walks up the pistil until she reaches the stigma, the receptive surface at the top. Once there, she carefully packs a pollen mass onto the stigmatic surface—thereby insuring pollination and a supply of seeds for her offspring once they hatch.

From the point of view of a yucca plant, a visit from *T. maculata* is sort of a good news/bad news story. The good news is that yucca moths are extremely efficient pollinators. They conscientiously collect large amounts of pollen and deliver it directly to another yucca flower, ensuring cross-fertilization and preventing interspecific hybridization. Moreover, many less refined pollinators actually eat some of the pollen grains they collect, eliminating the chance for that pollen to fertilize another flower; yucca moths don't eat at all as adults and thus deliver all pollen intact. Thus, only yuccas visited by yucca moths have any chance at all to produce a bumper crop of yucca seeds. The bad news is that the eggs a yucca moth lays in the ovary eventually hatch into cigar-shaped, almost legless caterpillars that can gobble down as many as two dozen seeds before dropping from the flower into the soil to pupate.

Overall, the interaction seems to benefit both parties involved. Yucca moths can get a guaranteed food supply for their offspring, not to mention a secluded place for sexual encounters, for only a few hours of work. Although seeds do get eaten, most caterpillars consume only a few seeds over their lifetime, so infested plants still produce plenty of seeds to ensure future generations of yucca plants for yucca moths to enjoy. Moreover, the plants can enjoy the benefits of reliable sexual reproduction without having to produce other forms of floral rewards, like nectar, to attract their pollinator. All the yucca moth requires is a few fruits for her labors. It's not altogether surprising that *T. maculata* expects to be paid for her services—a no-nonsense type, she is, after all, the original pistil-packing mama.

References

Addicott, J. F., J. Bronstein, and F. Kjellberg. 1990. Evolution of mutualistic life-cycles: yucca moths and fig wasps. In *Insect Life Cycles, Genetics, Evolution, and Co-ordination*, ed. F. Gilbert, 143–61. London: Springer Verlag.

Aker, C. L., and D. Udovic. 1981. Oviposition and pollination behavior of the yucca moth, *Tegeticula maculata* (Lepidoptera: Prodoxidae) and its relation to the reproductive biology of *Yucca whipplei* (Agavaceae). *Oecologia* 49:96–101.

Allan, P. B. M. 1943. *Talking of Moths*. Newtown, Eng.: Montgomery Press.

Burkhardt, D., and I. de la Motte. 1987. Physiological, behavioural, and morphometric data elucidate the evolutive significance of stalked eyes in Diopsidae (Diptera). *Ent. Gen.* 12:221–33.

Casey, T. M. 1981. A comparison of mechanical and energetic estimates of flight cost for hovering flight in moths. *J. Exp. Bull.* 91:117–29.

Clausen, C. P. 1940. *Entomophagous Insects*. New York: McGraw–Hill.

Covell, C. V. 1984. *A Field Guide to the Moths of Eastern North America*. Boston: Houghton Mifflin.

Forbes, W. T. M. 1954. *Lepidoptera of New York and Neighboring States*. Part 3, *Noctuidae*. Cornell University Agricultural Experiment Station Memoir 329.

Heinrich, B. 1979. *Bumblebee Economics*. Cambridge, Mass.: Harvard University Press.

———. 1983. Insect foraging energetics. In *Handbook of Experimental Pollination Biology*, ed. C. E. Jones and R. J. Little, 187–234. Cincinnati: Van Nostrand Reinhold Co.

Hinton, H. E. 1974. Lycaenid pupae that mimic anthropoid heads. *J. Ent.* (A)44:65–69.

Holland, W. J. 1903. *The Moth Book*. New York: Doubleday, Page and Co.

Klots, A. 1951. *A Field Guide to the Butterflies*. Boston: Houghton Mifflin.

Lucas, W. J. 1895. *The Book of British Hawkmoths*. London: L. Upcott Gill.

McMasters, J. H. 1989. The flight of the bumble bee and related myths of entomological engineering. *Am. Sci.* 77:164–69.

Opler, P., and G. Krizek. 1984. *Butterflies East of the Great Plains*. Baltimore: Johns Hopkins University Press.

Plath, O. E. 1934. *Bumble Bees and Their Ways*. New York: Macmillan.

Rees, C. J. C. 1975. Form and function in corrugated insect wings. *Nature* 256:200–203.

Riley, C. V. 1872. The luna silkworm. In *Fourth Annual Report of the Noxious, Beneficial, and Other Insects, of the State of Missouri*, 123–25. Jefferson City, Mo.: Regan and Edwards.

Schweitzer, D. 1934. Notes on the biology and distribution of the Cucullinae (Noctuidae). *J. Lep. Soc.* 28:5–21.

Tomlin, A. D., and J. J. Miller. 1989. Physical and behavioral factors governing the pattern and distribution of Rhipiphoridae (Coleoptera) attached to wings of Halictidae (Hymenoptera). *Ann. Ent. Soc. Amer.* 82:785–91.

Utrio, P. 1983. Sugaring for moths: why are noctuids attracted more than geometrids? *Ecol. Ent.* 8:437–45.

Chapter **7**

Water Sports

AQUATIC SPRINGTAILS

That all collembolans have a spring in their step is not so much a reflection of youthful vitality as it is a function of basic anatomy. Most members of the order Collembola come equipped with a furcula, a forked spring that originates near the tip of the abdomen and extends forward underneath the body. The fork is secured in place by a clasp, called the tenaculum, on the third abdominal segment. When the fork is forcibly released from the clasp and slaps against the ground, the springtail is launched skyward to dizzying heights, at least from the point of view of a springtail. A springtail only five millimeters in diameter can spring more than one hundred millimeters (four inches) into the air.

Although, like insects, springtails have six perfectly serviceable legs, they have no wings. Were it not for the furcula, collembolans would be permanently earthbound and, lacking anything in the way of sharp teeth, claws, or noxious secretions with which to defend themselves,

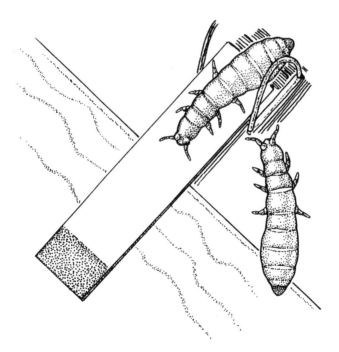

Aquatic springtails: "Just remember, use your furcula and don't look down."

helpless victims for any predator passing by. As it is, they can jump to safety (or at least out of immediate danger) with style and panache.

Despite their high-flying mode of locomotion, most collembolans lead a low-profile existence, favoring such out-of-the-way places as leaf molds, fungi, or dead trees as residences. There are, however, about a dozen species of springtails that literally have a "spring" in their step in that they live on the surface of springs—or creeks, rivers, lakes, streams, ponds, and other such bodies of fresh water. Aquatic springtails look more or less like their terrestrial counterparts, with a few notable exceptions. The terminal segment of the furcula, the mucro, is paddle-shaped, as befits an appendage designed to propel objects through water. One other refinement that helps to keep collembolans afloat is the placement of the claw, which in most collembolans is at the tip of the leg. In aquatic collembolans, the claw is higher up and off the surface of the water, where there is less risk of breaking the surface tension that supports the springtail. Finally, the entire body of the aquatic springtail is encased in a waterproof coating that serves as a sort of life jacket to keep it afloat.

Podura aquatica is perhaps the most familiar of the admittedly obscure aquatic springtails. It's found throughout North America in all kinds of freshwater habitats. Reddish brown to black in color, *P. aquatica* is often so numerous that aggregations form colorful and conspicuous flotillas on water surfaces. Eggs of *P. aquatica* hatch underwater, but after an immature springtail breaks through to the surface it spends the rest of its life there, never again venturing below decks.

Sminthurides aquaticus is more colorful in both appearance and habits than *P. aquatica*. Pink to violet in color, adults measure only about a millimeter across. The second and third antennal segments of the males are specially modified as grasping organs. When courting, a male grabs a willing female, who is generally substantially larger than he. She then hoists him up over her head, literally sweeping him off his feet, and carries him around for a few days such that he never touches the water. After mating is completed, he is released and she busies herself with egglaying. Curiously, it appears that any individual female *S. aquaticus* is capable of producing offspring of only one sex. Why this is the case is, at the moment, anyone's guess. After several weeks of feasting on fungi, dead leaves, and algae, interspersed with three molts, *S. aquatica* eventually reaches adulthood. The tiny males can look forward to walking on water for an average of four to five weeks, while the larger and heartier females live up to four months or more.

One of the earliest accounts of the peculiar lifestyle of aquatic springtails was penned in 1743 by one Charles DeGeer. The paper on springtails, his first scientific publication, was written when he was a callow youth of twenty years. From a wealthy family whose fortune had come from successes in the iron-smelting business, DeGeer had the luxury of leisure time in which to rear silkworms and observe insects. He continued his scientific studies throughout his life, eventually publishing the massive *Memoires pour servir a l'histoire des Insectes,* seven quarto volumes containing descriptions of over fifteen hundred species. Sales of the first volume of the *Memoires* were so sluggish that, in frustration, DeGeer burned many of the unsold copies. Subsequent volumes in the series were given away at no cost to the few hardy souls who had purchased the first one. Contemporary authors of popular books about insects can certainly sympathize.

FAIRYFLIES

Charles Darwin was not an easy man to impress—after all, during his five-year voyage on the HMS *Beagle*, he visited four out of six continents and witnessed a tremendous variety of bizarre and amazing adaptations in animals and plants to all kinds of lifestyles. Occasionally, though, it was the ordinary that puzzled him. In his book *Origin of Species*, for example, he described an insect he'd read about whose ordinary appearance belied an extraordinary way of life: "All the members of the great order of Hymenopterous insects are terrestrial, excepting the genus *Proctotrupes*, which Sir John Lubbock has discovered to be aquatic in its habits; it often enters the water and dives about by the use not of its legs but of its wings; yet it exhibits no modification in structure in accordance with its abnormal habits."

The hymenopterous insects to which Darwin referred actually blow a lot of theories out of the water. The mymarids, or fairyflies, are definitely in competition for the title of smallest insects on earth. Full-grown, an adult fairyfly measures about half a millimeter in length (or

Fairyflies: "If anyone calls me Tinkerbell again . . ."

about ⅟₅₀ of an inch, for the metrically impaired). Even though it's actually smaller than some one-celled protozoans (like amoebas), it's equipped with all the requisite insect paraphernalia—six legs, four feathery little wings, two well-developed antennae, head, thorax, and abdomen full of all the normal organs. It's almost impossible to imagine how so many parts can be packed into so small a space.

Size is not the only unlikely thing about fairyflies. Their lifestyle is, to say the least, offbeat. As Sir John Lubbock discovered to his great surprise in 1864, they swim underwater. Swimming underwater is not a surprise in itself—lots of bugs and beetles do it. However, unlike the milling masses, mymarids swim not with their legs but with their wings. Probably the reason this feat is possible is that, for such a small animal, the viscosity of air is so great that it's not appreciably different, from the tiny animal's point of view, from the viscosity of water. What works in one fluid works equally well in the other.

Aquatic life for a minuscule animal poses some formidable operational problems. *Caraphractus cinctus*, for example, lays its eggs inside the underwater eggs of diving beetles in the family Dytiscidae. The first obstacle to pursuing an aquatic existence for a tiny fairyfly is the surface film. For massive human beings, the surface tension of water is, if anything, just an amusing diversion that makes bubble-blowing possible. For the minute mymarids, the surface film is like a brick wall. Not only can they walk *on* it, they can walk *under* it from the other side. They usually enter and leave where an emergent plant has broken the surface for them.

Once making her way through the surface film, a female fairyfly swims through the water, beating her wings about two times per second until she finds a likely looking submerged plant. Walking up and down the stem, she searches for the eggs of diving beetles, which are usually inserted into plant tissue. When she finds an egg, she inserts her ovipositor through the plant and into the host egg, depositing two or three of her own. The fairyfly egg expands significantly immediately after it is laid, suggesting that it squeezes through the tiny ovipositor like (in the words of one investigator) "sand through an hour glass." So goes the day of its birth. The larva doesn't have any mandibles with which to chew but, since all it has to deal with is egg yolk, it is quite content to suck raw egg. In summer, development is complete in anywhere from eight days to a month.

The adult, which does have mandibles, chews its way out of the host egg. Usually, males emerge first and stake out diving-beetle eggs from which female fairyflies are about to emerge. Fairyflies can mate both under and out of water. After about a day, the fertilized fairyfly begins laying eggs, leaving the water not to get air but only to search for more host eggs in virgin waters. How fairyflies breathe underwater is something of a mystery. They have a fully developed tracheal system, the system of air pipes that insects use for breathing, but tracheae can only transport oxygen in air, not water, and the fairyflies don't carry around an air supply, as do many aquatic species. They are small enough that they may be able to get an adequate air supply simply by diffusion through their exoskeleton.

If nothing else, fairyflies are to be commended for making do with what they have and for coming up with inventive new uses for standard-issue equipment. After all, fairyflies use waterwings to swim, not merely to stay afloat, as does a less inventive and less well-endowed terrestrial species found at parks, beaches, and swimming pools.

FISHING SPIDERS

With all their gear to manage—tacklebox, lures, lines, rods, and the like—fishermen might sometimes wish for another set of hands. Fishing spiders manage quite well with their eight legs. The vast majority of members of the order Araneida are resolutely terrestrial, as arthropods go. Most spiders risk getting wet only if inadvertently caught in a sudden thunder shower or flooded basement. Members of the family Pisauridae, however, are never far from the water and in fact depend upon water for their livelihood. Of course, within the family there are many variations on the nautical theme. Species in the genus *Dolomedes*—large, brown, hairy spiders—feed primarily on insects that have had the misfortune to fall into a body of water. *Dolomedes*, sometimes called swamp spiders, spend their days perched on a bit of floating vegetation in ponds, marshes, and swamps, dangling their front legs over the side like kids rolling up their trouser legs and dabbling their toes in the water. No idle pastime, this—*Dolomedes* dips its feet in the water in order to detect minute surface vibrations that give away the location of a struggling insect downed in the pool. Once it locates

Fishing spiders: "Should I use a fly or a spoon?"

191

its prey, *Dolomedes* swiftly sinks its chelicerae, or jaws, into the body of the victim, which then dies not of drowning (as it might have feared) but rather of slowing dissolving due to the powerful digestive enzymes injected by the spider.

Often *Dolomedes* doesn't wait for dire fate to intervene—instead of relying on an insect to commit an act of clumsiness, the spider will take action on its own. When alerted to the presence of a predaceous water bug or fish nearby, *Dolomedes* will dangle its front legs in the water as a lure, like a fisherman baiting a hook with an angleworm. In this case, however, the worm turns, and the powerful jaws and fast-acting venom can combine to overcome even tadpoles and fish attracted to its legs.

When they're not fishing, pisaurids tend to family matters. Their behavior in this respect has earned them a more redemptive name as well. Pisaurids are known as nursery web spiders for their distinctive maternal behavior. Female pisaurids, like many spiders, construct an elaborate silken egg case to house their developing young, but, unlike most spiders, they don't simply lay them and leave them. Female pisaurids tenderly cradle the egg sac, still attached by a silken thread to their spinnerets, gently but firmly in their chelicerae for the two to three weeks it will take the eggs to hatch. The egg sac is so large relative to the size of the spider that she has to literally walk "on tiptoe" to avoid dropping it. *Dolomedes* mothers must periodically immerse the sac in water to prevent the eggs from desiccating.

Living the life of a fisherman is not without its problems; one might say from the spider's point of view there's a catch to it. Fishing spiders, like their human counterparts, are basically terrestrial creatures. They're not equipped for life underwater—they can't breathe underwater and they can't even eat underwater, since the water dilutes their venom so much that it ceases to work as it should. Thus, most fishing spiders keep at least one of their eight feet firmly in contact with some part of the ground. If they submerge, it's only for brief periods and they always securely anchor to some stationary object with their back legs.

The European water spider, however, has come up with a creative solution to the problem and boldly goes where no spider has gone before. *Argyroneta aquatica* is aptly called the diving bell spider. A hungry spider first constructs a silken platform attached to an underwater aquatic plant. After the platform is complete, *A. aquatica* heads back up to the surface and collects an air bubble with its hind legs and abdomen. Climbing back down the vegetation, the spider then crawls underneath the platform and releases the bubble. Trapped by the platform, the bubble remains underwater. The spider repeats this procedure up to half a dozen times, bringing more air down below and reinforcing the silken net until it has completed a bell-shaped silken container of air. Once ensconced in the diving bell, *Argyroneta aquatica* extends its legs to feel for minute water vibrations. Whenever a potential prey swims by, it darts out of the bell and snags it, hauling it back under the bell to complete its meal at leisure. Thus, *Argyroneta aquatica* is the only spider able to dine while underwater, although never in a nice place—always in some dive.

GIANT WATER BUGS

Giant water bugs, aquatic insects in the family Belostomatidae, are unusual not only among insects but among animals in general when it comes to proper parenting. For several members of the family, child care is exclusively the responsibility of the father. After mating with a male, the female deposits her eggs on the back of her mate and swims away, never to see her children again (if she ever did, she'd probably eat them). The male tends the eggs on his back, stroking them with his hind legs to provide them with oxygen and to prevent fungus from growing on them. This can go on for as long as two weeks, at which time the eggs hatch and the nymphs swim off.

Entomologists were slow to recognize the sex-role reversal. Nineteenth-century chauvinists were convinced that female belostomatids somehow could contort themselves in such a way as to lay eggs on their own backs. It was a female scientist, one Florence Slater, who figured out the story in 1899, although, indoctrinated as she was in Victorian morality, she assumed the male was humiliated by the whole process. She noted when a male was attacked, "he meekly received the blows, seemingly preferring death to the indignity of carrying and caring for the eggs."

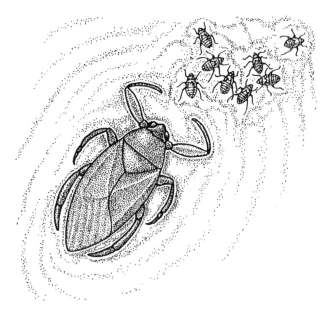

Giant water bugs: "On the bright side, even if I can't save enough money for tuition, most of them will be eaten long before they're old enough to register."

Male belostomatids, however, have a few angles figured out that Victorian entomologists didn't consider. A male, for example, won't let just any female lay eggs on his back; only those with whom he has just mated are granted the privilege. And he won't let even his own mate lay all of her eggs at one time. She can only lay two or three at a time before the male demands to mate again. In order for a female to lay her full complement of eggs, she'll have to mate with the same male up to a hundred times or more (an arrangement that one author calls "something of a zoological record"). Caring for the kids for a week or two seems like a small price to pay for ongoing romance. Moreover, the repeated mating insures the male that he's the father of all the eggs he's carrying; the female hardly has the time (or, one supposes, the energy) to have affairs on the side with other males.

When not tending the family, water bugs of both sexes are busy tending to their own voracious appetites. Like most aquatic bugs (members of the order Hemiptera), giant water bugs (such as *Lethocerus americanus*, which reaches a length of 2½ inches and a width of one inch) can actually bring down frogs, fish, snakes, and even wading shorebirds. The nickname "toe biter" refers to the fact that giant water bugs occasionally tackle even larger prey in the form of unsuspecting barefoot humans wading through ponds or quiet pools. Just when you thought it was safe to come out of the water, though, be advised that toe biters are very good flyers and often fly to electric lights a considerable distance from shore at night. It's not a bad rule of thumb to leave large, ovoid, brown, flat bugs over an inch long alone at night.

Carrying the burden of child care (literally) does have its disadvantages for a male water bug. When he's covered with eggs, he can't get up to fly, which cuts out some of his options in escaping from enemies or finding a better fishing hole. Moreover, belostomatids breathe by extending respiratory organs, called air straps, located at the tip of the abdomen, up through the water's surface. Air is pulled in through the straps to a chamber under the wing. Since the egg mass on his back can more than double his weight, a male can't exactly float freely up to the surface to renew his air supply. Some cling to aquatic vegetation just below the surface to allow themselves easy access to oxygen. It's undoubtedly more difficult to hunt for food, too, if you have to bring the whole family along with you. It must be a happy day in the life of a male giant water bug when the eggs hatch and the nymphs finally fend for themselves. Thus when a father giant water bug can at last say "get off my back," he's not being peevish—he's just being a good parent.

ONE-HOUR MIDGES

If you sometimes feel the day just isn't long enough to get everything accomplished that you set out to do, pity the poor one-hour midge. *Clunio marinus* is one of about seventy species of chironomid midges that live by or in the seashore. This choice of locations in and of itself is fairly unusual as insect homesites go. The vast majority of the class Insecta is resolutely terrestrial or else confined to bodies of fresh water; a marine lifestyle is only for the proud and the few. But *Clunio marinus* distinguishes itself even from the few by choosing to develop as a larva not in sandy beaches just a few feet from terra firma but rather at the bottom of the briny deep in sheltered bays. Far from other forms of insect life, *Clunio* larvae graze contentedly at ocean bottom on algae and diatoms.

Adult *Clunio marinus*, only two to three millimeters ($\frac{1}{10}$ inch) in length, can be found gliding on the surface of open sea from northwest Spain all the way up to northern Norway, above the Arctic Circle. Larval development, which depends on temperature, is therefore quite variable and ranges from two to twenty weeks. Adult lifespan, how-

One-hour midges: "Forget it, buddy! I wouldn't give you the time of day!"

ever, is fairly uniform over the entire range of the species. Adult *C. marinus* live on average approximately thirty minutes, with a few Methuselahs actually surviving for as much as two or three hours. Thus, the name "one-hour midge" can even at times be something of an exaggeration.

If you only have thirty minutes to accomplish everything in your adult life, you can't afford to waste even a minute of it, say, looking for love in all the wrong places. Complicating long-range planning is the fact that the marine environment is an extremely variable place, what with daily and seasonal fluctuations in water depth and temperature. Moreover, *C. marinus* can lay eggs only when the sea bottom is exposed, which is only for a few hours at low tides. Thus, development and eclosion (emergence of adults) are closely tied to tides. Since tides are influenced by the moon, love and sex in *C. marinus* are, as for so many lovers, linked to moonlight. From Spain through Helgoland, an island in the North Sea, *Clunio marinus* displays a semilunar rhythm of emergence, developing and emerging in synchrony with the full and new moon.

C. marinus apparently uses a pair of internal clocks to keep in synch with the sea—one that counts out two weeks and one that counts the hours in the day for pupae waiting to eclose (it would be a shame, for example, to emerge at 4:00 in the afternoon if all the other one-hour midges in the neighborhood were early risers who came out at 6:00 A.M.). The two-week clock in the temperate and subtropical regions is set by moonlight, but north of about forty-nine degrees north latitude the physical movement of the water is a more reliable cue than is the attenuated moonlight.

Internal clocks have always held great fascination for humans, the majority of whom must keep little external clocks strapped on their wrists in order to make it through the average day. The internal clocks of *Clunio marinus* are believed to be located in the brain and regulate physiological processes by way of neuroendocrine hormones. It's not surprising that *Clunio marinus* leaves nothing to chance in timing its emergence into adulthood; if it's even a few minutes late, this marine insect could miss the boat completely.

PHANTOM MIDGES

When it comes to using your head, the Chaoboridae or phantom midges win all awards hands down. The chaoborids are mosquitolike flies whose larvae, like those of mosquitoes, are legless aquatic worms. Unlike mosquito larvae, however, which by and large content themselves with nibbling sedately on inanimate pond scum, phantom-midge larvae pursue a more active lifestyle. They are voracious predators on crustaceans, rotifers, insects, and other aquatic life with the misfortune to be smaller in diameter than the open mouth of a phantom-midge larva (a shade over two millimeters or so). The legless larvae, somewhat limited in options, subdue and secure their prey not with limbs but with their heads. The antennae of phantom-midge larvae are highly developed and prehensile. When a planktonic prey item drifts by, the antennae wrap around and secure it and *Chaoborus*, no gourmet by any standards, ingests it whole.

Chaoborus doesn't exactly chase down its prey either. Most phantom-midge larvae remain suspended motionless in the water and literally "hang out" until dinner is served. Two design innovations assist them in their endeavors. First of all, phantom midges are virtually transparent (hence the names "phantom midge" and "glassworm") and would be completely invisible except for their dark-pigmented eyes and a pair of silvery spots on the fore and aft sections of the body. These spots correspond to buoyancy bladders, air-filled organs that allow chaoborids to float up or down in the water column. The so-

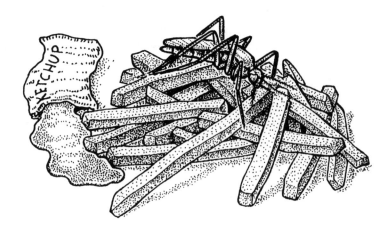

Phantom midges

called aeropneustic species float up at the water's surface all day; hydropneustic species spend the daylight hours nestled in mud at lake or pond bottom and move up to open water under cover of darkness.

The fifteen species of phantom midges in North America can be found in almost any kind of standing water, including ponds, lakes, temporary pools, and snow melt puddles. For almost nine months out of the year, chaoborids pass their time as eggs waiting to hatch. By late March to early May, the eggs hatch and the phantom-midge larvae make up for months of inactivity by assiduously eating. They're capable of consuming up to twenty-five water fleas a day, given the opportunity. After four molts in as many weeks, the larva pupates. For most insects, the pupa is a resting phase; chaoborid pupae, however, are very active, swimming freely and making up for a complete lack of jointed legs with paddles on their anal fins.

Adult phantom midges closely resemble mosquitoes except where it really counts—that is, they don't feed at all, so they don't bite humans. Males, distinguished from the females by their feathery antennae, typically form mating aggregations to which females fly for the business at hand. Once mated, females lay their eggs either in a jellylike mass on the surface of the water or among leaves and debris at the water's edge. By late May or early June, the cycle is complete and the eggs settle in for the long overwintering haul.

Just because phantom midges don't *bite* humans doesn't mean they don't *bother* humans. When emerging flies form mating swarms, they can number in the millions and stop traffic, obscure windows, and just about choke people by sheer volume. In Africa, near Lake Nyasa, people turn this mass emergence to their advantage. *Chaoborus edulis*, the local phantom midge, is collected en masse and compressed in a chunk called a "Kunga cake," which is eaten with great enthusiasm. This particular delicacy is unlikely to gain much popularity in U.S. fast-food cuisine, although the flies are undoubtedly a rich source of protein. If attitudes change in the future, though, it may someday be possible to order a "cheeseburger with a large order of flies" to go.

PITCHERPLANT MOSQUITOES

John B. Bogart, city editor of the *New York Sun* from 1873 to 1890, knew what was newsworthy. As he explained it, "When a dog bites a man, that's not news, because it happens so often. But if a man bites a dog, that is news." If such is indeed the case, then "Plants Eat Insects" must be the headline of the century. While over 300,000 species of insects routinely eat plants, only a handful of plants turn the (dinner) tables on their erstwhile consumers.

Among these lean, green, killing machines are pitcher plants—about sixty or seventy species in the family Nepenthaceae and about fourteen species in the family Sarraceniaceae. Pitcher plants are aptly named in that they all possess pitcher-shaped foliar structures that, like a pitcher, hold water. Around the opening of the pitcher is a fringe of downward-pointing hairs. Inside the pitcher itself are specialized tissues that secrete enzymes that break down animal proteins, as well as other substances that act as surfactants—that is, they break up the surface tension of the water that collects in the pitcher. This particular combination of features constitutes a one-two punch for insects unwary enough to slip

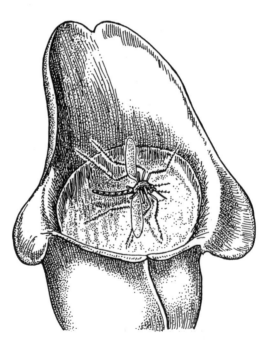

Pitcherplant mosquitoes: The pitcher of contentment

into the pitcher. The downward-pointing hairs prevent the insect from climbing up and out. The surfactant enzymes insure that the hapless insect will drown (rather than support itself on the water surface), and, as it drowns, the digestive enzymes slowly dissolve away its body parts. To add insult to injury, the plant actually depends on enzymes released by the dying insects themselves to break up the bodies. Not having mouths or teeth for tearing, or even appendages for holding forks and knives, pitcher plants must rely on chemistry to cut their meat for them.

Some pitcher plants have recruited an unusual ally to assist them in the tedious chore of disassembling insects into their component parts. *Sarracenia purpurea* produces a substance that is irresistibly attractive to females of the mosquito *Wyeomyia smithii*. *W. smithii* is found throughout North America, just about everywhere *S. purpurea* is found. The mosquito is, by mosquito standards, unusual in many ways. Unlike most familiar mosquitoes, a female *W. smithii* has the good taste to lay a batch of eggs without taking a blood meal (and in fact, in the northern part of its range, *W. smithii* are strict vegetarians). She is also far more discriminating than most mosquitoes as to where she lays her eggs. While other female mosquitoes don't bat an eyelash (as it were) about depositing their eggs in rain gutters, flower pots, old tires, sewage lagoons, and other unsavory places in which to raise children, *W. smithii* will only lay her eggs in the security of *Sarracenia* pitchers.

Like many mosquitoes, *W. smithii* spends its larval stages scavenging for microbes and other microscopic aquatic animal life. By consuming microbes, *W. smithii* does the plant a favor. Like plants, bacteria can only utilize dissolved proteins. The bacteria in the pitchers, then, are like unexpected company for dinner, from the pitcher plant perspective—there's less dissolved protein to go around for everyone. Rather than setting an extra place, *W. smithii* simply consumes the unwanted guests before they can hit the hors d'oeuvres. *W. smithii* helps out in other ways, too. By respiring, and in the process expiring carbon dioxide, the larvae provide the pitcher plants with fuel for photosynthesis—the process by which plants convert carbon dioxide and water into more plant tissue. This fuel boost is no small matter for a plant that can be overgrown by sphagnum moss in the bogs it frequents.

For its part, the plant provides the mosquito with a steady diet and a place to live. The pitchers remain full of water all year long, including through winter cold and summer drought. Overall, the arrangement is mutually beneficial and remarkably tidy—one might even say it's "pitcher-perfect."

SNAIL-KILLING FLIES

Although snails are not universally regarded as edible, much less a delicacy, the French hold escargot in high esteem. Snails have even greater admirers among the sciomyzid flies. Larvae of the sciomyzid flies feed exclusively on molluscs (loosely speaking, the shelled invertebrates) and, among these, most species greatly favor snails and slugs. They seek them out both on land and in water. The larvae are not truly aquatic in that they must keep in contact with air. As a result, they float just below the surface film, gulping air and staying afloat by virtue of water-repellent "float hairs" that ring the two air holes at their tail ends. These floats are so effective they can keep a larva near the water surface even when its mandibles are anchored in a large dying snail.

While some of the aquatic species can kill over a dozen snails before pupariating (that is, pupating inside their last larval skin), other terrestrial species are less prone to gourmandise, restricting their feeding to only three or four over a lifetime. These guys, while concealed inside the shell of their host, pick and choose carefully among internal organs so as to keep their host alive and fresher longer. When they pupariate, so as not to be disturbed, they construct a wall out of a cementlike substance to block off the entrance into the shell of the now-dead snail. One species in this group, *Sciomyza aristalis*, completes its larval development in only a single individual snail. Adult flies lay eggs on the outside of the shell and the hatching larva nestles in between the snail

Snail-killing flies: "Somehow, the thrill of pursuit is gone when you're preying on snails . . ."

and shell, consuming soft tissue until the snail dies, at which point the sciomyzid pupariates. This species never asks for second helpings—no larva has ever been spotted attacking a second snail.

Feeding on snails is not without hazards. Those sciomyzids attacking opisthobranch, or gill-breathing, snails are particularly at risk. These snails have a hinged lid, called an operculum, built into their shells that can close and seal up the snail. Although sciomyzids can crawl in through the flexible edges, occasionally one gets snapped in half by a slamming operculum. Other sciomyzids consume their molluscs in less risky ways. *Atrichomelina pubera* has been known to seek out dead, decaying, putrescent snails.

Since many close relatives of the sciomyzids eat decaying material, feeding on dead snails may be how the whole group got started on live molluscs in the first place. The scavengers in the group have the same float hairs as the aquatic forms, presumably to keep them from drowning in liquefied snail innards. Then there are the slug killers. These larvae hatch from eggs and lie on the ground with the upper two-thirds of their bodies casting about in hopes of touching slug skin. When they do, they crawl right up and find an opening—often into an eye tentacle or a mouth. The slugs die slowly, and most slug killers end up dispatching between two to ten slugs before they call it a larval period. Finally, some sciomyzids content themselves with snail eggs or molluscan caviar (a delicacy even the French have not yet adopted).

Adult sciomyzids, called marsh flies, are rather nondescript, ordinary-looking flies whose appearance belies the strange habits of their offspring. Most breed continuously and are so long-lived that they are still laying eggs when their daughters are beginning to lay eggs. In these species, adults hibernate through the winter. Other species, however, breed throughout the winter even at temperatures near freezing. Still others, associated with temporary ponds that dry up in summer, pass not the winter as hibernating adults but rather the long hot summer.

The biology of the Sciomyzidae is of major importance not only to a few obsessed entomologists or the occasional snailophobe but to the world in general. Sciomyzids are about the only deadly enemies of the snails that transmit schistosomiasis, parasitic infections caused by pathogenic organisms called flatworms or flukes. In Hawaii, where there are no native sciomyzids, snails that carry liver flukes, which infest cattle and then the people who eat beef, ran rampant until sciomyzids were introduced to control them, rendering Hawaiian beef safe again to eat. Although people were skeptical at first that these nondescript flies could do the job, sciomyzids proved conclusively that biocontrol in this case is no fluke.

SPONGILLAFLIES

Sponging meals off friends is one way to get yourself a reputation as a parasite. The reputation is perhaps more deserved for insects in the family Sisyridae, who make their living sponging meals off sponges. Sisyrids, or spongillaflies, are the only members of the order Neuroptera (or suborder Planipennia, depending on which taxonomist you consult) that grow up underwater, frequenting ponds, streams, and other bodies of fresh water. Like lacewings, dustywings, mantisflies, antlions, and other close relatives, spongillaflies are predaceous. Although the aquatic environment provides a tempting variety of seafood and shellfish from which to choose, spongillaflies are underwater gourmets who restrict their diet to nothing but the very finest freshwater sponges, species in the family Spongillidae.

The larvae are well equipped for their meal of choice. Their very long, hairlike mandibles are grooved along their lower surface; when each mandible is pressed next to the adjoining maxilla (the next mouthpart in line), a hollow tube is formed. The pair of hollow tubes is

Spongillaflies

plunged into sponge tissue and the contents sucked up, without even so much as a squeeze of lemon or dollop of tartar sauce.

Female spongillaflies, small, delicate brownish insects that resemble in passing miniature lacewings, lay their eggs on any of a variety of objects overhanging water. These objects include tree leaves, dead twigs, or branches in nature, and docks, pipes, loose boards, and other human contrivances where convenient. The egg clusters are carefully covered by the female with tiny white silken sheets. After about a week, hatching larvae drop onto the surface of the water, where they must contend with surface film, brought about by the surface tension of water. The larvae are abundantly spined, with one pair on each of eight abdominal segments and a circle of spines on the ninth segment. One or more of the posterior spines generally breaks through the film, allowing the larva to drift bottomward in search of sponges. Once on a sponge, they rarely leave, inserting their mouthparts for one- or two-minute meals every five minutes or so.

After two molts, spongillafly larvae not only leave their sponge, they leave the water as well, climbing onto shore, dock pilings, fishing nets, or boat hulls. After several hours, the larvae spin a cocoon using their abdominal spinnerets. It's a painstaking process—up to an hour to spin the net and another four to eight hours to complete the cocoon. Inside the cocoon, the larva pupates and, around sunset of the fifth or sixth day, emerges as an adult.

One might think that, since sponges are sessile (that is, anchored to one spot on the ground) and lacking a nervous system (to coordinate any escape behavior), feeding on them would be for any average predator, accustomed to chasing down and subduing prey, a piece of (sponge) cake. There are, however, some substantial hazards associated with sponge consumption. The tiny first instar spongillafly larvae, less than half a millimeter (1/50 inch) in length, face a unique problem. Sponges are filter feeders that depend on actively circulating water currents through their bodies so that individual cells lining the central cavity can engulf food particles. Water enters the sponge through many tiny openings called ostia and then leaves, minus its particles of food, through a large central opening called an osculum. Enormous volumes of water get pumped rapidly through a sponge in a day (large species can handle up to 1,500 liters or about 375 gallons). Spongillafly larvae feeding inside the central cavity of the sponge must deal with strong currents of water, so even the tiny first instar larvae are equipped with strong hind tarsal claws, to keep from becoming mere flotsam or jetsam.

There are other hazards faced daily by a spongillafly. The eggs of the spongillafly are attacked by both fungi and egg-sucking aquatic mites in their moist environment; the first instar larvae are prey to all kinds of plankton-feeding predators and even to carnivorous aquatic plants; the third instar larvae after exiting the water are eaten by ants, spiders, and centipedes; and the pupae in the cocoon are a special favorite of *Sisyridovora*, a pteromalid wasp that, as the name suggests, lays its eggs only inside the cocoons of spongillaflies—its grub offspring feast freely on spongillafly en papillote. In order to live long enough to see second instar, then, young spongillaflies must of necessity keep up with "current" events.

WATER BOATMEN

More than most insects, water boatmen, members of the family Corixidae, live by the philosophy that, if you have six legs, you may as well make the most of them. Each of their three pairs of legs is modified to accommodate an underwater lifestyle. Like many other aquatic members of the order Hemiptera, water boatmen have hind legs equipped for swimming. Elongate and flattened like oars, the hind legs are equipped with a long fringe of hairs that increases the surface area and enhances the rowing action. The middle two legs are long and slender and are tipped with two claws; these serve as anchors to secure corixids to aquatic vegetation whenever they're called upon to dock. The forelegs, however, are unique in the world of water bugs. Short and stubby, they terminate not in the customary series of three or four long slender tarsal segments but instead in one short segment that looks for all the world like a hairy spoon. These legs actually *are* spoons of a sort. Water boatmen use them to scoop up mud and ooze and to strain out small forms of plant and animal life—muckraking, as it were. Ooze-eating

Water boatmen: "Row, row, row your boatman . . ."

distinguishes corixids (or at least differentiates them) from the rest of the aquatic bugs who are, to a man (or bug), unreconstructed flesh-eaters (as opposed, one supposes, to "foul"-eaters).

The mouthparts of corixids reflect their unusual diet as well. The typical predaceous waterbug possesses a three- or four-segmented beak enclosing four stylets, two of which pierce flesh and two of which form a channel for sucking up vital fluids of hapless prey. The beak of the ooze-eating water boatman is short, stubby, and not visibly segmented; it seem to be used mostly for rasping and grinding up bits of muck and mire.

The front legs of male water boatmen have yet another unusual feature. They come equipped with a row of pegs on the femur, the segment adjacent to the tarsus. The water boatman stridulates—produces sound—by scraping the pegs against the sharp-edged side of its head. The tune might appropriately be called "Peg of My Heart," since it seems to serve the function, among others, of attracting females for mating.

Overwintering is usually in the adult or nymphal stage, although at least one species in Canada overwinters as an egg. In spring, after mating, females lay their eggs, generally in vegetation but occasionally on the bodies of slow-moving crustaceans. The developing nymphs molt five times before adulthood; for *Sigara alternata*, a denizen of roadside ditches all over northern North America, the process takes about six weeks before it reaches its full size of about ¼ inch. Corixids are excellent swimmers and, by trapping air bubbles on hairs on their undersides or in spaces under their wings, they can stay active underwater for long periods of time, recharging periodically by breaking the water surface headfirst.

Nevertheless, corixids spend much of their time on or near the bottoms of freshwater ponds and lakes, where they're close to their beloved ooze. As a result they're easy targets and are favorite prey of bass, perch, bluegill, crappie, and many other fishes. Actually, the eggs are considered quite a delicacy by yet another vertebrate predator, *Homo sapiens*. In Mexico, the eggs are prepared and eaten in a variety of ways. People in the water-boatman-egg business place reeds or sticks in the water and pull them out once they're laden with the oval stalked eggs. Cultivating water boatman eggs is probably a tough way to make a living—you might even say it's a difficult roe to hoe.

208

WATER PENNIES

Owners of streams or lakes throughout North America may be fortunate enough to count water pennies as part of their liquid assets. Far from being negotiable currency, water pennies are the immature stages of beetles in the family Psephenidae. For want of a better name, the adults are known as riffle beetles and are indeed found predominantly along the shores of fast-running shallow streams (in so-called riffle areas) and on wave-swept beaches of lakes. Adult *Psephenus herricki*, the only species of psephenid widely distributed throughout the eastern United States, are small, flattened, rather broad-shouldered blackish brown beetles about ⅕ inch (five to six millimeters) in length. As such, they can easily be mistaken for any of a number of aquatic beetles, including elmids (also known as riffle beetles, but a little more cylindrical in shape than psephenids) and dryopids (the long-toed water beetles, whose distinguishing feature is obvious by the name if not by close inspection).

There's no mistaking the larval stage of psephenids, however. The larva is basically round and flat. John Henry Comstock aptly coined the name (as it were) "water penny" to describe them; not only are they flat and round, they are even a sort of tarnished copper color. Flat is indeed the operative word here—with a cross-sectional profile of

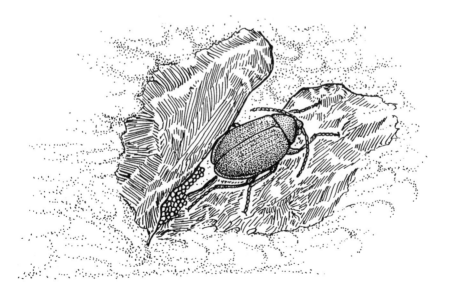

Water pennies: "I just hope none of the kids turns out to be claustrophobic."

209

only one millimeter ($\frac{1}{25}$ of an inch), water pennies put pancakes to shame. The larva of *Psephenus herricki* resembles nothing so much as a two-dimensional turtle. The head, six legs, and gills are covered by a segmented broad carapace, rendering these and most other body parts virtually invisible from above.

Pinching pennies is a regular occurrence in streams and waterways—psephenids prefer to rest wedged into tight nooks, crevices, and crannies of stony stream beds. The larvae are most comfortable when wedged in on all sides—a behavior known as thigmotaxis (or orientation to contact). These tenacious grubs can maintain their position flattened against rock faces even in swift-moving currents; once they gain a purchase, these pennies stick. Their bodies, although peculiar in appearance, are actually ideally constructed for clinging to rocks in fast-moving water. Water pennies usually align themselves with the long axis of their bodies parallel to the current, mostly on the downstream side of rocks. Water flows in under the carapace through lateral slots in between segments; after passing over the gills, it exits through the posterior end. This flow is induced by sequential uplift of the four abdominal plates (or tergites) in a wavelike fashion. The induced flow reduces turbulence around the water penny in much the same way that slots on an airplane wing reduce air turbulence.

Hydrodynamics aside, the unique design of the water penny makes it relatively immune to most predators. The clawed legs are very efficient at maintaining a grasp on rock faces and the carapace not only protects most vulnerable body parts but can even form a suction seal with the substrate, making removal an energy-consuming or even futile enterprise.

For their part, water pennies are inoffensive creatures, content to graze on algae of various descriptions. A hardy lot, they can withstand long periods without food and can even survive exposure out of water if streams run dry, as long as a thin film of moisture coats their gills. Larval development is thought to take two years to complete; eggs hatch in June and third or fourth instar larvae overwinter. About three more larval instars are completed in the following year and pupation takes place the year after, usually on a rock surface with the last larval skin forming a protective seal. Adults emerge from June through September in most of their range.

Adult lives are short (from two days to a week) but eventful. While adults are not known to feed, they do engage in what has been described by Murvosh (1971) as a

peculiar mating ritual. This occurs above the water line on the lee and sides of wave-splashed stones in riffles. The beetles are usually running very rapidly around the wet sides of the stones and appear to be very "excited." Occasionally, two or more will bump or run into each other and become tangled up for a second or more. They separate and scurry off in different directions. This is repeated over and over. The beetles are constantly running into each other even on large rocks. . . . What appear to be attempts at copulation occur at this time. Most are unsuccessful. . . . Copulation was timed in one pair and lasted 7 sec. At irregular intervals the beetles will stop running and stand motionless on the rock at the water's edge with the head end facing the water. . . . All of the adults on a single rock have been seen many times to line up at the same time in such a position and face the water. Fifty adults on a single boulder in Mill Creek were once seen doing this. The beetles will then begin scurrying about the rock again, usually all at the same time. This behavior is repeated continuously throughout the day.

The fun eventually comes to an end and females begin the business of egglaying in earnest. Curiously, riffle beetles can't swim and, although they do enjoy sitting on water-splashed rocks, they enter the water only to lay eggs. Adult females are as thigmotactic as the larvae and prefer to lay eggs, four hundred to six hundred at a time, crammed into tight crevices. Water pennies, then, are not to be envied—trapped between a rock and a hard place from the day they're born.

WATER SCAVENGER BEETLES

It's not surprising that, with over a quarter of a million described species, the order Coleoptera is renowned for setting records. For starters, it's the largest order of insects and probably the largest order of anything on the planet. It's also the order with the largest number of species that are aquatic as adults. Now, this is no small accomplishment, since the class Insecta is basically terrestrial; insects evolved on land and most of their unique anatomical features are designed for a landlocked life. Beetles, however, are not ones to ignore a challenge and routinely tough it out in all sorts of difficult environments, not the least of which are wet ones.

Among the many aquatic families of beetles is the Hydrophilidae (whose very name means "water-loving" and should give you a hint as to their lifestyle). Found as a rule in quiet ponds and slow-moving streams, they're known as water scavenger beetles due to a predilection for consuming decaying plant debris. Included in their ranks are some of the largest species of water beetles. *Hydrophilus triangularis*, for

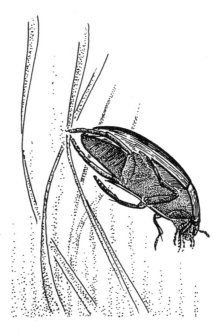

Water scavenger beetles: "I should have gotten a job in salvage."

example, a shiny black beetle with triangular yellow marks along its sides, tops out at an inch and a half or more in length. Like many hydrophilids, *H. triangularis* has a sharp spine on its underside projecting backward from the place where the forelegs join the body to just beyond the place where the hindlegs join the body. If flesh and spine align properly, an overenthusiastic collector with a precipitous grasp can receive a nasty jab for his or her efforts.

Hydrophilids have made relatively few dramatic adjustments to their underwater adult life. Their maxillary palps are a bit on the long side—they're even longer than the antennae—and may be particularly effective at detecting waterborne chemical cues. Like most aquatic beetles, water scavenger beetles are built for swimming. They're streamlined in shape and their hind legs are modified into oars for rowing—lengthened, flattened, and fringed with long hairs. Admittedly, oars don't have long hairs, but in this case, beetles have improved on human design. The hairs add to the thrust on the power stroke by increasing the surface area pushing against the water, then fold away neatly on the return stroke to decrease resistance. Like an oar blade, the far end of the leg, the tarsus, twists on the return stroke to cut down on drag. Unlike human oarsmen, hydrophilids stroke their legs alternately rather than together, so they swim in a sort of zigzag pattern that would not win them too many regattas. However, since the hydrophilids are scavengers and feed almost entirely on things that are already dead, speed is not at a premium.

While underwater, hydrophilids maintain an air supply for themselves in a silvery film held by a dense covering of water-repellent hairs on the underside of the thorax and abdomen. In most beetles, the spiracles—the air holes through which insects take in oxygen—are situated on the sides of the thorax; in hydrophilids, they're on the underside to hook up directly with the trapped air. The air film is recharged when the beetle swims to the surface and pokes an antenna through the water surface. Covered with water-repellent hairs that form a continuous layer with the thoracic hairs, the antenna carries a supply of air back underwater and serves as a conduit to the air storage facilities on the underside of the body.

When it comes time to reproduce, female water scavenger beetles engage in the time-honored practice of knitting. What they knit, however, is not six little booties for the bouncing baby grubs, but rather is a cradle with a built-in air supply. Accessory glands associated with the reproductive system produce a sticky fluid that is released through the end of the abdomen. Projecting off the end of the abdomen are two long flexible appendages called spinning rods, which draw out the fluid into thin silken strands and weave a cocoon directly on the air-filled surface of the abdomen. The cover is spun first, to trap an air supply, and then the base and sides are constructed. Eggs are deposited in the lower end of the structure, and the upper end is filled with crisscrossing silk strands to provide support. This cocoon is often anchored to a leaf and projects at one end above the surface film like a chimney, although in this case air flows in instead of smoke flowing out. Thus ensconced, the three to four dozen eggs have an air supply guaranteed to last as long as they need to hatch. Once hatched, the grubs, unlike their parents, are voracious predators.

In every family there are always a few members who can be considered a tad eccentric. In the case of the hydrophilids, the embarrassing relations are in the subfamily Sphaeridiinae. These counterculture upstarts are resolutely terrestrial. To make matters worse, they eat and live in dung. *Sphaeridium scarabeioides*, a red-spotted black species about a quarter of an inch long, is particularly partial to cattle droppings. It's unlikely they can ever return to an aquatic existence, since members of this subfamily lack swimming appendages. For the interim, then, *Sphaeridium* and its relatives will just have to stand pat—cow pat, at that.

References

Berg, C. L., and L. Knutson. 1978. Biology and systematics of the Sciomyzidae. *Ann. Rev. Ent.* 23:239–58.

Bradshaw, W. E. 1983. Interaction between the mosquito *Wyeomyia smithii*, the midge *Metriocnemus knabi*, and their carnivorous host *Sarracenia purpurea*. In *Phytotelmata*, ed. J. H. Brank and L. P. Lounibos, 161–89. Medford, N.J.: Plexus Publishing.

Brown, H. P. 1952. The life history of *Climacia areolaris* (Hagen), a neuropterous "parasite" of fresh water sponges. *Am. Midl. Nat.* 47:130–60.

Friedlander, C. P. 1977. *The Biology of Insects.* New York: Pica Press.

Hubbard, H. G. 1880. Habits of *Psephenus lecontei. Amer. Ent.* 3:73.

Istock, C. A., K. Tanner, and H. Zimmer. 1983. Habitat selection by the pitcherplant mosquito *Wyeomyia smithii*; behavioral and genetic aspects. In *Phytotelmata*, ed. J. H. Frank and L. P. Lounibos, 191–204. Medford, N.J.: Plexus Publishing.

Jackson, D. 1958. Observations on the biology of *Caraphractus cinctus* Walker (Hymenoptera: Mymaridae), a parasitoid of the eggs of Dytiscidae. *J. Roy. Ent. Soc. Lond.* 110:533–54.

Jacques, H. E. 1951. *How to Know the Beetles.* Dubuque, Iowa: Wm. C. Brown Co.

Klausnitzer, B. 1981. *Beetles.* New York: Exeter Books.

McCafferty, W. P. 1981. *Aquatic Entomology.* Boston: Science Books.

McShaffrey, D., and W. P. McCafferty. 1987. The behaviour and form of *Psephenus herricki* (DeKay) (Coleoptera: Psephenidae) in relation to water flow. *Freshwater Biol.* 18:319–24.

Matheson, R., and C. R. Crosby. 1912. Aquatic Hymenoptera in America. *Ann. Ent. Soc. Amer.* 5:65–71.

Miall, L. C. 1934. *The Natural History of Aquatic Insects.* London: Macmillan.

Murvosh, C. M. 1971. Ecology of the water penny beetle, *Psephenus herricki* (DeKay). *Ecol. Monog.* 41:79–96.

Neumann, D. 1986. Life cycle strategies of an intertidal midge between subtropic and Arctic latitudes. In *The Evolution of Insect Life Cycles*, ed. F. Taylor and R. Karban, 3–19. New York: Springer Verlag.

———. 1988. Temperature compensation of circasemilunar timing in the intertidal insect *Clunio. J. Comp. Physiol.* A 163:671–76.

Preston-Mafham, R., and K. Preston-Mafham. 1984. *Spiders of the World.* New York: Facts on File.

Waltz, R. D., and W. P. McCafferty. 1979. Freshwater springtails (Hexapoda: Collembola) of North America. *Purdue University Exp. Stn. Res. Bull.* 960.

Chapter 8

Animal Appetites

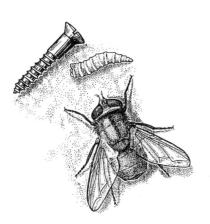

Beaver beetles

Bee mites

Elephant lice

Face flies

Fowl ticks

Horse flies

Mange mites

Rabbit fleas

Reindeer throat bot flies

Screwworms

Sheep keds

BEAVER BEETLES

Most Americans probably don't realize that the economic development of this great nation was made possible at least in part by a rodent. Actually, to be perfectly accurate, it was made possible by the skin of a rodent. In the eighteenth and nineteenth centuries, no well-dressed man felt complete without a beaver hat, a beaver cap, or a beaver collar. Accordingly, there was a tremendous demand for beaver skins, and North America, home to vast populations of *Castor canadensis*, the American beaver, suddenly became a land of opportunity for hunters, trappers, and fur traders. In the language of the Flathead-Salish Indians, the word *ska-le-oo*, meaning "beaver," was synonymous with "money." The Hudson's Bay Company sold over 270,000 skins in 1875 alone. Fortunes were made, towns were settled, and territories explored all because of beaver skins. Fashions, however, by their nature are changeable, and eventually beaver fell out of favor; demand for beaver skins dropped precipitously and, by the turn of the twentieth century, the market had shrunk considerably.

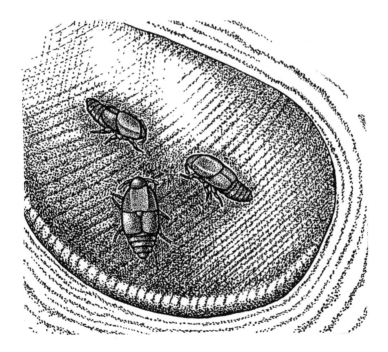

Beaver beetles: "Anyone up for a game of paddleball?"

Beaver skins have always been in great demand, however, by the less fashion-conscious beaver beetles. The beaver beetle, *Platypsyllis castoris*, is peculiar even by insect standards. Adults and larvae are found only on beaver skins; there, they can be found in large numbers. Accordingly, beaver beetles were familiar to hunters and trappers long before they were familiar to entomologists. When Westwood described them in 1869, he was so puzzled by their appearance that he placed them in their own order, the Acheiroptera. Although most entomologists concede today that they are in fact beetles, they're still causing headaches among coleopterists as to who their closest relatives are.

One reason for the confusion is that beaver beetles don't look much like typical beetles. They're very small (about three millimeters—a little over $\frac{1}{10}$ inch—in length), very flat, and totally lacking eyes and wings. While their appearance isn't consistent with coleopteran norms, it is consistent with norms for insects that lead an ectoparasitic existence. Reduction in sensory and locomotor apparatus is *de rigeur* for parasites that, living on their hosts as they do, have no need to look for or chase after food. They even have backward-pointing spines on the second and third pairs of legs; such spines are typical of parasitic insects such as fleas, which use the spines to keep themselves from being dislodged from among the dense hairs of their hosts.

While there are not that many holometabolous insects, or insects with complete development, that live as permanent ectoparasites on their hosts, there are some flies, fleas, and even a moth or two that manage nicely. What is truly remarkable about the beaver beetle is that it is a permanent ectoparasite even in its larval stages. As far as anyone has been able to determine, the only time a beaver beetle ever leaves a beaver body is to pupate and possibly to lay eggs. Females are thought to drop the eggs in the mud of the beaver lodge, although no one has actually witnessed them in the act, since they're very tiny and conditions for observation are less than ideal inside a beaver lodge in midwinter. Eggs hatch in about a month, depending upon temperature, and the young larvae immediately latch onto the closest available beaver, settling in preferentially around the head, neck, and shoulders. They use their sharp, pointed mandibles to pierce the skin and suck beaver blood. After three larval instars, beaver beetles at long last say farewell to their hosts and burrow into the soil on top of the lodge to pupate.

After about three weeks as a pupa, the adult beetle emerges and sets out in search of a new beaver. The adults are extremely sensitive to warmth and to beaver breath. Their reliance upon such cues is not surprising, considering that they lack eyes altogether and have antennae that can only generously be called stubby. Once on board a beetle, beaver beetles begin to feed. Their thin, platelike mandibles are not exactly built for piercing epidermis, so they may content themselves with lapping up fatty skin secretions instead of sucking blood.

Living on a beaver is not for the faint of heart (or dorsal aorta). Beavers routinely stay submerged for long periods of time in icy cold water. Accordingly, beaver beetles prefer to cling to the dense underfur of beavers, in which is trapped a layer of warm, dry air even when the beaver is submerged. Beavers also groom themselves constantly, with hind toenails specially split for the purpose; beaver beetles risk getting dislodged and tossed aside every time a beaver spruces up.

On the other hand, there are worse places to live. A beaver lodge is, all in all, a remarkable architectural achievement. It has a floor that can be raised or lowered according to water level, it is waterproofed against leakage, and, with as many as four or five entrances, it is even well-ventilated. Temperatures inside a beaver lodge remain a chilly but livable four degrees Centigrade even when outside temperatures drop as low as minus fifteen degrees Centigrade. These luxury homes attract quite a diversity of arthropod occupants. The uninvited guests include *Leptinillus validus*, another beaver beetle that spends its larval stages in the lodge, only visiting beaver skins for a quick snack, as well as the hair mite *Schizocarpus mingaudi*, which infests the skin, and *Prolabidocarpis canadensis*, which sets up housekeeping inside the ears of beavers. All told, at least twelve species of insects and arachnids are found exclusively on beavers in beaver lodges. With its architectural prowess, *Castor canadensis* makes life comfortable for these arthropods, who, when it comes to looking for a place to live, simply "leave it to beaver."

BEE MITES

Jonathan Swift was not really speaking about insects when he wrote:

> So naturalists, observe a flea
> Hath smaller fleas that on him prey;
> And these have smaller still to bite 'em;
> And so proceed ad infinitum.

He was actually discoursing metaphorically on the nature of literary criticism; what he said, though, applies very well to the honey bee and bee mites. One doesn't normally think of honey bees as having to worry about enemies—after all, colonies consist of thousands of individuals, most of whom come equipped with venomous stingers and an inclination to use them at the slightest sign of trouble. But the honey bee's biggest enemies are its smallest ones. There are at least three species of parasitic mites, less than a millimeter in length, that live on or around the bodies of bees, sucking their blood and causing major disruption to the order of things.

The most destructive species from the economic perspective of beekeepers, and from the I-want-to-live perspective of the honey bee, is

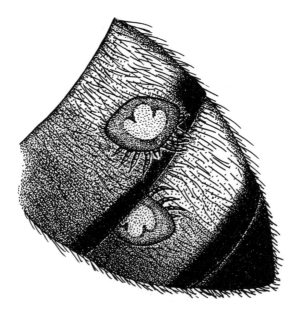

Bee mites: "Who do you have to know to get a seat by the wing?"

Varroa jacobsoni. It's a tiny reddish brown mite covered with dense fine hairs and it can be found, if one knows where to look, sucking the blood (or hemolymph) of mature larvae and adult bees. Female mites prefer to feed on adults, preferentially hiding under the segmental plates or sclerites of the abdomen or in the junction between the thorax and abdomen. Like all mites, they suck up fluids with their chelicerae, which they use to puncture the relatively thin cuticle between segments. Females ready to reproduce deplane the bee in the hive and enter a wax cell containing a grub, preferably the larger drone grub, between five and six days old. Although they may take a quick sip of grub blood, the mites generally burrow down into the mass of pollen and honey provided by the worker bees for the grub. There they remain immobilized until the grub seals its own fate by eating the brood food and releasing the mites. The mites then feed on the developing larva and pupa, laying eggs one at a time on the cell walls. A newly hatched mite molts once inside the egg and emerges in about two days, feeding as its mother does on the pupa. It molts once more into adulthood. Total development from egg to adult takes about a week for male mites and eight or nine days for female mites. The males, even smaller than the females, are relatively innocuous (but for the fact that they can father more *Varroa jacobsoni*); their mouthparts are modified for sperm transfer and they can't even eat. They mate inside the wax cell and wait for adult bees to pass by. Once the bee mite has latched onto an adult bee, it can live happily for up to two months in summer and five months in winter.

A honey bee colony that develops a varroa infestation is in big trouble; populations can build up quickly to eleven thousand or more, and drones can end up carrying over a dozen mites on their bodies. Entire colonies can be killed off, primarily due to the fact that the mites, which prefer drones, can eliminate all the males in a swarm, so a virgin queen remains a virgin and the colony collapses.

Although varroa can be found all over the world, such wasn't always the case. Before humans began transporting *Apis mellifera*, the European honey bee, all over the globe, varroa mites lived only on *Apis cerana*, the Asian hive bee. When the European honey bee, a superior honey producer, was introduced into Asia, it acquired the parasites of its Asian relative. The first occurrence of the mite in Europe was in western Russia, imported no doubt by beekeepers working with the Asian hive bee in eastern Russia. The mite was discovered in Romania in 1975, and Romania, as part of a foreign aid package, inadvertently shipped the mite off to Tunisia along with some honey bees, introducing varroa to the African continent. Japanese beekeepers moved mites accidentally to Paraguay in 1971, infesting the South American continent, where varroa can today be found throughout Brazil, Argentina, and Paraguay. The only commercial honey-producing areas largely free of varroa are the United States, Canada, Australia, and New Zealand. To keep itself varroa-free, the United States forbids importation of bees from any country other than Canada.

Varroa mites have a remarkable facility for spreading quickly once introduced into virgin territory. One study documented that the mites managed to extend their range seven miles (eleven kilometers) in three months without the assistance of humans. Only a year after the mite was first reported in Brazil, 520 colonies from 26 apiaries throughout Sao Paulo State were infested. It's almost enough to make one feel sorry for the Africanized "killer bees" that now inhabit Brazil—it's a situation of "kill or bee killed" there now.

ELEPHANT LICE

It's not altogether surprising that most people would have a hard time figuring out where to put an elephant—elephants are, after all, the largest land-dwelling animals on the planet. It is a little surprising, though, that entomologists have had so much trouble figuring out where to put the elephant louse, *Haematomyzus elephantis*. Clearly, size is not a problem. Topping off at a shade over three millimeters (a bit more than $\frac{1}{10}$ inch) at maturity, the elephant louse isn't even the largest known louse; the pig louse, *Haematopinus suis*, at about a quarter of an inch in length when full grown, is elephantine by comparison. Rather, placing the elephant louse is a conceptual problem and not a physical one.

Lice are, generally speaking, flat-bodied, dull-colored, wingless, largely sedentary, external parasites of warm-blooded vertebrates (this inventory of traits is at least part of the reason that being called a "louse" is not widely regarded as flattering). Insect taxonomists recognize two clearly different types of lice. The Mallophaga, or chewing lice, are noted (as the name suggests) for their chewing mouthparts. They use these mouthparts for chewing through skin flakes, wolfing down dried blood, and gobbling up other skin debris. Most are associated with birds (although at least one hundred species deign to dine

Elephant lice: "Now here's a cause I can support!"

225

on mammalian body tissues); the majority of mallophagans on birds (and hence the majority of mallophagans in general) have a pair of well-developed claws on the tips of their tarsi.

The Anoplura, in contrast, are known as the sucking lice. Unlike the masticating mallophagans, anoplurans have mouthparts modified for piercing epidermal tissues and sucking up blood. Anoplurans are by and large restricted to feeding on mammals; the legs, equipped with only a single (albeit stout) claw at the tip of the tarsus, are used for grasping hairs and staying in place (despite frantic efforts by irritated hosts to dislodge them).

The elephant louse, *H. elephantis*, at first glance seems to have traits in common with both the Mallophaga and the Anoplura. The shape of its genitalia (a trait that insect taxonomists spend a lot of time examining, not due to character deficiencies on their part but rather due to the fact that insect genitalia are often the only useful clues as to the identity of a species) shed no light on its affinities. It has only a single claw on its tarsi, as do all of the anoplurans—but then, the mammal-feeding mallophagans also have only one tarsal claw. It has chewing mouthparts, like the mallophagans—but it also has an esophageal pump, which suggests that it sucks up fluids like the anoplurans.

To make things even more complicated, *H. elephantis* has some features that are unlike anything else in louse-dom. Its tiny chewing mouthparts are situated on the end of an enormously elongated rostrum (one might even say "trunk"). After struggling with trying to find the place where elephant lice belong in the grand scheme of things, Ferris in 1931 took the easy way out—he created a unique category for *H. elephantis* and its only living relative, *H. hudsoni*, a parasite of wart hogs. He called this new taxon the Rhynchophthirina—loosely translated, the snout lice. There they stay, still argued over by a handful of entomologists determined to bring the lice into line.

One possible reason that elephant lice are so unlike other lice is that living on an elephant poses some impressive challenges. Lice generally feed on warm-blooded hosts, and those hosts keep their blood warm by growing a coat of insulating material like feathers or fur all over their bodies. This coat not only keeps hosts warm, it also provides handy handholds (or legholds) for ectoparasites, who can cling to hair or feathers with their strong claws. Elephants are among the exceptional mammals (whose exalted ranks also include humans and pigs) that are not noticeably hirsute; elephant lice actually have to hold onto their hosts by sinking their teeth into the skin. The elongated snout no doubt makes traveling a bit more comfortable and may also be helpful in penetrating the thick pachyderm skin.

All exciting events in the life of a louse are shared with the elephant host. Eggs are cemented onto the sparse hairs scattered over the body; the hatching nymphs as well as adults feed on elephant blood. While some lice are capable of living a few weeks off their hosts, an elephant louse separated from an elephant cannot survive more than a few hours at most. Elephant lice are apparently equally happy on both species of elephants—African elephants in Africa and Indian elephants throughout Asia. Elephant lice are not found with equal probability on any particular part of the elephant, however. They tend to gather on the capacious ears but can be found (much, no doubt, to the consternation of the elephant) in the groin area, in the armpits (legpits?), and around the base of the tail.

The elephant's baggy skin, with its ample supply of folds and wrinkles, actually protects the elephant louse from its worst enemy—the aggravated elephant. Unable to pick off the lice, an elephant can suffer a severe dermatitic reaction to their bloodfeeding and do itself serious damage rubbing itself raw trying to relieve the itchiness (probably, in the process, doing serious damage to the object against which it rubs as well). All in all, if an elephant could forget anything, a louse infestation is likely an experience most elephants would just as soon not remember.

FACE FLIES

A recitation of the taste preferences of *Musca autumnalis* would be enough to turn any human stomach, although its appetites are not surprising, considering it counts among its near relations the blood-sucking stable fly (*Stomoxys calcitrans*) and the garbage-feeding house fly (*Musca domestica*). So closely does it resemble the house fly in appearance that even experts can't always distinguish them. Unlike house flies, however, they don't associate much with people; they enter houses (often in large numbers) only to hibernate. Instead, like the stable fly, face flies tend to associate with large farm animals—cattle, mostly, but horses and other creatures when pressed. Unlike the stable fly, however, the face fly lacks sharp, piercing mouthparts and thus is unable to puncture cowhide to suck blood—although it is content to lap it up with its spongelike proboscis should a stable fly or any other fly break the skin first. Instead, the face fly concentrates on more accessible body fluids. It will not turn its nose (or proboscis) up at anything that oozes out of or flows from a bovine orifice and thus has been observed diligently lapping tears, nasal mucus, milk clinging to

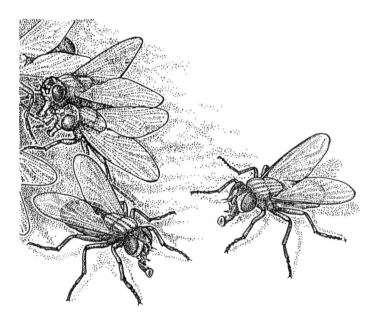

Face flies: "This place is packed—I'm going around to the service entrance."

the lips of nursing calves, saliva, placental fluids, genital discharges, and other things too horrible to mention.

Actually, face flies spend relatively little time feeding on their hosts. Most of their time eating is spent sucking more mundane fluids such as nectar or animal waste. Female face flies, however, need an extra shot of protein to produce a clutch of eggs, and bovine discharges fit the bill (of fare) nicely. Females lay eggs one at a time on the upper surface of a cow pat, preferably less than twenty minutes old. The eggs are well equipped for such a fate since they come equipped with a black respiratory mast or siphon, which projects out of the dung and acts like a snorkel, delivering fresh air to the developing embryo. The newly hatched maggots, less than a millimeter ($\frac{1}{25}$ of an inch) in length, are whitish, but they turn yellow by their second molt. Larvae burrow around underneath the crusty upper surface of the cow pat and in anywhere from three to seventy days, depending on temperature and humidity, leave the dung pat to pupate in the soil. The puparium of *Musca autumnalis* is rather distinctive in being a creamy white color—most fly puparia are shiny brown or black.

When pupation is complete, the emerging flies spend some time inflating and firming up their wings. They then head for a fence, a shrub, or any other nearby upright stationary object, where the sexes rendezvous. After mating, the flies start feeding their faces on faces. While face flies may not directly injure cattle, they certainly annoy them—as many as a hundred or more may congregate on eyes, on ears, on lips, or in the nostrils of a single cow. And while their mouthparts aren't as razor sharp as are those of the stable flies, they nonetheless possess small teeth that can tear sensitive eye tissue and, conveniently from the fly perspective, cause blinking and tear formation. Moreover, they can cause tremendous damage by acting as vectors for various bovine pathogens, including the bacterium *Moraxella bovis*, which causes bovine keratoconjunctivitis (pinkeye), and the nematode *Thelazia lacrymalis*, or eyeworm.

Thus, in 1976, less than fifteen years after *Musca autumnalis* first made an appearance in this country, it had caused an estimated economic loss of about $68 million. Where it came from is anyone's guess, since face flies were well established in Europe, Asia, North Africa, and the Middle East when they were introduced into the United States. So, when Winston Churchill said, "I have nothing to offer but blood, toil, tears, and sweat," in his first address to the House of Commons as prime minister, he might just have been reciting the menu at a British pub for face flies.

FOWL TICKS

Aristotle, the great philosopher and naturalist of the fourth century B.C., was, as a rule, objective and dispassionate in his voluminous writings—but when discoursing upon ticks he referred to them as "disgusting parasitic animals." Ticks have been called any number of names over the centuries (few any more flattering than Aristotle's pithy description), but it wasn't until the turn of the present century that fine distinctions among the various types of ticks were finally recognized.

Ticks basically belong to two families—the Ixodidae, or hard ticks, and the Argasidae, or soft ticks. Neither family is particularly endearing. The hard ticks, so-named due to the presence of a hard plate or scutum covering the backs of adult males, include in their ranks such disease vectors as *Ixodes* (the Lyme disease vector), *Dermacentor* (the vector of Rocky Mountain spotted fever), and *Amblyomma* (a vector of tularemia). Argasids may be soft, but they're hardly cute and cuddly. Among the eighty-five species of soft ticks, characterized by the leathery, wrinkled appearance of both male and female adults, are vectors of the spirochaete causing relapsing fever.

A particularly foul member of this group is the fowl tick *Argus persicus*. Fowl ticks, also known as adobe ticks, tampans, or blue bugs,

Fowl ticks: "Nothing beats an old-fashioned feather bed for comfort."

are reddish brown to slate blue in color. Like most soft ticks, the male and female are similar in appearance, although females tend to be about a millimeter longer and wider (at 8.5 millimeters by 5.5 millimeters). The truly curious can distinguish the sexes, however, by their genitalia—the genital orifice of the male is shaped like a half-moon while the genital orifice of the female, situated directly behind her mouthparts, is a simple slit. When fully engorged after a blood meal, a female can quadruple in thickness to about 3 millimeters ($\frac{1}{8}$ inch).

From the point of view of *Argus persicus*, the perfect meal is chicken—breast, wing, or thigh. The adults are nocturnal, crawling up to perches, sucking blood till replete and, like their legendary counterparts from Transylvania, retiring at the crack of dawn to hide during the daylight hours. When it comes to egglaying, fowl ticks put their feathered coopmates to shame. Females lay their large reddish brown eggs, twenty-five to one hundred at a time, in cracks and crevices; one female can lay over seven hundred eggs over the course of a lifetime.

After one to four weeks, the eggs hatch and the larvae seek out hosts both day and night. Once attached, they feed for five or six days, drop off, and crawl into a crevice to molt to the eight-legged nymphal stage. These nymphs are exclusively nocturnal, feeding for another ten to twelve days before molting to a second nymphal stage. After yet another weeklong series of nighttime snacks, the nymphs molt into adulthood.

Argus persicus is an unwelcome nocturnal visitor to chicken coops not only because of its blood-feeding habits but also because of the company it keeps. It is a principal vector for fowl tick fever (*Borrelia anserina*), poultry pyroplasm (*Aegyptianella pullorum*), and fowl plague (*Pasturella avicida*). Moreover, toxins in its saliva can cause permanent muscular weakness in the legs of infested birds. Determining whether ticks are involved in unexplained avian mortality can be difficult since *Argus persicus* spends so much of its time (particularly during daylight hours) hiding in cracks and crevices nowhere near its victims. So—mysterious deaths in a hen house that are otherwise inexplicable may well be the result of fowl (tick) play.

HORSE FLIES

Being hungry enough to eat a horse is a regular occurrence for flies in the family Tabanidae, known by both equestrians and entomologists as the horse flies. Female horse flies, most of whom require a meal of blood before they can begin to lay eggs, come equipped with knifelike mouthparts with which they pierce the hide of their warm-blooded prey, to start the warm blood flowing freely. They then use their labella, a spongy tonguelike organ, to soak it all up and in. Since horse flies can reach some hefty dimensions (one species has a wingspan reaching almost 2½ inches), they can take a rather hefty meal. Between the amount of blood actually lapped up by the fly and the amount that runs freely as a result of the deep puncture, a horse can lose almost half a cup of blood a day to horse flies. If horses aren't around, a horse fly can get hungry enough to eat cattle, hogs, camels, monkeys, dogs, and even humans; some species forgo a hot lunch and feed on cold-blooded lizards, turtles, or crocodiles.

Female horse flies find food by following moving objects; they pursue grazing or galloping mammals, humans on horseback, and have been observed chasing down moving cars, trains, and even ships a mile or

Horse flies: "I don't know, fairy tales always give me such an appetite."

more at sea, reaching flight speeds in excess of twenty-five miles per hour. Males horse flies, however, lead a much more sedentary existence. They don't feed on blood at all, opting instead for an occasional sip of nectar from a flower. Their primary occupation is finding female horse flies, or rather, letting females find them. At dawn and dusk, males congregate in large swarms around tall objects—treetops, grain elevators, fire towers, and the like—and wait for females to single them out. Male horse flies can easily be distinguished from females by virtue of the fact that their huge eyes are so enlarged that they actually meet along the midline of the head. It isn't clear whether they need such large eyes to look out for females or to check out their competition in the all-male swarms.

After mating, usually during the warmer parts of the year, females deposit layers of their waterproofed eggs in aquatic or semiaquatic environments. Horse fly maggots live in a variety of such places, including marshes, streams, swamps, bogs, lakes, beaches, springs, mud flats, and even rot-holes in trees. The maggots are distinctive in appearance—legless, tapered at both ends, often dirty white in color with black or brown rings around each body segment. Larvae of the larger species can reach two inches in length. While larvae of deer flies (tabanids in the genus *Chrysops*) are vegetarian, contentedly consuming leaf mold, rotting logs, and other debris, larvae of the genus *Tabanus* are voracious carnivores, attacking worms, snails, crustaceans, other insects (including other tabanids), and even vertebrates.

Larvae of *Tabanus punctifer*, for example, burrow down tail-first into the mud of ponds and lie in wait with their hooked mandibles flush with the surface. When a hapless toad or frog blunders across the waiting mouthparts, the maggot clamps down and drags the toad down under the mud, injecting a paralytic venom and sucking out the vital fluids. The legless maggots can exert remarkable force on the struggling toads; maximum resistance forces are up to thirty times their own weight and up to fifteen times the weight of the toad. In a world where the usual situation is toad-eats-worm, one supposes it was inevitable that the worm would one day turn.

MANGE MITES

Mange is something that shouldn't happen to a dog. Unfortunately, from the canine perspective, it happens with alarming frequency. Red mange in dogs is caused by a follicle mite called *Demodex canis*. Like other species in the family Demodicidae, *Demodex canis* is tiny in size (only a tenth of a millimeter or so in length, about ¹⁄₂₅₀ of an inch) and elongate in shape. This shape proves most suitable for permitting demodicid mites to occupy their favorite dwelling places—the narrow hair follicles in the skin of mammals. There, the mites are thought to feed on the waxy secretions produced by sebaceous glands. Thus, every want or desire of a follicle mite can be found in a follicle, and often all life stages—egg, larva, protonymph, deutonymph, and adult—happily can fit in a single follicle. The entire developmental period from egg to adult can take place in a follicle in just under a month.

About the only time a demodicid mite feels the urge to depart its hair is when it's time to find a mate. Mating for these mites is something of an acrobatic accomplishment. The male's genital organ is located on his back toward the anterior end of his body and the female's genital opening is on her underside, about a third of the distance between head and tail ends, situated between her fourth pair of stumpy little legs. To add to the anatomical obstacles, a follicle doesn't allow a lot of room for maneuvering.

Given the difficulties that mating seems to present for these mites, it's really remarkable just how ubiquitous they are. Mange mites have

Mange mites: "Just my luck—a Mexican hairless . . ."

been found in every breed of dog. Pedigree doesn't concern the mite, however, since mixed breeds are just as prone to harbor an infestation. In fact, there are those who believe that every *individual* dog is host to at least a few mange mites.

That not all dogs suffer from serving as mite hosts appears to relate to the vigor of the individual dog's immune system. Young puppies or older dogs suffering from malnutrition, parasitic infections, or other forms of debilitating disease are particularly susceptible to serious or even life-threatening outbreaks of mange. Characteristic of demodectic mange in dogs are two types of skin lesions. Squamous lesions, which are common on the head, particularly around the muzzle, eyes, and forefeet, are characteristically dry, scaly patches of hair loss. This is the form known as red mange (due to the raw, red appearance of the naked skin). Pustular lesions—moist, weepy blisters—often form after squamous lesions appear, probably as a result of secondary infection by *Staphylococcus pyogenes albus* and related skin bacteria.

Considering how widespread *Demodex canis* is, it's a little surprising that so little is known about how it moves around. It's not even generally agreed upon that the mites can travel from dog to dog (except possibly from nursing mother to puppies). And the mites are so highly specialized that they rarely if ever are found on any animal other than a dog. Before you breathe a sigh of relief, however, that other animals have been spared the indignity of having their hairs invaded by tiny creatures, you should be aware that most mammals have their own unique species of follicle mite. Bats, rodents, carnivores, horses, cattle, rabbits, primates, and even marsupials like the kangaroo are all known to have follicle mites to call their own. Humans are relatively unusual in that they are twice-blessed; not one but *two* species inhabit the hair follicles and sebaceous glands around the eyes, nose, and mouth.

The demodicid mites are so host-specific that one of the best ways to tell them apart is to identify the animal they were on. In those rare mammals that are host to two species, taxonomy then becomes a matter of splitting hair follicles.

RABBIT FLEAS

With their prodigious capacity for reproduction, rabbits should be accustomed to hearing the pitter-patter of little feet around the house. Around some rabbit nests, however, there is a bit more pitter-patter than can be accounted for by rabbit feet alone. *Spilopsyllus cuniculi*, the rabbit flea, is found only on European rabbits (*Oryctolagus cuniculus*) and in European rabbit nests. Generally, rabbit fleas prefer rabbit ears—not because they can get better television reception but because they are partial to warm and cozy quarters. A single pair of rabbit ears can house as many as three hundred rabbit fleas, although usually there are only a few dozen in residence. Rabbit fleas are not completely sedentary; they move to the inner ear when temperatures drop and sun themselves on the exterior of the ear on balmy days (in one ear and out the same one, as it were). In very cold weather, they abandon the ear altogether, opting for a rabbit fur coat to keep out the chill, as they bury themselves deep in body fur.

Mating and reproducing naturally affect a rabbit's life, but these activities have a profound effect on the life of a rabbit flea as well. When rabbit passions are inflamed, their ears get hot—several degrees hotter than they are under more ordinary circumstances. The increased temperature agitates the fleas, to the extent that agitated fleas on a

Rabbit fleas: "Oh, boy! They're playing the Bunny Hop!"

male rabbit can actually hot-foot it over to a new female host when male and female rabbits get together. After a female rabbit is mated, she ovulates and gets pregnant. Pregnancy in rabbits, as in humans, is accompanied by all kinds of hormonal changes. These hormone changes not only affect the behavior and physiology of the rabbit, they also affect the behavior and physiology of the rabbit fleas that ingest the rabbit hormones along with the blood.

Ingestion of hormone-charged blood by female fleas induces ovary development and egg formation in the flea. In males, the hormones cause the sperm cells to grow and the accessory glands to mature. That rabbit hormones can affect reproductive physiology in a different species is remarkable enough; even more remarkable, an additional dramatic change in fleas induced by rabbit hormones is the defecation rate. All this sexual stimulation greatly accelerates the rate at which fleas, particularly females, defecate. After ingesting the blood from pregnant rabbits, female rabbit fleas increase their defecation rate from once every half hour to once a minute.

Right after the host rabbit gives birth, the rabbit fleas move off the adult and onto the bunnies, preferring to congregate around the bunnies' tails. There, they mate, feed furiously, and then lay their own eggs in and around the nest debris. Only female rabbit fleas that have consumed bunny blood are deemed sexy enough to merit attention from male rabbit fleas. About fifty eggs are laid in the nest. These hatch in three days, and the wormlike larvae begin to consume the excrement thoughtfully provided by their courting parents just a few days earlier. About a week or two after the bunnies and larvae are born, adult fleas return to the host rabbit ears to await the next blessed event.

Oddly enough, despite the fact that rabbit fleas are so closely associated with rabbits in so many ways, they are unlike them in one very rabbitlike property. Although rabbits are known among mammals for their jumping prowess, rabbit fleas are far from spectacular when it comes to jumping in the flea world. *S. cuniculi* can jump only as high as about 50 millimeters. In contrast, the cat flea *Ctenocephalides felis* can leap as high as 330 millimeters. Rabbit fleas may not need such impressive locomotory skills, since all they'll ever need out of life can be found in a rabbit nest. Fleas in general are limited by the fact that their larvae are incapable of extensive movement, and fleas that feed on different species of mammals or birds that move around a lot may have trouble guaranteeing their offspring a well-provisioned nest in which to develop. Tuned in as they are to their host's reproductive patterns, rabbit fleas definitely have the jump on their relatives in terms of their own reproductive success.

REINDEER THROAT BOT FLIES

There's a general misapprehension that a reindeer's life, aside from the Christmas rush, is relatively free of strife—chew a little lichen, molt when the weather gets warm, and wait for the sun to go down to go to sleep (though admittedly, in the northern climates reindeer tend to favor, that can be a long wait indeed). But reindeer, like just about every other higher life form on the planet, have a few insect problems to contend with. Probably the most problematical is *Cephenemyia trompe*, the reindeer throat bot fly, which is found wherever reindeer are found—even in the northern arctic extremes of their range, places where most self-respecting insects wouldn't set one foot, much less six.

The reindeer throat bot fly is a member of the family Oestridae, a family full of medium to large, often hairy, flies with a passing resemblance to bumble bees. Like bumble bees, adult oestrids are partial to visiting flowers to partake of nectar on warm sunny days. Their herbivorous habits, however, are quickly shed when the time comes to

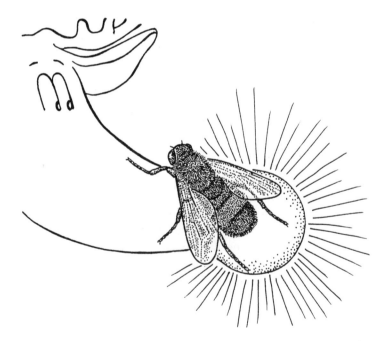

Reindeer throat bot flies: "Can you dim it, bub? I'm trying to work here!"

reproduce. The immature stages of oestrids, unlike the adults, are carnivorous and consume their meals from the inside out—all are endoparasites of mammals and are known as bots.

Gaining entry into a host is a problem of considerable dimensions for bot flies in general and some have come up with remarkably devious solutions. *Dermatobia horminis,* for example, lays its eggs on mosquitoes, which then fly off to find a warm-blooded host. Once the mosquito's sharp proboscis pierces the skin, the eggs hatch and the maggots then bore right in. *Cephenemyia trompe,* however, is considerably more direct about gaining entry. Eggs hatch inside the body of the female fly, who then ejects the larvae into the nostrils of the nearest reindeer. Not surprisingly, reindeer aren't too happy about this arrangement and are rendered rigid with terror (by some accounts) at the sight of a female bot fly hovering in front of their faces. Also not surprisingly, oestrids are among the faster-flying insects, having to dart in and out of a startled animal's nose before it can react and protect itself.

Once snugly ensconced in the nasal cavity, the larvae begin to feed on blood and soft tissues. Developing larvae move up the nostrils and generally complete development inside the nasal and pharyngeal pouches. All this crawling around understandably irritates the reindeer; infested animals tend to elevate their heads, sneeze, and cough repeatedly.

Generally, infestation by *Cephenemyia trompe* isn't fatal (although it can be if larvae take a wrong turn and end up in the lungs). In June, after development is complete (a process that can take nine to eleven months), the larvae leave the host the same way they came in—via the nostrils. The violent sneezing that this migration provokes assists in expelling the larvae. Once on the ground, pupation occurs in a few hours and the insect remains in the pupal stage anywhere from a little over two weeks to just under two months.

Considering that no effective control programs have been devised to eliminate the reindeer throat bot fly (a name that, in view of the actual habits, is either a misnomer or a euphemism), it's fortunate from the reindeer's perspective that infestation is rarely fatal. It's also somewhat surprising, given that reindeer throat bot flies are found wherever reindeer are found, that infestations aren't reported more often. After all, out of nine reindeer, only Rudolf showed up that Christmas Eve with a shiny nose.

SCREWWORMS

From the point of view of livestock, nothing can screw things up to the extent that screwworms can. Screwworms are species in genus *Cochliomyia*, whose closest relatives are blow flies, bluebottles, cluster flies, and other members of the family Calliphoridae. They actually are called screwworms because, if you try hard, you can see a resemblance between the maggots and a screw—flat at one end, tapered to a point at the other, and circled with elevated spines that could pass for the raised ridges on a screw. When this worm turns, however, it's bad news for anything with four legs, warm breath, and a fur coat.

After mating, female screwworm flies search the countryside for a cow, sheep, horse, mule, pig, goat, dog, fox, or even human being, one that's just slightly less than perfect—a nick here, a scratch there, any tiny wound or opening will suffice. Screwworms themselves can't break the skin of their host, but they're exceedingly adept at finding ready-made openings (even on occasion enlisting fellow arthropods by seeking out flea or tick bites). Once at a wound, a female fly can lay up to four hundred eggs, shingle-style, on the dry skin around the

Screwworms: "I wonder which is which?"

wound in under six minutes. After ten to twenty hours, the eggs hatch and the maggots begin to tear away at tissue with their sharp mouth hooks. At first, they restrict their feeding to the wounded area, but they quickly progress to healthy flesh, digging out deep pockets from which they must periodically withdraw in order to get air. As they feed, they produce a toxin that prevents the wound from healing, so infection quickly sets in. The resulting pus and foul odors actually attract more female flies to the site, who lay more eggs to cause even more problems for the infected animal. An unattended infestation of this sort can kill full-grown cattle in under two weeks (and that's no bull). When full grown (in four to ten days) maggots drop out of the wound to pupate in the soil for up to two weeks.

Depending on conditions, screwworms can complete a generation in three weeks flat and can run through eight to ten generations in a year. Not surprisingly, screwworms have typically been a major economic problem in livestock-producing areas. However, screwworms have proved to be vulnerable. First of all, they can't tolerate cold weather and can't live through the winter north of San Antonio, Texas. Infestations northward are the result of annual migrations. Second, since they can't penetrate skin, minimizing trauma to livestock can cut down on screwworm problems. Farmers are recommended to do their tail-docking, dehorning, shearing, branding, and castrating in the screwworm off-season and replace barbed wire with less aggressive fencing. Finally, the screwworm's sexual habits have proved its downfall.

Whatever else their shortcomings, female screwworm flies are nothing but monogamous—they mate only once in their lives. In 1962, an eradication program was initiated in which screwworms were raised in laboratories and exposed to sublethal doses of radiation. The radiation succeeded in sterilizing the male screwworms, which were released into areas where females were looking for Mr. Right. Since sterile males outnumbered normal males by about five to one, most females ended up mating with a sterile male and as a result laid infertile eggs. This so-called autocidal approach was simple but effective and has been in use ever since to keep the United States substantially free of screwworm problems.

Free for a while, that is. While in 1969, fewer than two hundred cases of screwworm infestation were reported, by 1976 the numbers had climbed to over ninety-five thousand. Investigators seeking to find an explanation for this veritable population explosion found a number of contributing factors: an outbreak of Gulf Coast ticks, which gave screwworm flies the openings they needed for getting under the skin of livestock; a massive influx of screwworm flies from Mexico, where autocidal controls were not widely used; and, finally, a major and completely unexpected problem with mass-rearing sterile flies for release. It turned out that the laboratory males, when released into the wild, were not as aggressive in finding females and not as successful in mating with them. Even though lab males outnumbered wild males in areas where they were released, they consistently lost out in the mating game. Once the problem was identified, the breeding program was duly adjusted to restore the competitiveness of the flies to be released. The effectiveness of the program was restored, proving once again that first-class males really do deliver.

SHEEP KEDS

If anyone is accustomed to having the wool pulled over its eyes, *Melophagus ovinus* is. *M. ovinus*, the sheep ked or sheep tick, spends its entire life buried in the fleece of domestic sheep. Sheep are its only known hosts, and everywhere lambs go, keds are sure to follow; they've been found breeding on sheep from every continent. Although they generally don't thrive in moist, tropical climes, they manage just fine in colder temperatures. Ensconced in their winter woollies, they flourish as far north as Lapland and Iceland and at elevations above ten thousand feet in the Peruvian Andes.

Even for an insect, *Melophagus ovinus* is really strange. Confusion about its common name is completely understandable; it looks a lot more like a tick (which it isn't) than a fly (which it is). It's dorsoventrally flattened, reddish brown in color, wingless, equipped with hooks on its legs, and apparently lacking antennae. It's so unflylike that it even lacks halteres, the knobby balancing organs that in other flies take the place of the mesothoracic (second) pair of wings. Sheep keds belong to the family Hippoboscidae, a family of flies highly modified for life as ectoparasites of birds and mammals. *M. ovinus* is a bit more modified than most of its immediate family. Most of the more than one hundred

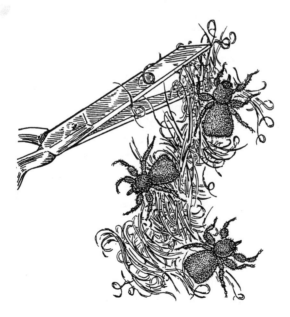

Sheep keds: "What happened? We're being fleeced!"

species in the family are equipped with a pair of fully functional wings and are able fliers. Some members of the family, like *Lipotena* species that live on forest deer, shed their wings once they land on a host. But *Melophagus ovinus* has absolutely no wings at all. Presumably, crawling in and around the tangled, matted fleece of domestic sheep is difficult enough without having to worry about dragging a pair of wings around with you.

Sheep keds probably never bemoan their loss since they never go anywhere that requires flying. Keds spend most of their time not in the long, coarse, outer hairs but in the short, soft, oily layer closest to the skin. According to Bequaert (1942), mating "is a matter-of-fact procedure, without any display of nervous excitement." After mating, the female develops only a single egg, which hatches internally. The larva undergoes its entire development inside the reproductive tract of its mother, feeding on milklike glandular secretions. Berlese in 1899 for chauvinistic reasons decided that the nutritive secretions are provided by the male in the form of abundant seminal fluids and sperm and that female secretions provide only a sort of glue to cause the emerging puparium to stick to fleece. Perhaps he was impressed by the fact that the coiled testes of male sheep keds are four to five times longer than the body. When full grown, the larva emerges and immediately pupates right in the fleece; about two to three weeks later, an adult ked emerges. In its four-month life, a female ked can produce on average only about a dozen offspring.

One of the first things a ked does upon emerging is eat. Sheep keds have unusually long mouthparts for penetrating thick fleece to reach tender skin. Capillary feeders, they probe the skin and then puncture it with a set of prestomal teeth that are successively everted and inverted; the entire mouthpart apparatus, or haustellum, twists on its long axis like an awl. Each blood meal consists of anywhere from eight to fourteen milligrams of blood; due to its extensible abdomen, a ked can almost double in size (to about a quarter of an inch) when engorged or pregnant.

As might be expected, sheep keds deep in fleece are rarely bothered by passing predators and parasites. Nonetheless, they're tough. Their chief enemy is the sheep, which can lick or bite out the parasites. Sheep danger, however, can be minimized by hiding out on the neck or head, where the teeth can't reach. A rather more serious threat, however, is the sheep shearer. Even if the keds are not removed with the wool, they are exposed and vulnerable on freshly sheared sheep skin. Probably, the sight or sounds of clippers is enough to send most keds into "shear panic."

References

Allen, J. R. 1979. The immune response as a factor in management of Acari of veterinary importance. In *Rec. Adv. Acarology*, ed. J. Rodriguez, 2:15–24. New York: Academic Press.

Askew, R. 1971. *Parasitic Insects*. New York: American Elsevier Publishing Co.

Bequaert, J. 1942. A Monograph of the Melophaginae, or ked-flies, of sheep, goats, deer, and antelopes (Diptera, Hippoboscidae). *Ent. Amer.* 22:1–208.

DeJong, D., R. Morse, and G. Eickwort. 1982. Mite pests of honey bees. *Ann. Rev. Ent.* 27:229–52.

Ferris, G. F. 1931. The louse of elephants. *Parasitology* 23:112–27.

Flynn, R. J. 1973. *Parasites of Laboratory Animals*. Ames: Iowa State University Press.

Gildart, R. L. 1982. *Montana Wildlife*. Helena: Montana Magazine.

Grzimek, B. 1975. *Grzimek's Animal Life Encyclopedia*. New York: Van Nostrand Reinhold Co.

Jackman, R., S. Nowicki, D. J. Aneshansley, and T. Eisner. 1983. Predatory capture of toads by fly larvae. *Science* 222:515–16.

James, M. T., and R. F. Harwood. 1969. *Herms's Medical Entomology*. 6th ed. New York: Macmillan.

Janzen, D. H. 1963. Observations on populations of adult beaver beetles, *Platypsyllus castoris*. *Pan Pacific Ent.* 39:215–28.

Lancaster, J. L., and M. U. Meisch. 1986. *Arthropods in Livestock and Poultry Production*. New York: Halsted Press, J. Wiley and Sons.

Marshall, A. G. 1981. *The Ecology of Ectoparasitic Insects*. New York: Academic Press.

Nutting, W., and C. Desch. 1979. Relationships between mammalian and demodicid phylogeny. In *Rec. Adv. Acarology*, ed. J. Rodriguez, 2:339–45. New York: Academic Press.

Oldroyd, H. 1964. *The Natural History of Flies*. London: Weidenfeld and Nicolson.

Roberts, F. S. H. 1951. *Insects Affecting Livestock*. Sydney: Argus and Robertson.

Rothschild, M., and B. Ford. 1964. Breeding of the rabbit flea (*Spilopsyllus cuniculi* (Dale)) controlled by the hormones of the host. *Nature* 20:103–4.

Soulsby, E. J. L. 1968. *Helminths, Arthropods, and Protozoa of Domesticated Animals*. 6th ed. Baltimore: Williams and Wilkins Co.

Williams, R. E., R. D. Hall, A. B. Broce, and P. J. Scholl, eds. 1985. *Livestock Entomology*. New York: J. Wiley and Sons.

Wood, D. M. 1964. Studies on the beetles, *Leptinillus valudus* (Horn) and *Platypsyllus castoris* Ritsema (Coleoptera: Leptinidae). *Proc. Ent. Soc. Ont.* 95:33–63.

Chapter **9**

Inhumanities

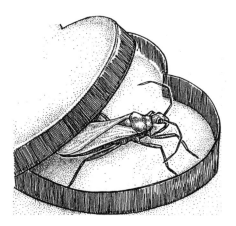

Asian tiger mosquitoes

Chigoes

Deer ticks

Eye gnats

Fire ants

Jersey mosquitoes

Kissing bugs

Puss caterpillars

Sweat bees

Tsetse flies

ASIAN TIGER MOSQUITOES

Unbeknownst to most people, it's a scientific fact that the United States of America was invaded by aliens in 1985. First discovered in Harris County, Texas, they've now been reported in eleven other states and have infiltrated several major urban areas, including Chicago. These aliens have repeatedly made contact with humans, but the vast majority of these people never realized what they were dealing with—for good reason, because most people don't stop to inspect the body scales on a mosquito before they flatten it.

The alien is *Aedes albopictus*, the Asian tiger mosquito, a species formerly restricted to China, Japan, South Korea, and other parts of Southeast Asia. The new import is a voracious biter, but its arrival in the United States is less than welcome for a more important reason; *Aedes albopictus* is a vector, or transmitter, of an incredible assortment of human diseases. Many deadly disease organisms are perfectly capable of wreaking havoc with a host's lungs, liver, heart, brain, or spleen, but they're incapable of moving on their own power from one host to another. Some blood-feeding insects, wittingly or not, provide transportation service to blood-borne microbes when they feed on one person, survive a slap and a swear word, and move on to the next. Whether or not a microbe will survive the trip depends a lot on the genetics and physiology of the potential insect vector. *Aedes albopictus*, by all appearances, was made to move microbes; it's the ultimate pathogen limousine service. The Asian tiger mosquito is an efficient vector of dengue fever, hemorrhagic fever, yellow fever, Japanese encepha-

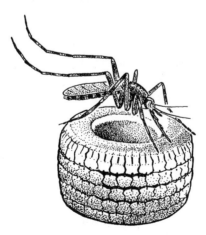

Asian tiger mosquitoes: Retiring to America

litis, eastern and western equine encephalitis, Venezuelan equine encephalitis, La Crosse encephalitis, and possibly St. Louis encephalitis. Dengue alone afflicts upward of 100,000 children a year in Southeast Asia.

Aedes albopictus is the first disease-bearing insect to invade America's borders for over three hundred years. The last interloper was *Aedes aegypti,* which is thought to have slipped past the border patrols as a stowaway on slave ships from Africa. Its arrival was followed by a massive outbreak of yellow fever, a viral disease transmitted by the mosquito, in which 500,000 Americans were infected and 100,000 died. *Aedes albopictus* has the potential to be an even bigger problem than its predecessor. Like *Aedes aegypti, Aedes albopictus* is a container breeder—that is, it lays its eggs in any small volume of water. The Asian tiger mosquito needs very little to feel at home; larvae have been found breeding in soda cans, chainsaw handles, sandboxes, discarded television sets, and even in the pool of water formed in a plastic lunchmeat wrapper. They have also been found breeding in treeholes, a discouraging development from the point of view of controlling them since treeholes are much more difficult to find and monitor than litter, unless you happen to be an Asian tiger mosquito.

Hopes that the Asian immigrant would be defeated by an old-fashioned bone-chilling winter were dashed when laboratory studies showed that the mosquito can tolerate subfreezing temperatures and even has a built-in diapause response to decreasing daylight hours. Thus, residents in states ranging from Maine and New Hampshire, west to Illinois and Iowa, and anywhere south may find themselves playing unwilling host to a new parasite. Westward, dry summer conditions may prevent the establishment of the mosquito, a situation that may make summer vacations in Idaho more attractive in coming years.

If you're wondering how a mosquito that rarely flies more than five hundred yards in its entire life managed to cross the Pacific Ocean in sufficient numbers to establish a beachhead in North America, look in your driveway. If you have recaps or used tires, you may have your answer. American dealers have been importing increasing numbers of used tires from Japan, India, Taiwan, and other countries where *Aedes albopictus* is no stranger. A used tire is the ultimate in luxury mosquito accommodations. Always full of water, dark, heat-retaining in winter, it's the ideal place from the mosquito point of view to raise a family. When the United States imported used tires from Asia, it also imported breeding populations of *Aedes albopictus.* Tire dumps and dealerships across the country have been the unwitting accomplices of Asian tiger mosquitoes in their conquest of North America. A Goodyear for *Aedes albopictus,* then, means a bad year for the rest of us.

CHIGOES

As far as dining habits go, the majority of fleas in the family Pulicidae like to eat and run (or at least eat and jump)—they board a host to take a brief blood meal and then debark. The cat flea (*Ctenocephalides felis*), for example, is said to spend as much as 90 percent of its time off its hosts. In contrast, however, *Tunga penetrans* is a flea who comes to dinner and never has the grace to leave.

Tunga penetrans is known variously as the chigoe, jigger flea, or sand flea. Although it's thought to be native to South America, it can currently be found as far north as southern Florida. It is also firmly established in Africa, where it was first reported in 1732. Early on, the chigoe's lifestyle is like that of most of its relatives. Eggs are laid in loam or sandy soil (hence, "sand flea"). The larvae feed on debris, pupate, and reach adulthood in one to two weeks. Adult *Tunga penetrans*, about a millimeter (1/25 inch) long, look for the most part like normal, everyday fleas, although they lack the prominent backward-pointing combs on the head and thorax and the head is larger relative to the size of the body than is the case for most other fleas.

Chigoes: "Ugh! Steel-toed work boots!"

251

Not only do chigoes look like other fleas, they even act like other fleas, at least for a while. Males and virgin females take sporadic blood meals from a multitude of hosts, including (aside from people) pigs, dogs, chickens, mice, and rats. Once a female is fertilized, however, the prospect of motherhood causes a drastic change in lifestyle. She feels the urge to abandon the vagabond life and settle down, which she does by burrowing into the epidermis of a luckless host.

Unfortunately, one of the preferred locations to set up permanent residence is between the toes or under the toenails of barefoot humans. Rarely, the skin of knees or elbows gets breached as well. How the female manages to excavate her way under the skin is something of an entomological mystery, since she is anatomically ill equipped for the task; she is, however, anatomically well endowed for remaining in place since backward-pointing spines on her abdomen lock her in position and make extrication nearly impossible. Once ensconced, females happily begin shooting out eggs and excrement to fall where they may. Pregnant and continuing to feed, a female can swell to the size of a pea. Meanwhile, her presence in the host causes swelling to the extent that the presence of a chigoe is characterized by a hard "bump," in the center of which are visible only the last two segments of the female's abdomen.

The main danger of chigoe infestation is bacterial infection. Ulceration can develop to the point that gangrene can set in. According to one account, a curious Capuchin friar in Hispaniola decided to allow a chigoe infestation to develop undisturbed "but unfortunately for himself, and for science, the foot entrusted with the precious deposit mortified, was obliged to be amputated, and with all its inhabitants committed to the waves" (Andrews 1977).

Chigoes, however, are completely preventable by the relatively uncomplicated prophylactic measure of wearing shoes (advice that generations of mothers repeatedly offer their children, anyway). If you insist on going barefoot on the beach, though, at least check to make sure your Caribbean vacation resort is not infested—it's best to be on your toes to keep everything else off them.

DEER TICKS

As deer season draws to a close, hunters reluctantly pack up their shotguns and shells and eagerly await the next season. For *Ixodes dammini*, however, it's open season on deer all year long. *Ixodes dammini*, the deer tick, is a small, brown, otherwise nondescript tick that has been making headlines of late all out of proportion to its size. This notoriety is not so much for the tick as it is for its fellow traveler; it has recently been discovered to be the principal vector of Lyme disease.

Lyme disease is a bacterial infection caused by *Borrelia burgdorferi*, a spirochaete like the organism that causes syphilis. As is true for spirochaete infections in general, Lyme disease presents a bewildering array of symptoms, generally beginning with a rash at the site of the bite and progressing to terrible headaches, sore throats, stiff joints, fatigue, fever, chills, and, if untreated, heart block and neurological complications. The first cases of what's known as Lyme disease showed up in Old Lyme, Connecticut, where they were misdiagnosed as, among other things, juvenile rheumatoid arthritis in children and rheumatic fever in adults. When a rash of similar symptoms began showing up in large numbers and then began hitting dogs and cats in the neighborhood, people got suspicious and an astute physician noticed the re-

Deer ticks: Deer tick who flunked spelling

semblance between what became known as Lyme arthritis (no doubt to the consternation of the local Chamber of Commerce) and a European ailment called erythema chronicum migrans, or ECM. Since ECM was a tick-borne disease, the search was on, and *Ixodes dammini* was soon found. Towns like Old Lyme on the east bank of the Connecticut River, where Lyme disease was rampant, had tick populations twelve to sixteen times higher than towns right across the river.

Finding *Ixodes dammini* was something of a surprise to acarologists, or people who spend their time looking for ticks in general. Prior to the 1960s, this particular tick was known only from a small island near Cape Cod, Massachusetts. It was named not for any damnable behavior on its part but rather in honor of a man named G. J. Dammin. However, like British rock music and granola, *Ixodes dammini* prospered in the sixties, largely because of the proliferation of white-tailed deer. Adult *Ixodes dammini* feed almost exclusively on white-tailed deer. Adult females take blood meals primarily in the fall but, when the weather warms up in early spring, they find venison on the hoof hard to resist. The females insert their sharp sucking mouthparts into the skin of the deer and remain attached for the duration of the meal. While males can and do feed this way, they're more apt to be found with their mouthparts embedded in the female's genital opening while she feeds. This isn't an odd form of sexual perversion on the part of males—their mouthparts are adapted for sperm transfer and they engage as the female engorges. Females then lay eggs that hatch in late summer. After that, from the human perspective, the trouble starts.

Like children of many species, larval ticks don't generally care for what their parents eat (although in a pinch they can accommodate). Their meal of choice is mouse blood, unwillingly provided by *Peromyscus leucopus*, the white-footed mouse. Should mice be in short supply, larval ticks will also take a blood meal from squirrels, cats, dogs, chipmunks, foxes, raccoons, opossums, and the unfortunate human being who traipses through the woods at an inopportune moment. After feeding only once, albeit for two straight days, larvae pass the winter in relative inactivity and molt the following year from May to July. As nymphs, they take a second blood meal, this one lasting three to four days, again from a variety of menu items. Finally, two years after they're born, nymphs molt into adulthood and focus their culinary attention on deer. Nobody really knows why adult deer ticks are so fixated on deer, while immature forms will feed on anything under the sun *and* in the shade.

Lyme disease has in less than fifteen years progressed from an unnamed collection of symptoms to the most commonly diagnosed tick-borne disease in the United States. One reason for the meteoric rise is

254

the amazing spread of the tick. Once known only from Massachusetts, it's been reported as far north as Maine, west to Wisconsin and Illinois, and south to Delaware and Maryland. Two factors may contribute to its spread—the fact that people travel with tick-bearing pets on their summer vacations, and the fact that white-tailed deer have undergone a major population explosion in recent years (deer, by the way, seem to be capable of harboring the spirochaete without succumbing to the disease). Some people have proposed eliminating white-tailed deer completely from areas populated by people. Whatever the eventual solution, you can be sure it will cost more than a few bucks.

EYE GNATS

Conscientious entomologists who keep their eyes open for *Hippelates* may be getting more than they bargained for. Members of the fly family Chloropidae, *Hippelates* gnats are irresistibly drawn to human body secretions. Nothing is too foul for these flies to resist—they revel in pus, sebaceous secretions, blood, and open, festering sores of all descriptions. For most *Hippelates,* however, the most readily accessible body fluids are those that bathe the eye, so *Hippelates* are generally known as eye gnats.

Aesthetically, eye gnats are hardly an eyeful. Among other things, they're tiny, barely a tenth of an inch in length. In general conformation, they are vaguely reminiscent of a house fly, with short, stubby antennae; stocky, shiny black bodies; and hairy abdomens. Unlike house flies, which have soft, spongy mouthparts for soaking up vile and disgusting fluids of all descriptions, eye gnats have sharp spines on their labella, with which they can (and do) rasp away at fluid-covered surfaces.

Eye gnats are, if nothing else, extremely annoying. Although they aren't known for launching a frontal assault, they make up in persis-

Eye gnats: "A doll! Rats! I need a *real* crybaby."

256

tence what they lack in directness. Eye gnats generally land in the vicinity of a potential host and make short sorties, either crawling or alighting briefly. Once at a mucus-rich feeding site, they are exceedingly tenacious and very difficult to dislodge. Females are particularly single-minded about feeding, inasmuch as they require protein for egg development. Although mucus or pus may seem unappetizing, it at least has the saving grace of being rich in protein.

The tastes of larval eye gnats are hardly more refined than those of the adults. *H. pusio*, which ranges over most of the United States, prefers to breed in animal dung or in soil contaminated with animal dung. It's not particularly fussy as to the source of the dung, although chicken manure does support faster larval development than human dung. Females lay their eggs on or just under contaminated soil. After a few days, the larvae hatch and begin to ingest the surrounding ordure. Interestingly, eye gnat larvae can only develop in soils that are naturally fertilized; soils enriched with chemical fertilizers won't sustain growth. After one or two weeks, the larva pupates in the soil, and after yet another week the adult emerges and sets out in search of human body fluids.

Considering their size, adult eye gnats are capable of covering an amazing amount of territory. They've been reported to fly more than four miles within six hours. They tend to annoy people most in areas that might be conducive to breeding—notably, areas with moist, well-drained soils. In California, these areas include, according to one account, "residential areas, sprinkled lawns, car washes, golf courses, school yards, wineries, irrigated areas, orchards, grapefruit plantings, date gardens, vineyards, crop fields, and densely packed shrubbery." Thus, it seems that the "good life" for a person—a well-kept yard, a well-maintained car, and enough money and leisure time to enjoy golf and fine wine now and then—is a life destined to be filled with eye gnats as well as simple pleasures.

Although *Hippelates* certainly enjoys human company, its habit of visiting excrement and feeding at open sores make it a less than desirable companion for humans. While its nuisance status is well defined, its importance as a disease vector is not easily confirmed. Eye gnats are suspected, though, of being involved in the transmission of a number of diseases. Among these is pinkeye, a contagious bacterial infection of the membranes of the eye. The association between pinkeye and eye gnats was noticed back in 1912, when a pinkeye outbreak coincided with an outbreak of eye gnats. The causative agent (the bacterium), however, has never been found on the body of the fly, so it can't yet be conclusively indicted as a vector.

The association between *Hippelates* and an even more serious disease, yaws, has been postulated for over four hundred years. Yaws is an infectious pantropical disease caused by a spirochaete called *Treponema pertenue*. It's manifested initially by the eruption of large weeping skin lesions. These sores appear initially on the leg, but, within three months, they extend over the rest of the body. The red, inflamed appearance of these lesions has earned yaws the name *framboesia tropica* (from the French for "raspberry") in some countries. Although the skin lesions can heal, relapses decades later can damage both skin and bone.

Yaws is potentially a crippling, life-threatening ailment. Although it now responds to antibiotic treatment, such was not always the case. There are many historical accounts of yawslike conditions, and in many of these accounts flies are mentioned as potential vectors. Perhaps the oldest indisputable account linking yaws with flies is that of de Sousa, who in 1587, in his visit to Brazil, noticed "mosquitoes which are called *nhitinga*, and which are very small and of the form of flies; these do not bite, but are very troublesome, because they settle on the eyes and in the nostrils, and will not let one sleep by day in the open unless there be a wind. They are very fond of sores, and suck the poison which is in them; and if they then go and settle upon any abrasion on a healthy person, they leave the poison in it, and then many people are seen covered with boubas" (Ransford 1983).

Over the next four centuries, there were many more accounts suggesting that flies and yaws are associated, and many more studies, as recently as 1965, attempting to prove scientifically that the association is causative. The *Treponema* that causes yaws was isolated from the vomitus of the flies over fifty years ago. The flight pattern and feeding habits of the flies, however, are not sufficiently well known to conclude without doubt that they are acting as vectors for yaws. The lack of conclusive evidence, despite over four hundred years of speculation, is certainly frustrating. Knowing how yaws is transmitted can provide insights into preventive measures designed to contain its spread; in the longstanding controversy over containing this disease, the eye gnat is certainly in the eye of the storm.

FIRE ANTS

Fireproofing your home is a good investment—in the long run, it saves time, money, heartache, and injury. A lot of people in the southeastern United States would like to fire-ant-proof the entire country for the very same reasons. The fire ant, *Solenopsis invicta*, is a relatively recent addition to the North American continent. Nobody is exactly sure when and how they got here—the best guess is that they arrived sometime around 1940 hidden in soil clinging to potted plants imported from western Brazil or Paraguay, where they're native. Since that time, fire ants have been spreading like wildfire, mostly through the warmer southeastern and southwestern parts of the country. In thirty-five years, they've managed to colonize some fifty-two million hectares of American soil.

The "fire" in "fire ant" refers not to its reddish color but rather to its fiery sting. If a fire ant is disturbed, it clamps onto the source of the disturbance with its powerful mandibles and then swings its abdomen up and over to inject venom, often into an incision created by the mandibles. The alkaloid-rich venom causes an intense burning sensation, followed by swelling at the site of injection. A blister then forms, which fills with pus as the cell-destroying venom goes to work. These blisters can take days to heal and often, after healing, leave scars. Some

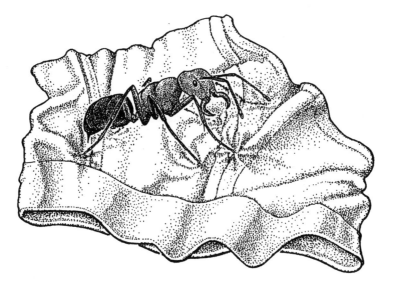

Fire ants

unfortunate victims can suffer a systemic reaction to the venom, characterized by nausea, vomiting, dizziness, allergic reaction, and even, in some cases, death.

The "*invicta*" in *S. invicta* is from the Latin for "conqueror," and *S. invicta* is indeed designed for conquering continents. Newly emerged queens take off on a nuptial flight; after mating, they return to the ground, shed their wings, and pursue a terrestrial existence for the rest of their lives. The fertilized female excavates an underground burrow, constructing a vertical shaft a few inches deep, with horizontal cells extending outward at the top and bottom of the shaft. The "*Soleno*" in *Solenopsis*, from the Latin for "pipe" or "channel," refers to the burrowing habits of all species in the genus. Within a day or so, the female lays eggs in the cells. Hatching grubs are fed by the queen or else help themselves to unhatched eggs within easy reach. The fast-growing grubs complete four molts in just about a week and then pupate. After another week, adults emerge. Sterile females remain in the nest to assist the queen with rearing more grubs, and fertile adults take off for nuptial flights of their own.

The rapid reproductive cycle is a large part of the fire ant's formula for conquest. A generation can be completed in under three weeks. After three months, colonies (initiated by a single female) can contain 300 members; within a year, 11,000 members; and within three years 50,000 to 60,000 members. All of this population growth necessitates major home improvements. The nest is constantly being enlarged, and a three-year-old colony can have a dome that rises three feet from the ground and tunnels reaching three feet down to the water table. Throughout the life of the colony, new queens are constantly being produced, and a single colony can at any given time contain several hundred queens, all set to fly off at a moment's notice to found their own empires.

Fifty or sixty thousand is a lot of hungry mouths to feed, so it's not surprising that fire ant workers spend a lot of time foraging. Although occasionally fire ants damage seedlings and other small plants, small insects and other invertebrates are the mainstay of the fire ant diet. Fire ants even eat destructive agricultural pests, like boll weevils, in substantial numbers. Despite their depredations of the local insect populations, fire ants are generally not welcomed with open arms by farmers. They build their huge cementlike domes in the middle of crop fields and stream out biting and stinging whenever they are disturbed by the occasional inattentive cow or combine. The large mounds are a psychological obstacle as much as a physical one to farm workers familiar with the potent venom and nasty tempers of the ant inhabitants.

Human attempts to vanquish *S. invicta* have been largely ineffectual. Heady with success in a program to eradicate hog cholera, a bacterial disease, Congress in 1957 created a program with the express goal of eradicating fire ants from the 126 million acres that they had colonized. Over the next two decades, massive insecticide sprayings met with little success. Although the fire ants continued to expand their range, other nontarget species, ranging from crabs to quail, began to suffer the effects of the blanket sprayings. By 1978, the war was officially over; over $91 million had been spent by the federal government and over $64 million had been spent by state governments in a futile attempt to stem the fire ant tide. Today, control tactics more closely tied to the biology of the fire ant are being investigated; these include introducing into the United States predators and pathogens from the fire ant's native stomping grounds.

The fire ant eradication program proved to be an expensive lesson; one scientist referred to it as the Viet Nam of insect control efforts. All things considered, though, the lesson, if learned, was cheap at the price. After all, the savings and loan fiasco of the late 1980s could end up costing American taxpayers over $5 *billion*, a figure that makes one wonder what species presents the greater threat to the U.S. economy.

JERSEY MOSQUITOES

Every summer on the beaches or in the cities, residents of New Jersey inevitably feel that they are unjustly inflicted with more than their fair share of mosquitoes. Actually, these suspicions are grounded in truth; over forty species of mosquitoes call New Jersey home. Not all of these, however, make their presence known to humans. Three don't even bite at all, only half are even considered troublesome, and about a dozen merit Class A nuisance status. Among these dirty dozen are six species entirely lacking from landlocked states. Those species are partially or totally dependent upon the waters of New Jersey's salt marshes.

Salt marshes show up wherever poorly drained soil gets inundated by ocean water, either directly, as along New Jersey's extensive coastline, or indirectly, as along the several rivers that crisscross the state. These six species are well adjusted to the distinctive characteristics of salt marsh environments. Among the least loved and most conspicuous is *Aedes sollicitans*, the white-banded salt marsh mosquito, known at least in New Jersey as the Jersey mosquito. The species is hard to

Jersey mosquitoes: "I don't care if I *do* have hypertension, Doc, I just don't see how I'm going to cut down on my salt intake."

262

mistake for any other. Its proboscis, when not buried in human skin, can be recognized by its broad white band. The legs of *A. sollicitans* are similarly banded by white markings, and more yellowish white bands demarcate the back border of each abdominal segment. A broad yellow stripe runs ignobly down the length of the abdomen. The overall striping has earned *A. sollicitans* the sobriquet of the convict mosquito, a name not inappropriate given the antisocial behavior of the insect.

The salt marsh mosquito spends its winters as a spindle-shaped egg buried in salt marsh mud. If covered by water, eggs can hatch as early as March; if standing water persists for at least one to three weeks, the larvae, wormlike wrigglers, quickly complete development. Pupation under the right conditions takes only a day, so, within at least a week and at most a month, female mosquitoes are on the wing looking for blood. *Aedes sollicitans* can fly forty miles or more from its place of birth in search of erythrocytes, so distance from a salt marsh is no guarantee of safety. Within twenty-four hours, a female mosquito is ready to plaster the salt marsh mud with eggs. Since the salt marshes are continually supplied with eggs, the number of broods or generations depends on the number of times floodwaters rise high enough to immerse the eggs between early March and late October.

Despite what today's New Jersey residents might think, salt marsh mosquito populations aren't nearly what they once were. Around the turn of the century, a massive concerted effort was made to drain extensive areas of salt marsh. Good drainage guarantees that standing water won't stand for a period long enough to allow salt marsh mosquitoes to complete development. Moreover, the large expanse of salt marsh bordering the Hackensack River, known to an inordinate number of metropolitan New York types as the Meadowlands, has by virtue of its location become some of the most prime real estate in North America. Commercial development of the area has reduced salt marsh acreage from about twenty-seven thousand acres to less than ten thousand. Where salt marsh mosquitoes contentedly raised families a mere fifty years ago, Bruce Springsteen is now singing to sellout crowds in Brendan Byrne Arena. That's not only adding insult to injury, as far as the Jersey mosquito is concerned, it's pouring salt *out* of the wound.

KISSING BUGS

Even if Valentine's Day is close at hand, you would be advised *not* to take a kissing bug to lunch. The kissing bug, otherwise known as *Reduvius personatus*, is a member of the hemipteran family Reduviidae, the assassin bugs. Assassin bugs all share a stout, strong beak that they use with great effect to pierce things like insects, spiders, poultry, small rodents, and human skin. The kissing bug earns its name from its habit of flying into people's faces and inflicting exceedingly painful bites around the mouth and nose. The bite of a kissing bug is probably the most painful of all insect bites, although some people may have their own personal favorites. According to one account, the bite results in intense pain that usually affects a great deal of the body, followed by swelling and, in the worst cases, faintness, vomiting, and other long-lasting and unpleasant effects.

Among assassin bugs, *Reduvius personatus* is less ruthless than most. It only bites humans in self-defense when they clumsily wander into its line of flight. Unfortunately, the habits of the kissing bug tend to

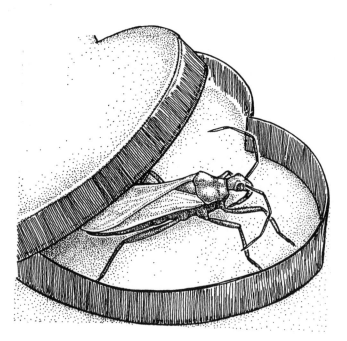

Kissing bugs

bring it into frequent contact with humans. *Reduvius personatus* is also called the masked bed bug hunter; its preferred prey is *Cimex lectularius*, the bed bug. Since bed bugs can most reliably be found in the beds of human beings, *Reduvius personatus* is attracted to lights and enters houses in search of a meal. The "masked" part of masked bed bug hunter doesn't refer to any characteristic color pattern—they're uniformly black or dull brown—but rather to the fact that, once hatched, the nymphs are covered with a sticky viscid substance to which dust and lint adhere. Since females lay their eggs singly in dusty corners, the body, legs, and antennae of baby bed bug hunters are covered almost immediately with dust. Thus camouflaged, unless they're moving, they've virtually invisible.

While *Reduvius personatus* feeds on human blood only when it's inside a bed bug, other assassin bugs avoid the middleman to feed directly on the source. All members of the subfamily Triatominae feed directly on the blood of vertebrates. The bloodsucking conenose, or Mexican bedbug, *Triatoma sanguisuga,* has perfected the art of blood feeding such that, when it's feeding, its bite is painless and its human host is totally unaware of its presence (a form of painless extraction that antedates modern dentistry). However, when its life is threatened, it can inflict the same sort of painful bite that *Reduvius personatus* can.

From Mexico to Argentina, the kiss of a kissing bug could be the kiss of death. Many triatomines can transmit Chagas' disease, or American trypanosomiasis. The primary symptom of Chagas' disease is one-sided swelling of the face, called the "sign of Romaña." Chagas' disease can lead to persistent fevers, anemia, loss of nervous control, and death due to myocarditis. Chagas' disease is transmitted by triatomines by virtue of the fact that they almost invariably defecate as they feed. Infected feces are then easily transferred by fingers to the eyes, nose, or mouth, where infection can set in. At least sixteen species of triatomines can act as vectors of Chagas' disease, and over seven million cases can occur in Central and South America in any given year. So whoever wrote "a kiss is just a kiss" clearly wasn't thinking about kissing bugs.

PUSS CATERPILLARS

Sometimes entomology and etymology seem at odds. Take for example, the word "caterpillar," technically defined as the immature stage of any member of the order Lepidoptera, the butterflies and moths. The word conjures up an image of a long, crawling, cylindrical, often greenish, and generally repulsive wormlike creature. The word actually derives from the Latin for "hairy cat." As for hairy, the vast majority of caterpillars are totally naked or else equipped with tiny hairs at scattered intervals that only an entomologist could appreciate. As for "cat," well, irrespective of how you feel about cats, this term can only be regarded as an insult to felinehood everywhere.

There is one family of caterpillars, however, that truly lives up to its Latin roots. Caterpillars in the family Megalopygidae, unlike the majority of their ilk, are covered with a dense coat of long silky hairs. Not inappropriately, they're known as puss caterpillars. The hairs of *Megalopyge opercularis* are reddish brown and swept up into a crest

Puss caterpillars: "Maybe you should think of changing the title, you know, to broaden its appeal?"

266

along its back. Physical appearance aside, puss caterpillars act pretty much like the vast majority of caterpillars. *M. opercularis* spends its days munching on the foliage of various trees, including hackberry, oak, sycamore, and maple. Resting on a branch or tree trunk, the reddish brown caterpillar can be difficult to spot, despite the fact it can reach an inch or more in length at maturity. *M. opercularis* is equally hirsute as an adult; the moth is chunky, cream-colored, and covered with long hairs. As adults, members of this hairy clan are known as flannel moths.

In one respect, however, puss caterpillars are similar to pussycats. When disturbed, like cats, they arch their backs and raise their hairs. This is not merely theatrics or idle threats on the part of the puss caterpillars; raising the soft, silky hairs exposes a series of otherwise concealed hollow spines all over their bodies. These spines are filled with a toxic venom that, if injected, can cause intense burning pain, itching, and swelling, and, in severe reactions, paralysis, fever, and nausea. Puss ("u" as in "put") caterpillars might thus more appropriately be known as puss ("u" as in "us") caterpillars, since oozing pustules are characteristic of the skin reactions. Recognizing dermatitis brought about by puss caterpillars can be easy since the rash that forms occasionally takes on a perfect teardrop-shaped outline of the caterpillar. In South America, where they occur in considerable numbers, they're known by the name (among others) of "fire caterpillar."

All told, there are only eleven species of Megalopygidae in North America and only three routinely encountered north of subtropical Texas and Florida. Megalopygids, however, aren't the only caterpillars you have to worry about bumping into. Caterpillars in at least ten families are known to cause toxicity upon contact. In fact, there's even a name for it—"erucism" is technically defined as toxicity resulting from contact with a caterpillar (a useful term no doubt invented by someone too embarrassed to admit that he had to take a few days off work because he touched a caterpillar). South American natives have exploited erucism for their own ends, using the caterpillars for poisoning their arrows, and even for what one author describes as "libidinous ceremonies." This all just goes to show that there's more than one way to skin a caterpillar, even a furry one.

SWEAT BEES

If anyone can make the best of blistering hot summer weather, maybe the sweat bees can. Sweat bees are members of the family Halictidae, a group of small to medium-sized bees recognized by entomologists by their distinctive wing venation but by almost everyone else by their distinctive habit of seeking out and landing on the exposed portions of perspiring people. It's not really clear what they think they'll find there—salt, perhaps, to supplement their low-salt vegetarian diet—but they're always willing to get their licks in during sunny, hot summer weather. Members of one group of sweat bees, in the genus *Nomia*, are known as alkali bees due to their predilection for settling in areas characterized by clay-rich alkali soils—so it may be the salt of the earth that attracts them there.

What distinguishes halictids, along with a couple of other families, from the more familiar honey and bumble bees is literally on the tips of their tongues; halictids are so-called short-tongued, as opposed to long-tongued, bees. The short-tongued bees have a much simpler social life than do the long-tongued honey and bumble bees. In general, a

Sweat bees

fertilized female hibernates through the winter in an underground burrow. Come spring, she emerges and constructs a subterranean nest composed of a burrow with chambers branching off either side. An egg is laid in each chamber and provided with a mass of pollen and nectar. In a month to six weeks, the all-female offspring emerge and repeat the process; however, since there are no males around to provide sperm, the virgin females, for genetic reasons, can lay eggs destined only to be male sweat bees. Meanwhile, their mother is still laying fertilized eggs, often in chambers constructed and provisioned by her own daughters. The female offspring produced by the foundress with the help of her virgin daughters will, when mature, emerge to mate with their own nephews and any other males in the vicinity (which makes, no doubt, for interesting genealogies).

Some sweat bees benefit from the sweat of other brows; those in the genus *Sphecodes* are known as cleptoparasites. Instead of going to the trouble of excavating their own burrows, they wait until other sweat bees have constructed and provisioned one. Then they move in, kill the rightful owner-occupants, and lay their own eggs so their grubs can partake of the pirated pollen masses. Some species are so dedicated to this parasitic existence that their bodies entirely lack the hairs typically used by bees for securing pollen grains. A hardworking, honest sweat bee like *Dialictus zephyrus*, for example, in contrast will collect pollen and nectar from more than two dozen plant families.

Sweat bees on the wing can often be recognized by both size and color—species in the genera *Augochloropsis*, *Augochlorella*, and *Augochlora* are half an inch or less in length and brilliant metallic green (whence cometh the "chlor" in their name, as in "chlorophyll"). Species in the parasitic genus *Sphecodes* have a bright red abdomen, and many species in the genera *Halictus* and *Lasioglossum* have a shiny metallic black head and thorax. Sweat bees, then, have mastered the secret of getting a nice shine in the summer sun without even working up a sweat.

TSETSE FLIES

If you've ever had trouble getting out of bed in the morning and wondered if you had sleeping sickness, don't lose any more sleep over it—unless you live in one of the three regions comprising a band that cuts across middle Africa to which sleeping sickness is currently confined. Sleeping sickness is the result of pathogenic infection by any of a group of microscopic organisms called trypanosomes. Infection begins with intermittent fever and swollen lymph glands and ends with an often fatal inflammation of the brain. Along the way, sleeping sickness is associated with lethargy, as the name implies, but also with irritability, irresponsible behavior, extreme sensitivity to cold, "morbid craving for meat," mania, and secondary infection.

As a limbless, unicellular protozoan lacking a nervous system, trypanosomes would have difficulty trekking across central Africa, much less the rest of the world, were it not for the mobility provided by its constant associate and two-winged insect vector, the tsetse fly. The tsetse was so named by the Tswana tribe in imitation of its high-pitched

Tsetse flies: "I hate this part—she always wakes up."

buzz. Five species in the genus *Glossina—palpalis, fuscipes, tachinoides, morsitans,* and *pallidipes*—are the major vectors of the disease, although in all likelihood any of the twenty-two species in the genus could transmit the disease if called upon to do so. Tsetses are often placed in their own family, the Glossinidae, although some experts feel they are close to stable flies in the family Muscidae.

Tsetses are about ⅓ to just over ½ inch in length and range in color from yellowish to blackish brown. There are two distinguishing features that set them apart from other pestiferous flies—their long, needle-like, biting mouthparts, which project outward from the head like bayonets from a bulb-shaped base (which earned them the name *Glossina,* from the Latin for "tongue"), and their wings, which fold like scissors over their backs. The celebrated tsetse "tongue" consists of two channels, one for sucking up the warm blood of vertebrates and another for pumping saliva into the wound. Anticoagulants in the saliva keep the blood from clotting and clogging the delicate food channel. Unlike mosquitoes, which daintily plug into capillaries, tsetses use their rasp-like labellum to saw through the skin and create a pool of blood from which they pump up dinner.

Tsetses would be just another bunch of annoying biting flies but for the fact that they rarely dine alone. Flies feeding on an animal infected with trypanosomes pick them up on their proboscis and can transmit them directly, acting as a flying contaminated hypodermic needle, or indirectly, by playing host to the trypanosomes themselves. Depending on the species, trypanosomes can undergo portions of their life cycle in the proboscis, salivary glands, gut, or any combination of organs of the tsetse.

The association between tsetse and trypanosome was not really nailed down until the turn of the century. It was an army doctor named David Bruce (who earned an odd sort of immortality as the namesake of *Trypanosoma brucei,* which causes sleeping sickness in livestock) who figured out the connection. The famous African explorer and missionary David Livingstone incorrectly presumed that the fly injected some sort of venom to cause disease. He sent home to Britain the first specimen ever to reach Europe, although its head dislodged in transit and was glued back on upside down on arrival. Thus it graces the frontispiece of his 1857 book, *Missionary Travels.*

Although the tsetse's feeding habits have created nothing but grief and suffering, there's much in its home life to commend. *Glossina* takes maternal care a step beyond most insects. Immature *Glossina* develop one at a time inside their mother's body in a structure that is called a uterus. There, they are nourished by a rich fluid released into the uterus from "milk glands." After one to three weeks, depending on temperature, larval development is complete; the maggot is "born" and quickly burrows into the soil to pupate inside its last larval skin. In another three to four weeks, an adult tsetse emerges. Very few insects (indeed, very few animals at all) are capable of giving birth to almost fully grown offspring (generally a talent ascribed only to Greek gods and goddesses). After their young are born, female tsetse flies emit a characteristic sound of almost six minutes' duration—called by one investigator the "post-partum blues," perhaps in recognition of the lost childhood of their offspring.

The tiny tsetse fly has been a veritable scourge of Africa for generations. It proved to be a major obstacle to European development of the continent (and in fact European "advances" such as steamship travel, punitive military raids, forced labor marches, and road construction assisted the tsetse greatly in expanding its sphere of influence). It's even mentioned in the Bible (Isaiah 7:18-25). *Glossina* may have enjoyed dominion over the earth even earlier. Its ancestors are known from the Carboniferous Era 230 to 260 million years ago. It's been suggested that the vertebrates on which they fed were reptiles and that the proto-tsetses were responsible for the extinction of dinosaurs. Not bad for an animal not even as big as a dinosaur's toenail.

References

Andrews, M. 1977. *The Life that Lives on Man.* New York: Taplinger Press.

Darsie, R. R. 1986. The identification of *Aedes albopictus* in the Nearctic region. *J. Am. Mosquito Control Assoc.* 2:336–40.

Delgado Quiroz, A. 1978. Venoms of Lepidoptera. In *Arthropod Venoms,* ed. S. Bettini, 555–611. New York: Springer Verlag.

Florida Entomologist. 1983. Vol. 66 (1). Issue devoted to fire ants.

Ginsberg, H. S., and C. P. Ewing. 1988. Deer ticks, *Ixodes dammini* (Acari: Ixodidae), and Lyme disease spirochetes, *Borrelia burgdorferi* in Maine. *J. Med. Ent.* 25:303–4.

Greenberg, B. 1973. *Flies and Disease.* Vol. 2. Princeton: Princeton University Press.

Hall, S. S. 1987. The invader. *Hippocrates* (Sept.–Oct.): 36–45.

Horsfall, W. R. 1962. *Medical Entomology: Arthropods and Human Disease.* New York: Ronald Press.

James, M. T., and R. F. Harwood. 1969. *Herms's Medical Entomology.* New York: Macmillan.

Lofgren, C., W. Banks, and B. Glancy. 1975. Biology and control of imported fire ants. *Ann. Rev. Ent.* 20:1–30.

Meeham, J. 1988. Catching the bug. *Arthritis Today* (May–June): 43–47.

Mitchell, C., B. Miller, and D. Gubler. 1987. Vector competence of *Aedes albopictus* from Houston, Texas, for dengue serotypes 1 to 4, yellow fever and Ross river viruses. *J. Amer. Mosquito Control Assoc.* 3:460–65.

Nawrocki, S., and W. Hawley. 1987. Estimation of the northern limits of distribution of *Aedes albopictus* in North America. *J. Amer. Mosquito Control Assoc.* 3:314–17.

Ransford, O. 1983. *Bid the Sickness Cease: Disease in the History of Black Africa.* London: John Murray.

Reiter, P., and D. Sprenger. 1987. The used tire trade: a mechanism for the worldwide dispersal of container breeding mosquitoes. *J. Amer. Mosquito Control Assoc.* 3:494–501.

Richter, J., B. Farmer, and J. Clarke. 1987. *Aedes albopictus* in Chicago, Illinois. *J. Am. Mosquito Control Assoc.* 3:657.

Spielman, A., M. C. Wilson, J. F. Leure, and J. Peisman. 1985. Ecology of *Ixodes dammini*–borne human babesiosis and Lyme disease. *Ann. Rev. Ent.* 30:139–60.

Wilson, E. O. 1972. *Insect Societies.* Cambridge, Mass.: Harvard University Press.

Wilson, M. C., S. R. Telphord, J. Peisman, and A. Spielman. 1988. Reduced abundance of immature *Ixodes dammini* (Acari: Ixodidae) following elimination of deer. *J. Med. Ent.* 25:224–28.

Index

Buprestidae, 96
Bursaphelenctus xylophilus, 107
Burying beetles, 137–39
Butterflies: brush-footed butterflies, 81, 83; cabbage white butterflies, 38–39; Camberwell beauty butterflies, 80; comma butterflies, 82–83; gossamer-winged butterflies, 84, 166; grand surprise butterflies, 80; hop merchant butterflies, 83; mourning cloak butterflies, 80–81; question mark butterflies, 82–83; wings of, xv

Cabbage white butterflies, 38–39
Cabbageworms, 38–39
Cadra cautella, 22
Cadra figulilella, 22
California red scales, 26
Calliphoridae, 61–62, 240
Calocampa exoleta, 172
Camberwell beauty butterflies, 80
Cankerworms, 98–99
Cannibalism: of corn earworms, 42; of garden spiders, 69; of milkweed bugs, 77; of swordgrass caterpillars, 172; of winter moths, 172
Caraphractus cinctus, 189
Cardiac glycosides, 76–77
Carpet beetles, 25
Carrion flies, 139
Carrot rust flies, 124–26
Castelvetro, Ludovico, 66
Caterpillars: of Angoumois grain moths, 32; of buck moths, 155; of cabbage white butterflies, 38–39; of corn earworms, 41–42; of cutworms, 48; Eastern tent caterpillar, 103; fire caterpillars, 267; of harvesters, 167; of luna moths, 170; of Mediterranean flour moths, 21–22; puss caterpillars, 266–67; spiny elm caterpillars, 81; swordgrass caterpillars, 172
Cat fleas, 237, 251
Cecropia moths, 155
Celastrina ladon, 84–85
Cellar spiders, 8–9
Centruroides sculpturatus, 136
Centruroides suffusus, 136
Cephenemyia trompe, 238–39
Cerambycidae, 106
Cerambycid beetles, 106–8

Ceratocystis ulmi, 101
Chaetoccnema pulicaria, 50–51
Chagas' disease, 265
Chalcidoid wasps, 13–14
Chaoboridae, 198–99
Chaoborus, 198–99
Chaoborus edulis, 199
Cheese skippers, 10–12
Chemical compounds. See Insect chemicals; Insecticides; Plant chemicals
Chenopods (Chenopodiaceae), 50
Chewing lice, 225–26
Chicken (Gallus gallus), 231
Chigoes, 251–52
Chinch bugs, 79
Chironomid midges, 164–65, 196–97
Chloropidae, 256
Chrysomela crotchii, 117
Chrysomela interrupta, 117
Chrysomela lapponica, 117
Chrysomela scripta, 117
Chrysomelidae, 46, 49, 116–17
Chrysops, 233
Cigarette beetles, 18
Cimex lectularius, 265
Citrus crops, 71–72
Cleptoparasites, 269
Climaciella brunnea, 74
Climbing cutworms, 47
Clothoda urichi, 145–46
Clunio marinus, 196–97
Cluster flies, 240
Cobweb spiders, 143
Coccinellidae, 70–72
Cochliomyia, 240–42
Cockroaches: American cockroaches, 14; Asian cockroaches, 3–4; brown-banded cockroaches, 13–14; German cockroaches, 3–4, 102, 178; Oriental cockroaches, 14, 102; parasites of, 13–14
Cole crops (Cruciferae): and cabbageworms, 38–39; and flea beetles, 50, 51
Coleoptera, 212
Collagen, 62
Collembola, 185–87
Collembolans (springtails), xvi, 185–87
Colorado potato beetles, 49
Comma butterflies, 82–83
Comperia merceti, 13–14
Comstock, John Henry, 209
Confused grain beetles, xvii
Convergent lady beetles, 72

277

Hair mites, 221
Halictidae, 177–78, 268–69
Halictus, 269
Haplodiploid reproduction, 88
Hard ticks, 230
Harvesters, 166–68
Hawk moths, 161–63
Helicoverpa virescens, 42
Helicoverpa zea, 40–42
Hemaris, 161–63
Hemileuca maia, 154–55
Hemimetabolous development, 88
Hemiptera, 5, 78, 195, 207
Hemispherical scales, 26
Hemorrhagic fever, 250
Hide beetles, 25
Hippelates, 256–58
Hippelates pusio, 257
Hippoboscidae, 243–44
Hippodamia convergens, 72
Hog cholera, 261
Holometabolous development, 88, 220
Homoptera, 71, 112
Honey ants, 127–29
Honey bees, 66, 158, 159, 163, 222–24, 268
Honeydew, 20, 43–44, 123, 167
Hop flea beetles, 50
Hoplothrips karnyi, 88
Hop merchant butterflies, 83
Hops (*Humulus lupulus*), 50, 83
Hop-tree (*Ptelea trifoliata*), 113
Horse flies, 232–33
House flies, 228, 256
Hulme, Edward, 80
Hummingbird hawk moths, 161
Hydrophilidae, 212–14
Hydrophilus triangularis, 212–13
Hydroxydanaidol, 152
Hylurgopinus rufipes, 100–101
Hymenoptera, 111, 188
Hyphantria cunea, 102–3

Icerya purchasi, 71
Imported ensign wasps, 14
Imported willow leaf beetles, 117
Inchworms, 99
Insecta: compared to humans, xvi–xvii; rules for membership in, xiii–xvii; terrestrial origins of, 212
Insect chemicals: acetates, 134; and ant

behavior, 122, 134; of berothids, 124; honeydew, 20, 43–44, 123, 167; hydroxydanaidol, 152; of Mediterranean flour moths, 22; monoterpenes, 6; salicylaldehyde, 117; shellac, 27; toxins, 267; unsaturated aldehydes, 77. *See also* Pheromones; Venom
Insecticides: and boll weevils, 36; for bronze birch borers, 97; for cutworms, 48; and fire ants, 261; for flea beetles, 51; for Japanese beetles, 52; made from shellac, 27; nicotine used as, 18; for spider mites, 56. *See also* Biological control
Insidious flower bugs, 79
Internal clocks, 197
Isia isabella, 152
Ixodes, 230
Ixodes dammini, 253–55
Ixodidae, 230

Japanese beetles, 52–53
Japanese encephalitis, 250
Japanese silk moths. *See* Silkworms
Jersey mosquitoes, 262–63
Jigger fleas, 251–52

Kentucky bluegrass, 33–34
Kissing bugs, 264–66
Koebele, Albert, 71–72

Laccifer lacca, 27
Lacewings, 123, 204
La Crosse encephalitis, 250
Ladybird beetles, 71
Ladybugs, 70–72, 105
Larder beetles, 25
Large milkweed bugs, 75–77
Lasioderma serricorne, 18
Lasioglossum, 269
Lasius alienus americanus, 43–44
Leaf-footed bugs, 6
Leiobunum longipes, 64
Leiodidae, 131
Lepidoptera, 67, 98, 171, 266
Lepidosaphes ulmi, 104–5
Leptinillus validus, 221
Leptocoris trivittatus, 5–7
Lethocerus americanus, 195
Leucophaea maderae, 14
Lice, 225; booklouse, 16; chewing lice,

282

Trialeurodes vaporariorum, 19–20
Triatoma sanguisuga, 265
Tribolium confusum, xvii
Trichogramma spp., 42
Triungulin, 176–77
Trypanosoma brucei, 271
Trypanosomes, 270, 271
Tsetse flies, 270–72
Tularemia, 230
Tunga penetrans, 251–52
Tunnel-making cutworms, 48
Tutankhamen, 17
Two-spotted spider mites, 54–56
Two-spotted treehoppers, 112–13

Uloboridae, 67
Umbelliferae plants, 125–26
Unsaturated aldehydes, 77
Utetheisa bella, 151
Utetheisa ornatrix, 151

Variegated cutworms, 47
Varroa jacobsoni, 223–24
Vedalia beetles, 71
Venezuelan equine encephalitis, 250
Venom: of Dolomedes, 192; of fire ants, 259–61; of horse flies, 233; of scorpions, 135–36; of spiders, 9; of walkingsticks, 115
Venturia canescens, 22
Vetchworms, 40

Walking sticks, 114–15
Wasps: chalcidoid wasps, 13–14; eulophid wasps, 105; imported ensign wasps, 14; paper wasps, 74; parasitic wasps, 13–14, 20, 22, 42, 95, 105; pteromalid wasps, 206

Water boatmen, 207–8
Water pennies, 209–11
Water scavenger beetles, 212–14
Webspinners, 145–46
Webster, F. M., 32
Wedge-shaped beetles, 176–78
Western equine encephalitis, 250
Wheat (Triticum): and Angoumois grain moths, 31–32; and bluegrass billbugs, 33–34
Wheeler, William Morton, 122, 128, 133
White-banded salt marsh mosquitoes, 262–63
White-footed mouse (Peromyscus leucopus), 254
White-tailed deer, 254–55
Willow leaf beetles, 116–17
Willow trees, 116–17
Wings: of Asian cockroaches, 4; of bumble bees, 157–58; construction and use of, xiv–v; lacking in immature stages, xv; lacking in some adult insects, xvi; of sheep keds, 243–44; of thrips, 88
Winter moths, 171–72
Wolf spiders, 143
Woolly aphids, 167
Woollybears, 103
Wyeomyia smithii, 201

Xanthopan morganii var. praedicta, 162

Yaws, 258
Yellow fever, 250
Yellow woollybears, 152
Yucca moths, 179–80
Yucca plants, 179–80

Zimmerman pine moths, 110

A Note on the Author

MAY R. BERENBAUM, professor of entomology at the University of Illinois at Urbana-Champaign, studies the chemical interactions between herbivorous insects and their hostplants, and the personal interactions between humans and their arthropod companions on planet Earth. A Fellow of the American Association for the Advancement of Science and a recipient of a Guggenheim Foundation fellowship, Berenbaum also is the coauthor of over seventy-five articles and book chapters. The present volume is a companion to her *Ninety-nine Gnats, Nits, and Nibblers,* and both are part of her effort to improve people's attitudes toward insects.

A Note on the Illustrator

JOHN PARKER SHERROD is a biologist-illustrator who has been a technical assistant at the Sections of Economic Entomology and Biodiversity at the Natural History Survey at the University of Illinois at Urbana-Champaign. He is currently a scientific illustrator in the Ichthyofaunal Program in the Department of Biology at the University of New Mexico, Albuquerque.